MW00720878

THE NORTHWEST GOLFER

(Fourth Edition)

A GUIDE TO EVERY GOLF COURSE WHERE THE PUBLIC IS WELCOME IN OREGON & WASHINGTON

Cover Photo
The Resort at the Mountain's Foxglove Course
Welches, Oregon

OTHER BOOKS BY KIKI CANNIFF

NORTHWEST FREE – Volume One;
   The Best Free Historic Attractions in Oregon & Washington

A CAMPER'S GUIDE TO OREGON & WASHINGTON;
   The Only Guide to the Region's Non-membership RV Parks
   and Improved Tent Campgrounds

FREE CAMPGROUNDS OF WASHINGTON & OREGON;
   A Detailed Guide to the Region's Hundreds of Cost-free
   Campgrounds

UNFORGETTABLE PACIFIC NW CAMPING VACATIONS;
   Your Guide to Oregon & Washington's Most Spectacular
   Camping Regions

THE NORTHWEST GOLFER

(Fourth Edition)

A GUIDE TO EVERY GOLF COURSE WHERE THE PUBLIC IS WELCOME IN OREGON & WASHINGTON

By KiKi Canniff

Ki² Books
Published by Frank Amato Publications, Inc.
P.O. Box 82112
Portland, OR 97282
(503) 653-8108

Published in 1996 by:
Frank Amato Publications, Inc.
PO Box 82112 • Portland, Oregon 97282
(503) 653-8108

Printed in Canada

10 9 8 7 6 5 4

Library of Congress Cataloging-in-Publication Data

Canniff, KiKi
The Northwest Golfer; A Guide to Every Golf Course Where the Public is Welcome in Oregon & Washington (Fourth Edition) by KiKi Canniff.
p.   cm.
Includes index.
ISBN 0-941361-12-8 $14.95
1. Golf courses – Washington (State) – Directories.   2. Golf courses – Oregon – Directories.   3. Washington (State) – Guidebooks.   4. Oregon – Guidebooks.   I. Title.

TABLE OF CONTENTS

INTRODUCTION

This book describes every golf course in Oregon and Washington where the public can play without purchasing a membership. Besides public courses, it includes all of the region's semi-private courses that provide regularly scheduled times for public play. In all, the book covers 328 locations; some locations have more than one course.

Unless you're looking for membership in a private club, this is the only guide an Oregon or Washington golfer will ever need. It's an ideal addition to your golf gear, or keep it in your glove box so that no matter where you go you can always find the nearest course. A quick-reference tee line at the beginning of each listing lets you instantly determine if a course is right for your schedule and/or budget.

HOW THIS BOOK IS LAID OUT

The Northwest Golfer is divided into two sections. The first section covers all of Oregon's courses; the second details Washington's courses. Each section begins with a brief introduction, and a map showing how the state has been divided into these four regions: Coast, I-5 Corridor, Central and Eastern.

Each region begins with a map of the area, which is followed by a breakdown by page number making it easy to access each city's listings. For ease of use, the cities have been arranged in the same north to south order as they appear on the map.

WHAT YOU WILL FIND IN EACH COURSE LISTING

Throughout the book, course listings begin with complete contact information. This is where you'll find the name of the course, its location, and reservation phone number.

Opposite this information you'll see a custom tee line showing the number of holes offered, its total yardage, the men's par, and the price category.

The price category is defined by one to four dollar signs. A single dollar sign calls your attention to a bargain course, two shows you it's moderately priced, three denotes a higher-priced course, and four a deluxe course. The actual dollar amounts used to categorize the courses is based on the lowest rate available to every golfer. The exact breakdown is as follows:

> $ shows that you can play for less than $10.00,
>
> $$ means the fee is between $10.00 and $19.00,
>
> $$$ says the fee is between $20.00 and $29.00, and
>
> $$$$ shows that you will pay more than $30.00.

Once you have determined that this course fits your needs, read the full listing and you'll learn what the terrain is like, when it is open, whether or not they take reservations, and what makes each course special.

You'll find out exactly how much they charge for green fees and rental equipment, whether or not they have discount days or special times when you can play for reduced fees, the women's par, and if juniors and/or seniors can play for cheaper rates. Unless otherwise noted, junior rates are for those 17 and under, and senior rates are for golfers 65 and older.

Facilities are also covered. If the course has a putting green, driving range, practice area, or offers lessons, this book lets you know. It will tell you whether you'll find a snack bar, restaurant, lounge, accommodations, or on-site camping facilities. You'll also find out whether they offer banquet facilities, serve alcohol, or provide help with tournament planning.

At the end of each listing you'll find concise, easy-to-follow directions.

LOCATING A FAVORITE COURSE

An alphabetical list by golf course name appears, grouped by state, within the index at the back of this book. This will help you to locate any course you know by name, but not necessarily by location. Cities are also grouped by state within the index, providing an easy way to quickly find local courses.

The author has made every effort to include all of the region's courses, and worked directly with each course's staff to provide accurate information. If any information contained herein is incorrect, or a course with regular public times has been overlooked, please send details to the author, KiKi Canniff, at P.O. Box 186, Willamina, Oregon 97396.

SECTION ONE

OREGON'S
PUBLIC GOLF COURSES

AN INTRODUCTION
TO OREGON'S COURSES

Oregon is a great place to golf, with its variety of terrain, professional course designs, and spectacular mountain views. Public golf courses, along with semi-private courses that offer regular public hours, total 144. Eight of these locations sport more than one golf course.

The Portland Area has three multiple course sites; there are two more just a short drive away. In Portland, Glendoveer and Heron Lakes each offer two 18-hole courses; West Linn's Sandelie has both an 18-hole and 9-hole course. East of Portland, The Resort at the Mountain beckons with three 9-hole courses and some of the finest greens in the region. South of Portland, at Wilsonville, Charbonneau also has three 9-hole courses.

In Central Oregon you'll find two 36-hole courses, plus one with a total of 54 holes. Black Butte Ranch's two 18-hole courses are surrounded by trees and provide sensational views of snow-capped mountains. West of Redmond, Eagle Crest Resort also offers two 18-hole courses. The first was designed by Bunny Mason and opened in 1986; the second opened in 1993 and was designed by John Thronson.

Sunriver sports three 18-hole courses, all created by well-known designers. Fred Federspiel and Robert Trent Jones II each designed one; the new course, which opened in 1995, was designed by Robert Cupp.

Oregonians saw three other new courses open during 1995. The Greens at Redmond, which provides 9 holes designed by Robert Muir Graves, Eagle Point's Stoneridge Golf Club, and Aurora's Langdon Farms. The latter two each sport 18 holes. In 1996 two established 9-hole courses plan to open a second 9, Wildwood, northwest of Portland, and the Tukwila OGA Course at Woodburn.

Several new courses were built, and others modified, in recent years. In 1994, Applegate Golf opened in Grants Pass, Bay Breeze in Tillamook, and a second 9 was added to both Gresham's Persimmon Country Club and the Crooked River Ranch Golf Course.

In 1993, Golf Digest declared Sandpines Golf Resort, at Florence, to be the best new public course in the United States. That same year the Quail Valley Golf Course was built at Banks, Creekside Golf Club opened in Salem, Meadow Lakes made its debut in Prineville, and Medford saw the addition of two new courses, Quail Point and Stewart Meadows. To a state that already had a plethora of great courses, this was like adding icing to a cake.

To make it easy to find local golf courses, this section has been separated into the four regions shown on the map below. Each of these regions has its own section which begins with a map of the area. This is followed by a table of contents in which the cities, along with their page numbers, appear in the same north to south order as they are on the region's map.

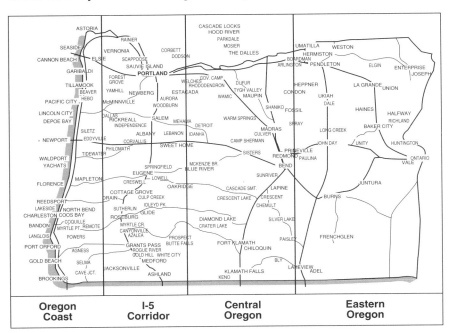

| Oregon Coast | I-5 Corridor | Central Oregon | Eastern Oregon |

Golfers in Oregon can play within view of the Pacific Ocean or surrounded by snow capped mountains, tee off on fairways shadowed by thick forests or within view of a clear mountain stream, sink a putt in the high mountain desert or beside a wetland frequented by migrating waterfowl. These are just a few of the special treats you can enjoy while golfing in Oregon.

What appears on the following pages is sure to make any golfer anxious for a day on the fairways.

THE OREGON COAST

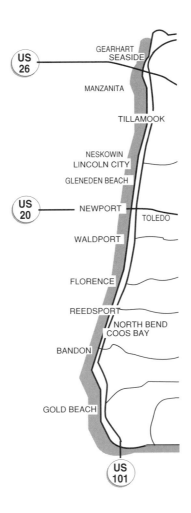

US 26
GEARHART
SEASIDE
MANZANITA
TILLAMOOK
NESKOWIN
LINCOLN CITY
GLENEDEN BEACH
US 20
NEWPORT
TOLEDO
WALDPORT
FLORENCE
REEDSPORT
NORTH BEND
COOS BAY
BANDON
GOLD BEACH
US 101

Oregon Coast
Table of Contents

GEARHART

GEARHART GOLF LINKS
Marion Avenue
Gearhart, OR
(503) 738-3538

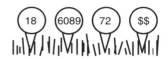

Established in 1892, Gearhart Golf Links is the oldest golf course in the Pacific Northwest. Its second 9 was added in 1913. Built on softly rolling dunes, this links-style course is situated just off the Pacific Ocean. The slope is 114 and the ratings 68.7 for men and 72.7 for women. Open year round, from dawn to dusk, reservations are advised. The women's tees cover 5,882 yards for a par of 74.

Green fees remain the same all week long, $13.00 for 9 holes or $25.00 for 18. Annual discount cards are available for juniors and seniors. Clubs can be rented for $4.00, handcarts $2.00 per 9 holes, and motorized carts $15.00 for 9 holes or $25.00 for 18. Facilities include a restaurant with a liquor license, banquet facilities, and a full-service pro shop. Lessons are available and they provide help with tournament planning.

Directions: Leave Highway 101 in Gearhart and head west to Marion Avenue.

THE HIGHLANDS
1 Highlands Rd.
Gearhart, OR
(503) 738-5248

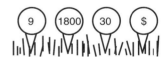

The ocean view is great at this year-round course and the terrain is one of gently rolling hills. Opened in 1986, reservations are needed one week in advance for weekend and summer play.

Green fees at The Highlands are very reasonable, $8.00 for 9 holes or $15.00 for 18. Clubs rent for $3.00, handcarts $2.00 per 9 holes, and motorized carts $10.00 and $15.00. They have a large pro shop and offer help with tournament planning. Lessons are available.

Directions: Take the Del Ray Beach exit off Highway 101 and follow the signs.

SEASIDE

SEASIDE GOLF CLUB
451 Avenue U
Seaside, OR
(503) 738-5261

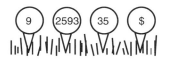

This course was built in 1921 and is open year round, weather permitting. It is situated on the site of the old Ben Holiday house with its historic race track. The view is pretty, the terrain flat, and you can hear the ocean from a few tees. Every hole has a river view and the course crosses the river twice. The slope is 102 and the ratings 62.9 for men and 65.0 for women. From the ladies' tees the distance is 2,500 yards. Reservations are not given.

You'll pay $8.00 to play 9 holes on weekdays, $16.00 for 18. On weekends and holidays it'll cost you $9.00 and $18.00. Clubs can be rented for $5.00, handcarts $1.50, and motorized carts $10.00 per 9 holes. They have a restaurant and lounge with a liquor license, plus a pro shop, banquet facilities and putting green. The new covered driving range offers both mat and grass tees.

Directions: The Seaside Golf Club is located at the south end of town.

MANZANITA

MANZANITA GOLF COURSE
Lakeview Drive
Manzanita, OR
(503) 368-5744

Manzanita is a wonderful little oceanside village with a year-round golf course. The course was designed by Ted Erickson, and opened in 1987. It offers tree-lined fairways, easy walking, and a pleasant game. On the 5th hole there's a 60 foot drop to the fairway below. The slope is 97 to 102, and the ratings 61.8 for men and 63.2 for women. The ladies' tees have a par of 33 for a total distance of 2,100 yards. Reservations are required.

Green fees are $12.00 for 9 holes or $22.00 for 18. You can rent clubs for $5.00 and handcarts for $1.00. They offer a full-service pro shop and a driving range that is open May thru September.

Directions: Leave Highway 101 on the Manzanita turnoff, follow Laneda Avenue to Carmel and turn left to the course.

TILLAMOOK

ALDERBROOK GOLF COURSE
7300 Alderbrook Rd.
Tillamook, OR
(503) 842-6413

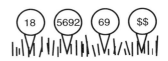

Alderbrook was started in 1924 and offers a great view of Tillamook Bay. Its terrain is fairly level with one hill affecting two holes; the 15th hole has a 25% uphill drive for a par three. Open year round, reservations are not required. The slope is 103 to 105, and the ratings 66.8 for men or 68.9 for women. From the ladies' tees the distance is 5,272 yards for a par of 71.

If you play 9 holes at Alderbrook the green fees are $10.00; 18 holes will cost you $18.00. Juniors can play during the week for $6.00 and $10.00. You can also purchase an annual membership. Rental clubs include handcarts and cost $5.00. Handcarts are $2.00 and motorized carts $12.00 for 9 holes or $20.00 for 18. Credit cards are welcome. They have a restaurant where beer and wine are served, plus a snack bar and full-service pro shop. You can get help with tournament planning and lessons.

Directions: Head north on Highway 101, go past the cheese factory and turn right on Alderbrook Road. From there it's 2 miles.

BAY BREEZE GOLF & RANGE
2325 Latimer Rd.
Tillamook, OR
(503) 842-1166

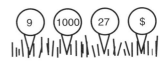

Bay Breeze offers plush bent grass greens plus plenty of water hazards and sand traps. The longest hole is 140 yards and the shortest 75, so it's a good place to use your irons. Built in 1994, it was designed by Mike Lehman. Reservations are not given.

Green fees are just $6.00 per 9 holes. Clubs rent for $3.00 and handcarts $1.00. Motorized carts are not available. Facilities include a covered, lighted driving range plus a putter's stage, lunch bar, and full-service pro shop. Credit cards are welcome, and you can get help with tournament planning and lessons. At the driving range you'll pay $2.00 to $5.00 for a bucket of balls.

Directions: Follow Highway 101 to the Tillamook Cheese Factory and turn right on Latimer Road.

NESKOWIN

HAWK CREEK GOLF COURSE
Highway 101
Neskowin, OR
(503) 392-4120

Hawk Creek sits in a beautiful coastal valley surrounded by forest. Open year round, a stream meanders across the fairways and the terrain is predominantly level. Protected from the wind, you get a wonderful ocean view, but winter often finds the grounds too wet to play. Reservations are advised on weekends and holidays.

Green fees remain the same seven days a week; 9 holes will cost you about $12.00. Clubs rent for $5.00, handcarts $2.00, and motorized carts $10.00 per 9 holes. Facilities include a limited pro shop with a snack bar that sells beer and wine. Help with tournament planning is available.

Directions: Located on the east side of Highway 101.

NESKOWIN BEACH GOLF
Hawk Avenue
Neskowin, OR
(503) 392-3377

This coastal course is found 10 miles north of Lincoln City. Built in 1932, it is one of the oldest courses along the coast and floods

completely during the winter. This flooding makes it lush and green all summer long. A creek comes into play on half the greens; it crosses the 5th hole twice. The view from the 7th hole is spectacular.

At Neskowin Beach you'll pay $12.00 to play 9 holes or $20.00 for 18. Off season those rates drop to $10.00 and $18.00. Gas carts rent for $10.00 per 9 holes, handcarts are $2.00, and clubs $5.00. Facilities include a snack bar serving beer and wine, plus a pro shop where lessons can be arranged.

Directions: Leave Highway 101 at Neskowin, drive thru the rest area and turn right.

LINCOLN CITY

LAKESIDE GOLF COURSE
3245 Clubhouse Dr.
Lincoln City, OR
(541) 994-8442

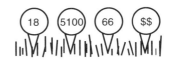

Situated between the coast mountains and Devil's Lake, this course has a rolling terrain with some hills. It offers year-round playability and each hole is unique. Lakeside provides a challenge for golfers of all skill levels. The 10th hole has a double dog leg and water along one side all the way to the green for a par of five; the 16th hole has you shooting over water for a par of three. Originally built in 1926, reservations are strongly advised on this exciting course. You'll find three tees at each hole.

Green fees are $18.00 for 9 holes or $30.00 for 18. Golfers age 18 and under play for $12.00 and $20.00 during the week; those 60 and over pay $16.00 and $27.00. During the winter everyone plays at discount rates. Credit cards are welcome. Clubs rent for $5.00 and $10.00, handcarts $2.00, and motorized carts $15.00 and $25.00. They have a limited driving range with mat tees and a complete health club with racquetball and tennis courts. You'll also find a restaurant and lounge with a liquor license, banquet rooms, and a full-service pro shop where you can arrange lessons and get help with tournament planning.

Directions: Located off Highway 101 in north Lincoln City.

21

GLENEDEN BEACH

SALISHAN GOLF LINKS
Salishan Lodge
Gleneden Beach, OR
(541) 764-3632

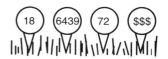

Salishan Lodge is a terrific place for a golfing vacation. Its wooded Scottish-style course is beautifully laid out and open year round. Built in 1965, the original designers were Fred Federspiel and John Gray; it was remodeled in 1996 by John Gray and Bill Robinson. The slope is 128 for a rating of 72.1, and the back nine has spectacular ocean views. Reservations are taken two weeks in advance. Three sets of tees are available.

July thru October green fees are $30.00 for 9 holes or $50.00 for 18. During May and June it'll cost you $25.00 and $40.00, and the rest of the year $15.00 and $25.00. Juniors play for half price during the week and lodge guests also receive discounts. Clubs are $10.00 for 9 holes or $15.00 for 18, handcarts $3.00 and $5.00, and motorized carts $15.00 and $26.00. You'll find resort facilities, a nice restaurant, pro shop and driving range. They provide help with tournament planning and lessons. The driving range has mat tees and you get 30 balls for $2.00.

Directions: Salishan is located just south of Lincoln City on Highway 101.

NEWPORT

AGATE BEACH GOLF COURSE
4100 N. Coast Hwy.
Newport, OR
(541) 265-7331

The Agate Beach Golf Course was built in 1931. It is open year round, fairly level with a slightly rolling terrain, and easy to walk. Surrounded by forests, they keep it well manicured and provide excellent putting surfaces. The slope is 109, and the ratings 65.8 for men, 68.7 for women. The total distance from the ladies' tees is 2,894 yards for a par of 38.

Green fees are $12.00 for 9 holes or $24.00 for 18. Clubs rent for $5.00 and $7.50, handcarts $1.50, and motorized carts $10.00 per 9 holes.

Facilities include a restaurant that serves beer and wine, a pro shop, and driving range. The range is for irons and offers grass tees. You can get a small bucket of balls for $2.50 or a large one for $4.00. Lessons are available.

Directions: Agate Beach is located at the north end of Newport, on Highway 101's east side.

TOLEDO

OLALLA VALLEY GOLF
1022 Olalla Rd.
Toledo, OR
(541) 336-2121

Built in 1967, this course is 7 miles inland and a good place to go when fog socks in the coastal towns. Open year round, it's challenging, hilly, and has enough water to keep you on your toes. The 8th green is heart-shaped, and the women's par 37 for a total distance of 2,587 yards. Call two days in advance for weekend tee times.

Green fees are $10.00 for 9 holes or $20.00 for 18 all week long. Punch cards get you 15 rounds for $100.00. Juniors, age 18 and under, can play 9 holes for $5.00; seniors, age 65 and over, can buy an annual membership for $400.00. Clubs rent for $5.00 per 9 holes, handcarts $2.00, and motorized carts $10.00. Credit cards are welcome.

You'll find a full-service pro shop, putting green, banquet facilities, and a restaurant that serves beer and wine at Olalla Valley. You can also get help with tournament planning.

Directions: Olalla Valley is located 1.5 miles off Highway 20, near Toledo.

WALDPORT

CRESTVIEW HILLS GOLF
1680 Crestline Dr.
Waldport, OR
(541) 563-3020

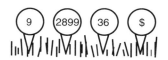

You'll get a view of the ocean from Crestview's 8th hole, and the 5th hole is one of the prettiest on the coast. This course has fairly small, but well-manicured greens and a hilly terrain. The slope is 114, and the ratings 66.0 for men and 69.5 for women. From the ladies' tees the total distance is 2,604 yards. During the summer this course is open at 7:00 a.m., and in the winter 8:00 a.m. Reservations are recommended on weekends.

Green fees are $8.00 for 9 holes and $16.00 for 18 on weekdays. On weekends it'll cost you $9.00 and $18.00. Juniors, under 18 years of age, can play for $5.00 any day of the week. You can rent a half set of clubs for $2.50 or a full set for $5.00, handcarts are $1.00, and motorized carts $9.00 per 9 holes. They have a full-service pro shop and a snack bar where beer and wine is available.

Directions: Take Highway 101 south of Waldport 1 mile to Range Drive and head east 1 mile to the course.

FLORENCE

OCEAN DUNES GOLF LINKS
3345 Munsel Lake Rd.
Florence, OR
(800) 468-4833

Ocean Dunes is described as "a wee bit of Scotland." Built on rolling sand dunes and bordered with rhododendron, beach grass and other native plants, the slope is 124 and the ratings 68.5 for men and 69.5 for women. The original 9 holes were built in 1962, the second in 1989. Open year round, reservations are available two weeks in advance. The back nine offers a panoramic view of the Florence area, and the women's par is 72 for a total distance of 4,881 yards.

Green fees are $15.00 for 9 holes or $28.00 for 18. Seniors can purchase a discount card and juniors pay lower rates on weekdays as well as after 1:00 p.m. on weekends and holidays. Clubs can be rented for $5.00 and $8.00, handcarts $2.00 and $3.00, and motorized carts $10.00 and $18.00.

Facilities include a snack bar offering beer and wine, plus a pro shop and driving range. The range is for irons only, and a bucket of balls cost $1.50 to $3.00. Lessons can be arranged.

Directions: Located 3 miles north of Florence. Leave Highway 101 on Munsel Lake Road and go 2 miles.

SANDPINES GOLF RESORT
1201 35th St.
Florence, OR
(800) 917-4653 or (541) 997-1940

This Rees Jones designed course received Golf Digest's 1993 award for the best new public course. It has been compared to Pebble Beach and Spyglass Hill. Giant sand dunes, deep man-made lakes, Monterey pines and cypress trees make it both challenging and beautiful.

The slope ranges from 111 to 129 for men with ratings of 65.8 to 74.0. The women's slope is 123 to 129, the ratings 71.1 to 75.7. Four sets of tees are available. Spring and summer hours are 7:00 a.m. to dusk; in the fall and winter they open up at 8:00 a.m. Reservations are given up to 2 weeks in advance.

You'll pay $25.00 to play 9 holes at Sandpines year round. In the winter 18 holes are $35.00; the balance of the year it's $40.00 midweek and $45.00 on weekends. Juniors, 17 and younger, can play for $20.00 and $30.00. Twilight rates begin at 2:00 p.m. on weekdays and allow unlimited play for $20.00; on Sundays after 1:30 p.m. you pay $25.00. Credit cards are welcome.

Clubs rent for $7.50 per 9 holes and handcarts $2.00 and $4.00. Motorized carts are $18.00 and $26.00, except during the winter when you pay just $10.00. Facilities include a snack bar offering beer and wine, plus a full-service pro shop and driving range. They can help you arrange tournaments and provide lessons. The driving range charges $3.00 for a bucket of balls.

Directions: Located at the north end of town.

REEDSPORT

FOREST HILLS COUNTRY CLUB
1 Country Club Dr.
Reedsport, OR
(541) 271-2626

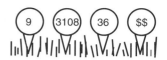

Forest Hills is relatively flat, has some hills, and is surrounded by woods. Open from 8:00 a.m. to dusk year round, it's very walkable with great putting greens. You'll find four sets of tees, adding variety to 18 holes. Reservations are taken 7 days in advance. The women's par is 37 for a total length of 2,774 yards.

Weekday green fees are $10.00 for 9 holes or $18.00 for 18; on weekends it's $12.00 and $20.00. Clubs rent for $5.00 and $8.00, handcarts $2.00 and $3.00, and motorized carts $10.00 and $18.00. Memberships are available.

You'll find a restaurant and lounge with banquet facilities and a liquor license, plus a driving range and discount pro shop. Lessons and tournament planning are available. The driving range offers grass tees, and you get a small bucket of balls for $2.00 or a large one for $3.00. The driving range is open from 8:00 a.m. until two hours before dusk.

Directions: You'll find signs on Highway 101 directing you to this Reedsport course.

NORTH BEND

KENTUCK GOLF & COUNTRY CLUB
675 Golf Course Ln.
North Bend, OR
(541) 756-4464

This is the most southern 18-hole course along the Oregon coast. The terrain is flat with small greens surrounded by woods. Open year round, the slope is 99 for a rating of 64.9. At the clubhouse you get a great view across Coos Bay and North Bend. The total distance from the ladies' tees is 4,469 yards.

Weekday green fees are $8.00 for 9 holes or $14.00 for 18. On weekends you'll pay $9.00 and $16.00. Juniors play for $7.00 and $12.00 all week long. Credit cards are not accepted for green fees. Clubs rent for $5.00, handcarts $1.00, and motorized carts $8.00 for 9 holes or $15.00 for 18. Facilities include a small restaurant where you'll find cold beer and wine.

Directions: Located 3 miles east of the Bay Bridge.

COOS BAY

SUNSET BAY GOLF COURSE
11001 Cape Arago Hwy.
Coos Bay, OR
(541) 888-9301

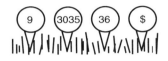

Every hole at Sunset Bay has at least one water hazard. This not only keeps the game interesting, but also creates a beautiful setting. The course is situated in a scenic valley and has several elevated greens and tees. Bordered by dense forest, it is fairly easy to walk. This course was designed by John Zoller and built in 1969. Reservations are not required.

Weekday green fees are $8.00 for 9 holes or $15.00 for 18. On weekends and holidays it's $9.00 and $16.00. Juniors, 12 and under, save $2.00 on weekday green fees. You can rent clubs for $3.00, handcarts $1.00 and $2.00, and motorized carts are $10.00 and $19.00. They have a pro shop and snack bar.

Directions: Located just south of Sunset Bay State Park.

BANDON

BANDON FACE ROCK GOLF
3235 Beach Loop Dr.
Bandon, OR
(541) 347-3818

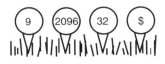

If you enjoy an oceanside game of golf, you'll really enjoy this course. It's right across the street from the Pacific Ocean, and the

9th tee is 200 yards from the sea. A relatively flat course, Bandon Face has a year-round creek running through it. One of the most challenging 9-hole courses in the Pacific Northwest, it was built in 1929 and is open year round. Reservations are not required, but they occasionally close for tournaments so you might want to call ahead. The distance from the women's tees is 1,915 yards.

Green fees are $8.00 for 9 holes and $13.00 for 18 on weekdays, $9.00 and $14.00 on weekends. You can rent clubs for $4.00, handcarts $2.00, and motorized carts $8.00 for 9 holes or $13.00 for 18. Annual memberships, as well as men's and ladies clubs, are available. You'll find a clubhouse with an ocean view, a restaurant and lounge with a banquet room and liquor license, and a full-service pro shop on site. Lessons, and help with tournament planning, are also available.

Directions: At Bandon take Sea Bird Lane off Highway 101 and head west toward Beach Loop Drive and the course.

GOLD BEACH

CEDAR BEND GOLF COURSE
34391 Squaw Valley Rd.
Gold Beach, OR
(541) 247-6911

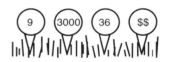

Built in 1969, this year-round course offers four sets of tees and two flags on each green. The slope is 115, and the ratings 67.6 for men and 70.8 for women. Cedar Bend is scenic; the terrain is flat and surrounded by large trees. Small streams affect most holes, and Cedar Creek cuts through the course. Reservations are requested May thru September. The women's tees have a par of 37 for a total distance of 2,605 yards.

Green fees are $13.00 for 9 holes, or $18.00 for 18, seven days a week. On weekdays juniors can play for $5.00 and $7.00, and seniors for $12.00 and $17.00. You can rent clubs for $5.00 for 9 holes or $7.00 for 18, handcarts are $2.00, and motorized carts $12.00 and $18.00.

Facilities include a lounge with a seasonal liquor license plus a snack bar, full service pro shop, and driving range. The driving range has mat tees and charges $1.50 for a small bucket of balls or $2.00 for a large one. They accept credit cards for green fees and can offer help with tournament planning.

Directions: Located 12 miles north of Gold Beach.

OREGON'S I-5 CORRIDOR

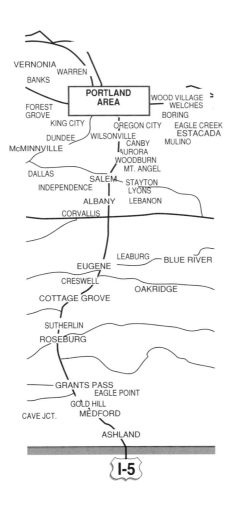

Oregon's I-5 Corridor
Table of Contents

VERNONIA

VERNONIA GOLF CLUB
15961 Timber Rd. E.
Vernonia, OR
(503) 655-1461 or (800) 644-6535

The Vernonia Golf Club course is nestled in timber, along the Nehalem River. It's quiet, beautiful, and a pleasure to play, but if your ball leaves the course, it's gone. The drainage is excellent, so the greens are dry when other courses are too wet to play. You'll find a few hills, but the course is easy to walk. The slope is 113 and the ratings 66.8 for men, 68.8 for women. Built in 1928, it's open year round from dawn to dusk. Tee times are necessary on weekends and holidays.

Weekend green fees are $9.00 for 9 holes or $17.00 for 18. On weekdays it's $8.00 and $15.00. During the week golfers under 18, and those over 60, can play for $7.00 and $13.00. Credit cards are accepted for green fees. Clubs rent for $5.00 and $7.50, handcarts $2.00, and motorized carts $10.00 per 9 holes. Facilities include a snack bar where you'll find cold beer and wine, plus a banquet room and full service pro shop. Lessons, and help with tournament planning, are available.

Directions: Vernonia is northwest of Portland via Highways 26 and 47. At Vernonia turn left on Timber Road and follow to course.

WARREN

ST. HELENS GOLF COURSE
57246 Hazen Rd.
Warren, OR
(503) 397-0358

This course offers a beautiful view of Mount St. Helens, Mt. Hood and Mt. Adams. The terrain is gently rolling and open year round. Built in 1959, it offers two sets of tees for those looking to play 18 holes. The women's tees have a total distance of 2,668 yards.

Monday thru Thursday you can play 9 holes here for $7.00 or 18 for $13.00. Seniors play for $6.00 and $11.00. Friday thru Sunday everyone pays $9.00 and $17.00. Clubs rent for $5.00, handcarts $2.00, and motorized carts $10.00 per 9 holes. They have a practice area, full-service pro shop, banquet facilities, and a snack bar where beer is available. Lessons, and help with tournament planning, can be arranged.

Directions: Warren is located about .5 mile south of St. Helens. To find the course leave Highway 30 on Church Road, drive 2 miles to Hazen Road and turn right.

BANKS

QUAIL VALLEY GOLF COURSE
12565 N.W. Aerts Rd.
Banks, OR
(503) 324-4444

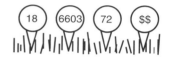

Designed by John Zoller, Quail Valley opened in 1993. It's a links-style course, flat with hills, and water comes into play on nearly half the holes. You'll find four sets of tees which vary from 5,519 yards to 6,603. Open year round, hours are 8:00 a.m. to dusk, 9:00 a.m. to dusk in the winter. Reservations are available 7 days in advance.

Monday thru Thursday green fees are $13.00 for 9 holes or $25.00 for 18. The rest of the week, and on holidays, they charge $14.00 and $27.00. Juniors, those 17 and younger, can play on weekday afternoons for half price. Clubs rent for $6.00 per 9 holes, handcarts are $1.50 and $3.00, and motorized carts $11.00 and $22.00.

Facilities include a restaurant and lounge where you'll find cold beer and wine, a full-service pro shop and driving range. At the range they offer grass tees and you get a bucket of balls for $2.50 to $6.00 depending on how many you need. Lessons, and help with tournament planning, are available.

Directions: Leave Highway 26 at the Banks/Tillamook exit; the course is 1.5 miles down this road.

PORTLAND AREA

(PORTLAND)

BROADMOOR GOLF COURSE
3509 N.E. Columbia Blvd.
Portland, OR
(503) 281-1337

This is a popular Portland course where reservations are necessary from March thru November. The course is very pleasant, and the terrain fairly flat with a few steep hills, lots of willow trees, lush greens, and a number of water holes. It is open year round, dawn to dusk, and has been in operation since 1931. The slope is 122 for men with a rating of 70.2, 110 and 69.9 for women. You can get reservations one week in advance.

For 18 holes, green fees are $18.00 on weekdays and $20.00 on weekends. November thru February you can play 9 holes for $6.00 or 18 for $12.00. Credit cards are okay for green fees. A special junior club allows members to play for half price. You can rent a half set of clubs for $5.00 or a full set for $10.00. Handcarts are $2.00, motorized carts $22.00.

Facilities include a restaurant and lounge with a liquor license, plus banquet rooms, a snack bar, full service pro shop, and driving range. They can provide help with tournament planning and offer lessons. At the driving range you'll find grass tees and can get a bucket of balls for $2.50 to $6.00.

Directions: Leave I-5 at the Columbia Blvd. exit and head east 2 miles; from I-205 take the Columbia Blvd. exit 2 miles west.

CLAREMONT GOLF COURSE
15955 N.W. West Union Rd.
Portland, OR
(503) 690-4589

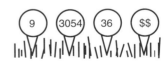

This year round course was built in 1989 and is easy to walk. It offers nice greens with plenty of lakes and sand traps in a country-like setting. Reservations are recommended. The first hole is a par three shot over water; the second hole is 554 yards for a par five.

It'll cost you $10.00 to play 9 holes or $18.00 for 18 on weekdays. On weekends you'll pay $12.00 or $22.00. Seniors, age 62 and over, can play 9 holes during the week for just $6.00. Clubs rent for $5.00 and handcarts $2.00 per 9 holes. Lessons are available.

Directions: Take Highway 26 west to the 185th Avenue exit, turn right and drive 1.5 miles.

COLWOOD NATIONAL
7313 N.E. Columbia Blvd.
Portland, OR
(503)254-5515

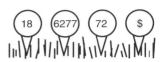

This pleasant tree-lined course is fairly flat and open year round. The women's tees have a par of 77 for a total of 5,673 yards. Both group and individual lessons are available, and they have a nice warm-up range. Foursomes need to call one week in advance if they want to play 18 holes. The course is occasionally closed for tournaments.

Weekday green fees are $9.00 for 9 holes or $16.00 for 18. On weekends it's $10.00 and $18.00. Juniors, under the age of 18, can play during the week for half price. Clubs rent for $6.00 and $10.00, handcarts $3.00 and $6.00, and motorized carts $11.00 and $20.00. They have a nice restaurant and lounge with a liquor license and banquet facilities, plus a full-service pro shop where you can get help with tournament planning.

Directions: Located about 18 blocks west of I-205 on Columbia.

EASTMORELAND GOLF
2425 S.E. Bybee
Portland, OR
(503) 775-2900

Eastmoreland's terrain is very hilly, and the course is bordered by Crystal Springs Lake. This is one of the top courses in the United States, and has been the site of the city championships since 1918. Open year round, they take reservations 7 days ahead in person, or 6 days by phone. The women's par is 74 for a total distance of 5,646 yards.

Weekday green fees are $9.50 for 9 holes or $18.00 for 18. On weekends it's $10.50 and $20.00. Twilight rates are offered Friday thru Sunday and begin two hours before dusk. Seniors, age 65 and up, can purchase a punch card that allows them to play for $7.25 and $14.50 on certain days. The junior punch card makes a 9-hole game just $3.00 on special days. A half set of clubs rents for $6.00 and a full set $15.00; handcarts are $2.00 and $3.00, and motorized carts $12.00 per 9 holes.

Facilities include a restaurant and lounge with a liquor license and banquet facilities. You can get help with tournament planning and arrange for lessons at the full-service pro shop. They have a lighted two-story driving range that stays open until 10:00 p.m. It's covered, offers mat tees, and a bucket of balls is $2.00 to $5.50.

Directions: Leave Portland heading south on Highway 99E, take the exit marked Reed College, and cross over the highway.

GLENDOVEER GOLF COURSE
14015 N.E. Glisan St.
Portland, OR
(503) 253-7507

(36) (6296) (73) ($)

You'll find two 18-hole courses at Glendoveer, with ratings of 67.4 to 73.5. The west course is just a bit shorter than the east course, with a total distance of 5,922 yards for men and 5,117 for women. Par for women is 75 on either course; on the west course it's 71 for men, 73 on the east course. The terrain is varied and heavily wooded.

Built in 1928, this is the oldest 36-hole course in the Northwest. Open year round, from daylight to dusk, reservations are necessary on weekends.

During the week green fees are $9.00 for 9 holes or $17.00 for 18. Seniors can play 9 holes for $6.00, juniors $3.50. On weekends everyone pays $10.00 for 9 holes or $19.00 for 18. Clubs rent for $6.00, handcarts $2.00, and motorized carts $22.00 for 18 holes.

Glendoveer has a great restaurant and lounge with a liquor license and banquet facilities. They also have a snack bar, driving range, and a full-service pro shop where you can arrange lessons and get help with tournament planning. The driving range has mat tees, is heated, and open year round.

Directions: Located on Glisan at 140th Street.

HERON LAKES GOLF COURSE
3500 N. Victory Blvd.
Portland, OR
(503) 289-1818

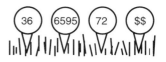

There are two 18-hole courses at Heron Lakes, Green-Back and Great Blue. Both were designed by Robert Trent Jones Jr. and are open year round from sunup to sundown. Reservations are given 7 days in advance, 6 days ahead by phone. Credit cards are not accepted for green fees. Course amenities include a restaurant that serves beer and wine, plus a full-service pro shop where lessons can be arranged and a driving range. The driving range is open from sunup to sundown and has grass tees.

Heron Lakes' Green-Back course has a flat terrain and is very walkable. The style is traditional with lots of trees and plenty of sand bunkers. With three tees on each hole, the slope is 113 to 124 and the ratings 69.4 to 71.4. Weekday green fees are $9.50 for 9 holes or $18.00 for 18. On weekends it's $10.50 or $20.00.

The Great Blue course is very challenging and has a total yardage of 6,916. It is Scottish-style, with rolling fairways, lots of water, and plenty of sand bunkers. With four tees on each hole, the slope is 120 to 132 and the ratings 69.4 to 73.6. This course charges $14.50 for 9 holes or $29.00 for 18 all week long.

Seniors, age 65 and older, with a City of Portland Senior Golf Pass can play 9 holes for $7.25. Juniors can get a card that lets them play 9 holes on weekdays before 4:00 p.m., and after 3:00 p.m. on weekends and holidays, for $3.00. Clubs rent for $14.00, handcarts $3.00, and motorized carts $12.00 per 9 holes.

Directions: Leave I-5 at the Delta Park/Expo exit #306-B and go west to the course.

PORTLAND MEADOWS GOLF
901 N. Schmeer Rd.
Portland, OR
(503) 289-3405

Portland Meadows is a bargain course. Located on the infield of the Portland Meadows Race Track, it's only open May thru September. Reservations are not taken, but the course occasionally closes for tournaments so you might want to check their schedule. An easy-to-walk course, the women's par is 35.

Green fees are around $5.00 for 9 holes on Mondays, Tuesday thru Friday $7.00, and weekends and holidays $8.00. Juniors and seniors play for reduced rates. Clubs rent for $5.00 and handcarts $2.00. Facilities include a limited pro shop where you can get help with tournament planning and a snack bar offering cold beer. At the driving range you get 35 balls for $3.00.

Directions: Take the Delta Park exit off I-5, turn right and follow to the race track.

ROSE CITY GOLF COURSE
2200 N.E. 71st Ave.
Portland, OR
(503) 253-4744

Rose City's setting is pretty with lots of trees and water on the back 9. It is the city's second oldest course and open year round. The slope is 118 and the ratings 70.6 for men, 71.6 for women. Reservations for 18 holes are available 7 days ahead in person, or 6 by phone. Call 24 hours in advance to get tee times for 9 holes. Three sets of tee add variety to the course. The women's par is 74 for a total distance of 5,619 yards.

The weekday green fees are $9.50 for 9 holes or $18.00 for 18. On weekends it's $10.50 and $20.00. Lower rates are offered in the winter. Seniors can use their Portland senior card, available from the city, for discount rates. It allows them to play 9 holes for $7.25. Juniors get to play 9 holes for $3.00. You can rent clubs for $7.50 and $12.00, handcarts $2.00 and $3.00, and motorized carts for $12.00 per 9 holes. Facilities include a full-service pro shop where you can get help with tournament planning and arrange for lessons. You'll find beer and wine at the snack bar.

Directions: The Rose City Golf Course is located just south of Halsey on 71st Avenue.

TOP O'SCOTT GOLF COURSE
12000 S.E. Stevens Rd.
Portland, OR
(503) 654-5050

Top O'Scott is open year round, from sunup to sundown, closing only in late May during the Memorial 3 Man Scramble. The course is fairly flat, but you'll find a few hills on the back 9. The women's par is 72 for a total length of 4,766 yards. Reservations are necessary on weekends and holidays.

Weekday green fees are $8.00 for 9 holes or $14.00 for 18. Seniors can play for $6.00 and $10.00. On weekends and holidays everyone pays $9.00 for 9 holes or $16.00 for 18. Clubs rent for $6.00, handcarts $2.00, and motorized carts $10.00 and $18.00. Lessons are available. Facilities include a pro shop where you can get help with tournament planning.

Directions: Located east of I-205; take the Sunnyside Road exit and follow to Stevens Road which will lead you to the course.

WILDWOOD GOLF COURSE
21881 S.W. St. Helens Rd.
Portland, OR
(503) 621-3402

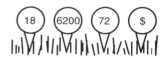

Designed by Bill O'Meara, and built in 1990, this course will open a second 9 in 1996. You'll find lots of elevated tee shots and water on almost every hole. The slope on the front 9 is 109 for a rating of 68.1. Open year round, you can tee off at 8:00 a.m. during the week or 7:00 a.m. on weekends. It's advisable to call at least two days ahead for weekend reservations.

Green fees during the week are $7.00 per 9 holes; on weekends it'll cost you $9.00. Clubs rent for $6.00, handcarts $1.00, and motorized carts $7.00 per 9 holes. Facilities include a snack bar where you will find cold beer, plus a full-service pro shop where you can get help with tournament planning and arrange lessons.

Directions: Located on Hwy. 30, 2 miles north of Cornelius Pass.

(BEAVERTON)

PROGRESS DOWNS GOLF
8200 S.W. Scholls Ferry Rd.
Beaverton, OR
(503) 646-5166

The Progress Downs course has lots of trees and rolling hills, but very little water and just a few bunkers. Built by the City of

Portland parks department in 1969, it has three tees per hole. Tee times are given out 6 days in advance by phone, 7 days in person. The women's par is 73 for a total distance of 5,626 yards.

Green fees for 9 holes are $9.00 during the week and $10.00 on weekends. For 18 holes you'll pay $17.00 and $19.00. Golfers under 18 can play 9 holes for $3.00 or 18 for $6.00. Those 65 and over pay $6.75 and $13.50. Discount rates are available during the winter. Clubs are $5.00 and $10.00, handcarts $2.00 and $3.00, and motorized carts $10.00 and $20.00.

Progress Downs has a full-service pro shop with a large selection of products. Amenities include a restaurant and lounge where liquor is served, banquet facilities, a swing analyzer, video and still action equipment, and other helpful devices. They can assist you with tournament planning and arrange for everything from individual to group lessons. At the driving range you'll pay $2.00 for a small bucket of balls, $4.00 and $5.50 for larger buckets. The range is open 6:00 a.m. to 10:00 p.m. and offers mat tees.

Directions: Take Highway 217 to the Progress/Scholls Ferry exit. The course is 4 blocks north of Hall.

(CLACKAMAS)

SAH-HAH-LEE GOLF COURSE
17104 S.E. 130th Ave.
Clackamas, OR
(503) 655-9249

Built in 1990, this course is located along the beautiful Clackamas River. The clubhouse is a renovated farm house that overlooks the entire course. Open from dawn to dark year round, reservations are available one week in advance. The level ground is easily walked and sports beautiful bent grass greens.

During the week it costs $7.00 to play 9 holes or $12.00 for 18; weekends it's $8.00 and $13.00. Golfers 60 and over, as well as those 15 and under, can play on weekdays for $6.00 and $10.00. Clubs rent for $4.00 and $6.00, and handcarts $1.00 per 9 holes. Motorized carts are not available. Facilities include a snack bar offering beer and wine, plus a full-service pro shop and covered driving range. This lighted range provides buckets of balls for

$2.50 to $5.50 and stays open until 9:00 p.m. in the summer. Tournament planning and lessons can be arranged.

Directions: Take I-205 to the Highway 212 exit and drive east 2 miles before taking a right on 130th Avenue.

(CORNELIUS)

FOREST HILLS GOLF COURSE
36260 S.W. Tongue Ln.
Cornelius, OR
(503) 357-3347

This year-round course offers a great view of Mt. Hood and a rolling terrain. Forest Hills was built in 1927. The slope is 122 and the ratings 69.7 for men, 71.7 for women. Par from the women's tees is 74 for a total length of 5,673 yards.

Green fees are $12.00 for 9 holes and $24.00 for 18. Juniors play for half price on weekdays and after 2:00 p.m. on weekends and holidays. Clubs rent for $7.00, and motorized carts $19.00. Facilities include a restaurant/lounge with a liquor license, plus banquet facilities, a driving range and full-service pro shop. They can help you with tournament planning and arrange for lessons. At the driving range you'll find both mat and grass tees, and will pay $2.50 for a small bucket of balls or $5.00 for a large one.

Directions: Leave Highway 26 at the Hillsboro/North Plains exit and drive through Hillsboro. After 3 miles turn right onto Tongue Lane and go 3 miles west to the course.

GHOST CREEK @ PUMPKIN RIDGE
12930 Old Pumpkin Ridge Rd.
Cornelius, OR
(503) 647-9977

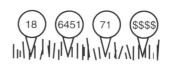

The fairways at Pumpkin Ridge weave their way through forests, and past wetlands and creeks. Designed for golfers of all levels, it has bent grass fairways, plenty of sand traps, and was designed to preserve the natural habitat for wildlife. Bob Cupp was the designer. It opened in 1992 and has already earned National recognition. With four sets of tees the slope ranges from 121 to

140, and the ratings from 69.2 to 73.8. Open year round, from dawn to dusk, reservations are needed one week in advance.

Green fees are $35.00 for 9 holes or $60.00 for 18 Monday thru Thursday, and $75.00 Friday thru Sunday. Twilight rates are available, and frequent players will save money by purchasing a Ghost Card. You can rent clubs for $20.00, handcarts are $3.00, and motorized carts $15.00 for 9 holes or $24.00 for 18.

Facilities include a restaurant/lounge with a liquor license, plus banquet facilities, a full-service pro shop, state-of-the-art indoor teaching facility, 25-station driving range, chipping and putting greens, and practice bunkers. The range is open dawn to dusk, has both mat and grass tees, and you get a bucket of balls for $3.00. Lessons are available, as is help with tournament planning.

Directions: Take Highway 26 west of Portland to Dersham Road exit #55, go right to Mountaindale Road, turn right and follow to Old Pumpkin Ridge Road and the course.

(GLADSTONE)

RIVERGREENS GOLF COURSE
19825 River Rd.
Gladstone, OR
(503) 656-1033

Rivergreens offers lush fairways, smooth greens, and is nestled along the banks of the Willamette River. Formerly 18 holes, it was recently transformed into a challenging 9-hole course. The setting is pleasant with a variety of trees and flowering bushes, and it's a good place to sharpen your short game skills. Open year round, this semi-private course offers annual memberships. Reservations are suggested, and children are not allowed.

Green fees are $7.00 for 9 holes or $12.00 for 18, seven days a week. Seniors, 60 and older, can play for $5.00 and $10.00. They don't rent clubs, but have a few motorized carts for disabled golfers. Handcarts are $2.00, and facilities include a practice green. Help with tournament planning is available at the pro shop.

Directions: Located .5 mile north of I-205's Oregon City exit, just off McLoughlin Blvd. (Highway 99E).

(GRESHAM)

GRESHAM GOLF COURSE
2155 N.E. Division
Gresham, OR
(503) 665-3352

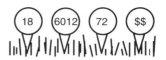

The Gresham Golf Course is open year round, is semi-flat, and has a nice view of Mt. Hood. Designed by Sam Wolsborn, it opened in 1965. The slope is 105 and the ratings 67.3 for men, 69.0 for women. Reservations are needed on weekends. The women's par is 72 for a distance of 5,284 yards.

During the week green fees are $10.00 for 9 holes, $18.00 for 18. On weekends it'll cost you $13.00 or $20.00. Juniors can play 9 holes for $6.50 on weekdays before 3:00 p.m. and weekends after 4:00 p.m. Golfers 65 and older can purchase a 12-game 9-hole weekday ticket for $92.00. You can rent clubs for $10.00, handcarts $2.00, and motorized carts $22.00.

You'll find both a grass and covered driving range. Open dawn to dusk, balls are $2.50 for a small bucket, $4.00 for medium, or $6.00 for large. Facilities include a restaurant and lounge with a liquor license, plus banquet rooms and a full-service pro shop. Lessons, and help with tournament planning, are available.

Directions: Located 12 miles east of downtown Portland via Division Avenue.

PERSIMMON COUNTRY CLUB
8015 S.E. Hogan Rd.
Gresham, OR
(503) 667-7500

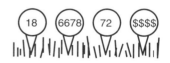

This semi-private club offers beautiful views of three mountains and is open year round, but closed Christmas Day. Designed by Bunny Mason, the second 9 opened in 1994. Four sets of tees are available with total yardages ranging from 4,852 to 6,678. The slope is 125 and the ratings 71.2 for men, 70.3 for women. Non-members can get reservations three days in advance.

Green fees are $45.00 on weekdays, $55.00 on weekends. Monday thru Thursday mornings they have a "Dew Sweeper" rate before 9:30 a.m. of $39.00 per person; if there are two of you that includes a cart. November thru March anyone can play during the week for $29.00 and on weekends for $39.00. Clubs are available for $10.00, handcarts $4.00, and motorized carts $22.00. Credit cards are welcome.

They have a restaurant and lounge, liquor license, banquet room, driving range, short game learning center, and a full-service pro shop. Lessons, and help with tournament planning, are available. The driving range stays open until dark and offers both grass and mat tees. You get a large bucket of balls for $6.00.

Directions: Leave I-84 at the Wood Village exit, turn right and drive 5 miles.

(HILLSBORO)

KILLARNEY WEST GOLF
1270 N.W. 334th
Hillsboro, OR
(503) 648-7634

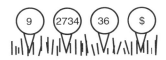

The fairways at Killarney West are narrow with lots of trees, two creeks, and a few small hills. It's easy to walk and has no sand traps. You'll find a water hole with a pond in the middle, lots of birds, and a quiet country setting. Reservations are necessary only on weekends and holidays. The women's par is 37.

Green fees are $6.00 during the week and $8.00 on weekends and holidays. Clubs can be rented for $5.00, handcarts $1.00, and motorized carts $8.00 per 9 holes. They have a small pro shop and a snack bar with a liquor license.

Directions: Located on the west side of Hillsboro, right off TV Highway; turn right on 334th and follow the signs.

MERIWETHER NATIONAL
5200 S.W. Rood Bridge Rd.
Hillsboro, OR
(503) 648-4143

This challenging course borders the Tualatin River and has some pretty tough par threes plus one par four that is said to be among the most difficult holes in the Northwest. The slope is 115 to 121, and the ratings 69.0 to 69.5 for men, 75.8 for women. Built in 1960, it's a fairly level course and open year round. The women's par is 74. They will soon be adding a 9-hole par three course.

Weekday green fees are $9.00 for 9 holes or $16.00 for 18. On weekends it'll cost you $10.00 and $16.00. Juniors, 16 and under, can play during the week for $4.50 and $8.00. Retirees, 62 and over, can enjoy unlimited play on weekdays for $85.00 per month. Clubs rent for $5.00 and $8.00, handcarts $2.00, and motorized carts $20.00.

They have a new clubhouse, restaurant/lounge with a liquor license, banquet room, covered driving range, full-service pro shop, snack bar, and 18-hole putting course. Lessons, and help with tournament planning, are available.

Directions: To find Meriwether, take Canyon Road west to the first stoplight past 239th, turn left onto Witch Hazel, go 1 mile to River Road, after 1 block turn left onto Rood Bridge, and follow for 1 mile.

ORENCO WOODS GOLF
Golf Course Road
Hillsboro, OR
(503) 648-1836

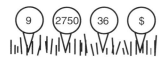

This hilly course is open year round. The slope is 114 and the ratings 65.8 for men, 69.3 for women. Three sets of tees add variety to the game. Facilities include a full-service pro shop, a snack bar serving cold beer, and a driving range. They take reservations for weekend play one week in advance.

Green fees remain the same 7 days a week, $9.00 for 9 holes or $17.00 for 18. On weekdays juniors and seniors can play 9 holes before noon for $6.50. You can rent clubs for $6.00, handcarts $2.00, and motorized carts are $10.00 per 9 holes.

The driving range is open April thru October, offers mat tees, and charges $3.50 per bucket of balls. Lessons are available.

Directions: Orenco Woods is found 2 miles south of Highway 26.

(LAKE OSWEGO)

LAKE OSWEGO GOLF COURSE
17525 S.W. Stafford Rd.
Lake Oswego, OR
(503) 636-8228

This family course has a club for men, ladies, juniors, senior men, and mixed seniors. They also have an enclosed driving range with 14 mats. The course has some hills, and first opened in 1970. During the summer golfers can begin at 6:30 a.m., in December and January at 8:00 a.m, and the balance of the year at 9:00 a.m. They close at dark. Reservations are taken only on weekends and holidays.

Weekday green fees are $6.00 for 9 holes or $11.00 for 18. On weekends and holidays they charge $7.00 and $12.00. Juniors and seniors can play 9 holes during the week for $5.00 or 18 for $9.00. Clubs rent for $3.00 and $4.00, handcarts $2.00 per 9 holes, and they have one motorized cart which is reserved for disabled golfers. You'll find a restaurant, full-service pro shop, and driving range. At the range you can get buckets of balls for $2.50 to $5.50, depending on how many you want. They also offer golf lessons and help with tournament planning.

Directions: Take the Stafford exit off I-205, turn left, and drive 4 miles to the Lake Oswego Golf Course.

(TIGARD)

SUMMERFIELD GOLF CLUB
10650 S.W. Summerfield Dr.
Tigard, OR
(503) 620-1200

Summerfield is a semi-private course that is only closed to the public prior to 11:00 a.m. on Tuesday, Wednesday, Thursday and Saturday mornings. Open year round, reservations are taken two days in advance. This executive course has a view of both Mt. Hood and Mount St. Helens. Two sets of tees add variety to your 18-hole game.

Green fees are $10.00 per 9 holes all week long. They have no rental clubs, but handcarts can be rented for $2.00 and motorized carts $9.00 per 9 holes. They also have a full-service pro shop where you can arrange for lessons.

Directions: Take I-5 south to the Carmen Drive exit, and follow to Duram Road. The course is about 1.5 miles from the freeway.

(WEST LINN)

SANDELIE GOLF COURSE
28333 S.W. Mountain Rd.
West Linn, OR
(503) 655-1461

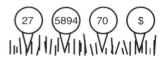

Sandelie has both an 18-hole and 9-hole course. The setting is quiet, and wildlife is often spotted. Its fairways are partly wooded, one green is bordered by a pond and another by a canyon, and the terrain ranges from flat to gently rolling. The 18-hole course has a slope of 99 for men and 109 for women, the ratings are 66.6 and 72.0. Open year round, daylight to dusk, reservations are advised. The women's par is 72 for a total of 5,406 yards.

During the week green fees are $9.00 for 9 holes, $18.00 for 18. On weekends it's $10.00 and $20.00. Seniors, 62 and older, can play on weekdays for $7.00 and $14.00. Clubs rent for $4.00 and handcarts $2.00. A snack bar and small pro shop are available.

Directions: Leave I-205 at Stafford Road, head south 1 mile to Mountain Road and turn left. The course is about 3 miles.

WOOD VILLAGE

HOUND HOLLOW GOLF
23010 W. Arata Rd.
Wood Village, OR
(503) 669-2290

Jim Colbert's Hound Hollow Golf Center opened in 1991 and is a links-style course. An executive 9, it is kept in good condition and open year round. Two sets of tees are available. The course operates from 7:00 a.m. to 10:00 p.m. during the summer and 8:00 a.m. to dusk in the winter. Reservations can be made one week in advance.

Weekday green fees are $7.50 for 9 holes or $12.50 for 18. On weekends you'll pay $8.50 and $17.00. Golfers 16 and younger, and those 62 and older, can play 9 holes before 4:00 p.m. during the week for $6.00. Clubs rent for a flat $4.00, handcarts $2.00, and motorized carts $9.00 per 9 holes. Facilities include a snack bar where you'll find beer and wine, plus a driving range and full-service pro shop. Lessons, and tournament planning help, are available. At the driving range you'll pay $2.50 to $6.00 for balls.

Directions: Leave I-84 eastbound at Wood Village and turn right. Go through two lights, make another right turn and follow signs.

WELCHES

THE RESORT AT THE MOUNTAIN
68010 E. Fairway Ave.
Welches, OR
(800) 669-4653

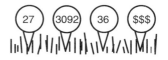

You'll find The Resort at the Mountain in a scenic valley at the edge of a Mt. Hood National Forest wilderness area. It includes three 9-hole courses with a Scottish theme and greens that are among the finest in the Northwest. The scenery is spectacular and the terrain includes hills, meadows, ponds, creeks and rivers. Reservations are needed at least two weeks in advance.

Their Pine Cone course was built in 1928 and is probably the most scenic. Thistle was built in 1966 and Foxglove in 1980. All three are open year round, weather permitting, and are mostly flat with at least one hill. The shortest course is 2,681 yards for a par of 34; the longest 3,351 yards with a par of 36.

Green fees are $20.00 for 9 holes on any course, whether or not you're staying at the resort. Resort guests can play 18 holes Monday thru Thursday for $25.00; Friday thru Sunday it's $30.00. Non-guests pay $30.00 for 18 holes Monday thru Thursday and $35.00 Friday thru Sunday. You can rent clubs for $8.00 per 9 holes, handcarts are $4.00 and motorized carts $16.00 and $26.00. This luxury resort has a fine restaurant and lounge with a liquor license, plus a complete conference center, full-service pro shop, tennis courts, and fitness center. Lessons are available.

Directions: Located 40 miles east of Portland via Highway 26.

FOREST GROVE

SUNSET GROVE GOLF CLUB
41569 N.W. Osterman
Forest Grove, OR
(503) 357-6044

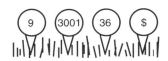

The Sunset Grove course has a rolling terrain, fairly small greens, wide fairways, two water holes, and a view of Mt. Hood off the 7th tee. It is open year round and reservations are advised. The women's par is 37 for a total distance of 2,715 yards.

Green fees are $7.00 for 9 holes during the week and $8.00 on weekends. Monday thru Friday juniors and seniors can play 9 holes for $6.00. Clubs are $3.50, handcarts $1.50, and motorized carts $8.00 per 9 holes. They have a limited pro shop and a snack shop where you will find cold beer and wine.

Directions: Located 2 miles north of town on Highway 47.

KING CITY

KING CITY GOLF CLUB
15355 S.W. Royalty Parkway
King City, OR
(503) 639-7986

The King City course is flat, narrow, and surrounded by trees and houses. A semi-private course, it is open year round, but closed to the public on Wednesday and Thursday mornings before 11:00 a.m. Reservations are advised. Many golfers consider King City's

7th hole one of the finest in the state. It's 415 yards for a par four and includes 5 traps; the lake sits 40 yards in front of the green. The women's par is 35 for a total distance of 2,347 yards.

Green fees are $10.00 per 9 holes. Seniors, 62 and older, play for $8.00 and juniors $7.00 any day of the week. Monday thru Thursday, between 2:00 p.m. and 3:00 p.m., anyone can play for $6.00. You can rent a half set of clubs for $5.00, handcarts are $2.00, and power carts $10.00 per 9 holes. You'll find a full-service pro shop, snacks, and a driving net. Ask at the pro shop for help with tournament planning or to arrange for lessons.

Directions: To get to the King City Golf Course, take the Tigard exit off I-5 and drive thru Tigard to King City. You'll find the course just past the city limits.

OREGON CITY

OREGON CITY GOLF CLUB
20124 S. Beavercreek Rd.
Oregon City, OR
(503) 656-2846

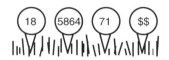

Built in 1922, this is Oregon's third oldest public course that is still in operation. It is also one of the best winter courses in the area. Because the terrain is mostly flat, and drains well, it is often playable when others are soggy. The slope is 107 and the ratings 67.3 for men, 70.8 for women. This course is open from dawn to dusk 365 days out of the year. Tee times are requested, and the women's par is 75.

Weekday green fees are $10.00 for 9 holes or $20.00 for 18. Weekend rates are $12.50 and $25.00. Juniors and seniors can play during the week for $7.00 and $14.00. Clubs rent for $5.00, handcarts $3.00, and motorized carts $15.00 and $25.00. You can arrange for lessons and tournaments at the pro shop where you'll also find a snack bar offering sandwiches and beer.

Directions: Located 1 mile south of Clackamas Community College, on Beavercreek Road.

BORING

GREENLEA GOLF COURSE
26736 S.E. Kelso Rd.
Boring, OR
(503) 663-3934

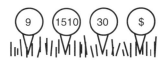

Considering its proximity to Portland, this course is a real bargain. Open from mid-February thru October, weekday hours are 8:00 a.m. to 7:00 p.m.; on weekends and holidays they open an hour earlier. This land was once a nursery and looks like a large park. It is well kept and has good drainage. You'll find very few hills here, nothing steep, and it's easy to walk. Two sets of tees make playing 18 holes possible.

During the week 9 holes will cost you $6.50; on weekends and holidays you'll pay $7.50. Clubs can be rented for $4.00 and handcarts $2.00. Motorized carts are not available, but they do have a limited pro shop.

Directions: Located 1.5 miles south of Boring, .5 mile west of the Mountain View course.

MOUNTAIN VIEW GOLF
27195 S.E. Kelso Rd.
Boring, OR
(503) 663-4869

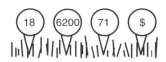

Mountain View is open year round. Built in 1964, it has a beautiful view of Mt. Hood, Adams, and St. Helens. Its rolling terrain presents a challenge to most golfers, and the 12th hole has a 200 foot vertical drop. If you haven't played this course recently, you'll discover they've changed the 13th and 14th holes. Tee times are recommended. The women's par is 73 for 5,348 yards.

Green fees during the week are $9.00 for 9 holes and $17.00 for 18, but juniors and seniors pay $7.00 for 9 or $12.00 for 18. Everybody pays $11.00 and $20.00 on weekends and holidays. Clubs rent for $5.00 per 9 holes and handcarts $2.00. Motorized carts are $11.00 and $20.00 during the week, $12.00 and $22.00 on weekends and holidays.

Amenities include a restaurant and lounge with a liquor license, plus banquet facilities, a driving range and pro shop. Lessons are available. At the driving range you can get a bucket of balls for $2.00 to $5.50.

Directions: Located 1 mile south of Boring.

EAGLE CREEK

EAGLE CREEK GOLF COURSE
25805 S.E. Dowty Rd.
Eagle Creek, OR
(503) 630-4676

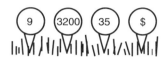

Eagle Creek opened in 1994 and eventually they plan to offer 27 holes. The terrain is flat with lots of oak and fir trees. You'll encounter lots of water, sandtraps and probably spot some wildlife during your game. The 5th hole is 617 yards, takes you over a pond for a par five, and has already gained a reputation for being one of the state's most difficult holes. Open year round, from dawn to dusk, reservations are required in the summer.

During the week you can play 9 holes at Eagle Creek for $5.00, 18 will cost you $10.00. On weekends the rates are $7.00 and $14.00. Clubs rent for $5.00 per 9 holes, handcarts $2.00, and motorized carts $8.00. They are building a new clubhouse with a view of Mt. Hood, and as they expand will offer more amenities. Tournament planning assistance is available.

Directions: Take Highway 224 to Eagle Creek and follow signs.

ESTACADA

SPRINGWATER GOLF COURSE
25230 S. Wallens Rd.
Estacada, OR
(503) 630-4586

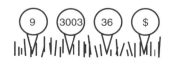

The Springwater course is situated in a picturesque spot with a great view of both Mt. Hood and Mount St. Helens. Open year round, it's flat, has good drainage, and is a good place for winter golf. The slope is 120 and the ratings 67.9 for men, 72.8 for women. From the ladies tees the total distance is 2,479 yards. Men and women each have two sets of tees, adding variety to an 18- hole game. From April to November tee times are required on weekends and holidays.

During the week green fees are $7.50 for 9 holes or $15.00 for 18. On weekends and holidays it'll cost you $9.50 or $19.00. On weekdays golfers over 60, and those in high school or younger, can play 9 holes for $6.00. Clubs can be rented for $4.00, handcarts $1.00, and motorized carts $8.00 per 9 holes. Facilities include a snack bar which offers beer and wine, plus a pro shop and practice green. Lessons are available.

Directions: The Springwater Golf Course is located 4 miles south of Estacada.

DUNDEE

RIVERWOOD GOLF COURSE
21050 S.E. Riverwood Rd.
Dundee, OR
(503) 864-2667

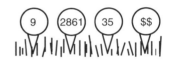

The Riverwood course is flat, open year round, and situated in a country setting with a view of Mt. Hood and surrounding wine fields. Built in 1932, this is the oldest established golf course in Yamhill County. You'll find two sets of tees, narrow fairways, and lots of trees, water and bunkers. The slope is 117 and the ratings 67.4 for men, 69.3 for women. Tee times are necessary March thru October, and spectators are not allowed on the course. They close only on Christmas Day.

Green fees are $10.00 for 9 holes or $19.00 for 18 all week long. During the week golfers 62 and over can play 9 holes for $7.50, and students age 9 thru high school play for $7.00. Clubs rent for $4.50, handcarts $1.50, and motorized carts $8.00 per 9 holes.

They have a restaurant open March thru October, and a year round snack bar, pro shop, banquet facilities and driving range. Beer and wine are sold on site, plus they offer golf lessons and help with tournaments. The driving range has both mat and grass tees depending on the weather and time of year.

Directions: Dundee is on Highway 99, between Newberg and McMinnville, and the course is well marked.

WILSONVILLE

CHARBONNEAU GOLF COURSE
32020 Charbonneau Dr.
Wilsonville, OR
(503) 694-1246

You'll find three 9- hole courses at Charbonneau. Each has a par of 31 and three sets of tees. The total distance on the North 9 is 2,113 yards, the West 9 is 2,007, and the East 9 is 2,148. Located south of Portland, this flat course has a nice view of Mt. Hood. Open year round, reservations are taken two weeks in advance.

Weekday green fees are $12.00 for 9 holes or $20.00 for 18. On weekends and holidays it's $12.00 and $22.00. Juniors, under 17, can play 9 holes during the week for $5.00. Clubs rent for $5.00 and $8.00, handcarts $1.00 and $2.00, and motorized carts $12.00 and $22.00. Facilities include a restaurant/lounge with a liquor license, plus a driving range and full-service pro shop. At the range you get a small bucket of balls for $1.75. Lessons, and help with tournament planning, are available.

Directions: Leave I-5 at exit #282B, turn left and follow the signs.

McMINNVILLE

BAYOU GOLF COURSE
9301 S.W. Bayou Dr.
McMinnville, OR
(503) 472-4651

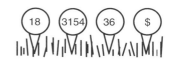

Bayou has both a short par three and a more challenging 9-hole course. That second course has a slope of 118 and ratings of 70.2

70.2 for men, 68.2 for women. Fairly flat, but challenging, it is situated on a gently rolling river delta with the South Yamhill River along its southern edge. A new tee on the third hole lets you choose to shoot across a pond for an additional challenge. The course is closed only on Christmas and Thanksgiving. Tee times are needed on weekends and holidays from April thru September.

Par 3 green fees are $5.00 for 9 holes or $10.00 for 18 all week long. On the longer course they are $10.00 and $18.00 on weekends and holidays, $9.00 and $16.00 the rest of the week. Juniors and seniors can play the big 9 weekdays before 4:00 p.m. for $7.00 and $13.00, and after 4:00 p.m. on weekends and holidays for $8.00 and $15.00. They can also play the par 3 anytime for $4.00 per 9 holes; children under 12 play for $3.00. Clubs can be rented for $3.00 and $6.00, handcarts $2.00 and $3.00, and motorized carts $10.00 and $18.00.

Facilities include a colonial mansion clubhouse that some believe is haunted by the founder's ghost, plus a snack bar that serves beer and wine, a banquet room, driving range, and full service pro shop. They offer lessons and can help you with tournament planning. The driving range is open March thru October, offers grass tees, and buckets of balls for $2.00 to $3.00.

Directions: Bayou is located 1 mile south of McMinnville, along Highway 99W.

CANBY

FRONTIER GOLF COURSE
2965 N. Holly
Canby, OR
(503) 266-4435

This is another one of those great places where golf is still cheap. Frontier is open March thru October, and a nice place to hone your skills. The flat terrain makes it easy to walk and the course is surrounded by farms. Deer occasionally wander across the fairways.

Green fees are $5.50 per 9 holes. Juniors can play 18 holes for $10.00 and seniors, older than 60, pay $4.00 for 9 holes or $7.50

for 18. Clubs rent for $2.00 and handcarts $1.50. They have a limited pro shop where you will find snacks, beer, and wine.

Directions: Leave I-5 at the Canby exit and follow signs toward the Canby Ferry; it's about 4 miles from I-5.

MULINO

RANCH HILLS GOLF COURSE
26710 S. Ranch Hills Rd.
Mulino, OR
(503) 632-6848

Ranch Hills is pretty with a creek winding its way through the middle of the course, and its own covered bridge. The terrain is flat and challenging, and the course open year round. Three sets of tees are available. Reservations are not needed, but you might want to check their tournament schedule. From the women's tees it's a total distance of 2,636 yards for a par of 37.

During the week you'll pay $8.00 per 9 holes; on weekends it'll cost you $9.00. Clubs are available for $3.50, handcarts $1.50, and motorized carts $10.00 per 9 holes. Facilities include a lounge and snack bar where you can purchase cold beer and wine. They also have a full-service pro shop and a covered warm-up range where you get a bucket of balls for $2.00. Lessons, and help with tournament planning, are available.

Directions: Head south out of Oregon City on Molalla Avenue. After 9 miles turn left on Passmore and follow signs.

AURORA

LANGDON FARMS GOLF CLUB
24377 N.E. Airport Rd.
Aurora, OR
(503) 678-4653

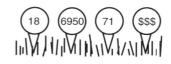

Langdon Farms opened in 1995, and was designed by John Fought and Bob Cupp. The slope is 125 and the rating 71.8.

Open year round, from sunup to sundown, reservations are available up to two months in advance. This easy-to-walk championship course offers large bent grass tees and a public resort atmosphere. Located in a farming community, the clubhouse is housed in a big red barn.

Green fees include the use of a motorized cart and vary depending on the season and time of day. Special discounts are available to seasonal cardholders, and they offer a nice twilight discount. Friday thru Sunday rates range from $20.00 to $60.00; the balance of the week it's $20.00 to $50.00. The cheapest rates are available November thru April, and credit cards are accepted for green fees. You can rent a set of Titlist clubs for $25.00.

Facilities include a restaurant/lounge with a liquor license, a full-service pro shop and driving range. The range has a large grass teeing area plus 28 lighted stalls. It's open until 9:00 p.m. in the summer but closes an hour earlier the rest of the year. The charge is $2.50 per 15 minutes. You can also get help with tournament planning and they can arrange lessons.

Directions: Leave I-5 at exit 282, just south of Wilsonville, go east 1/4 mile, turn right onto Airport Road and follow to course.

WOODBURN

TUKWILA OGA MEMBER'S COURSE
2990 S.W. Boones Ferry Rd.
Woodburn, OR
(503) 981-6105

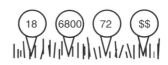

The first 9 holes at Tukwila opened in late 1994, the second in 1996. Designed by Bill Robinson, this year-round course operates dawn to dusk. The terrain is flat and easy to walk with some mounding. It contains several lakes, natural wetlands, a filbert orchard, and mature evergreens. Four sets of tees are available and reservations are taken one week in advance.

Non-member green fees are $18.00 for 9 holes or $32.00 for 18 on weekdays, $20.00 and $37.00 on weekends. Join the OGA, which is around $30.00 per year, and you can play for $13.00 and $22.00 during the week or $14.00 and $24.00 on weekends.

Juniors, age 17 and younger, can play 9 holes for $6.00 or 18 for $12.00. Clubs rent for $10.00, handcarts $2.00, and motorized carts $10.00 per 9 holes.

Facilities include a member clubhouse with cold beer, plus a golf museum, full-service pro shop, 12,000-square-foot putting green and a driving range. Help with tournament planning, and lessons, are available. At the driving range you get 30 balls for $2.00.

Directions: Leave I-5 at the Woodburn exit, turn left, go 1 mile to Boones Ferry Road, turn left again and follow the signs.

WOODBURN GOLF COURSE
Highway 14
Woodburn, OR
No Phone

This is one of the cheapest places to play golf in Oregon. It is open year round, flat, and easy to walk. This land was once planted as an orchard, and you'll find fruit trees scattered amongst the pines. The course was built in 1925 by a group of local businessmen who sold 100 shares to finance it. This is the only sand-green course in the state.

The Woodburn Golf Course operates on the honor system. Current fees are posted and are only a few bucks. You register and pay at the box on the east side of the clubhouse. Annual memberships are available. Facilities are limited, and the women's par is 37.

Directions: Located 1.5 miles west of I-5 via the Woodburn exit.

MT. ANGEL

EVERGREEN GOLF CLUB
11694 W. Church Road N.E.
Mt. Angel, OR
(503) 845-9911

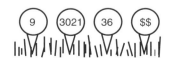

The terrain at Evergreen is rolling, but not hilly, making it easy to walk. It's well maintained and open year round. Built in 1962, the slope is 110 and the rating 68.6. The women's par is 37. You'll find lots of trees, a couple of small ponds, plus a beautiful view of Mt. Hood. Reservations are advised for spring and summer weekends. Men have this course all to themselves on Thursday mornings, women on Tuesday mornings.

Green fees are $11.00 for 9 holes and $20.00 for 18 during the week; on the weekends it'll cost you $12.00 and $21.00. On Mondays, Wednesdays and Fridays senior golfers play for $9.00 and $16.00. Clubs can be rented for $5.00, handcarts $2.00, and motorized carts $10.00 per 9 holes. Facilities include a restaurant and lounge with a liquor license and banquet rooms. You can arrange for lessons at the full-service pro shop, and get help with tournament planning.

Directions: Drive 1.5 miles east of town on Church Road.

DALLAS

SANDSTRIP GOLF COURSE
11875 Orrs Corner Rd.
Dallas, OR
(503) 623-6832

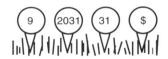

Sandstrip is fairly flat with some trees and water. Built in 1989, it was designed by John Zoller and Bruce Perisho. This is a challenging executive course with small greens. The slope is 91 and the rating 58.2. Open year round, tee times are needed only on weekends.

Green fees are $8.00 for 9 holes or $14.00 for 18. Juniors can play for $4.00 and $8.00, seniors for $7.00 and $13.00. Clubs are available for $3.00, handcarts $1.00 per 9, and power carts $7.00 for 9 holes or $14.00 for 18. They offer a full-service pro shop and a driving range. At the range you'll find both mat and grass tees and can get a small bucket of balls for $2.00 or a large one for $3.50. Ask at the pro shop for help with tournament planning or golf lessons.

Directions: Take Highway 22 to Highway 99S and drive 1 mile to Orrs Corner Road. The course is 3 miles west.

SALEM

AUBURN CENTER GOLF
5220 Center St. N.E.
Salem, OR
(503) 363-4404

Auburn Center Golf is only closed on Christmas Day. It has flat, tree-lined fairways that present a challenge to even the most accurate golfer. It is also one of the most reasonably priced courses around.

Seven days a week green fees are $6.00 for 9 holes, $10.00 for 18, or $13.00 to play all day. Golfers younger than 16, or older than 64, can play 9 holes for $5.00 or 18 for $8.00. Clubs rent for $2.00 and handcarts $1.50. Motorized carts are not available. Facilities include a snack bar, limited pro shop, and a miniature golf course.

Directions: Take the Market Street exit off I-5, head east to Lancaster, go south to Center Street, and east 1.5 miles.

BATTLE CREEK GOLF COURSE
6161 Commercial St. S.E.
Salem, OR
(503) 585-1402

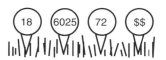

Battle Creek is in a flat, wooded area and has a creek flowing through it. The course slope is 117 and the rating 68.8. Three tees are available for each hole. This site was named for the 1846 skirmish between early settlers and neighboring Indians that happened nearby. Open year round, reservations are taken one week in advance.

Weekday green fees are $12.00 for 9 holes or $20.00 for 18. On weekends and holidays it'll cost you $13.00 and $22.00. Clubs rent for $3.00 and $5.00, handcarts $2.00 and $3.00, and motorized carts $10.00 per 9 holes. Facilities include a restaurant and lounge with a liquor license and banquet rooms. At the full-service pro shop you can get help with tournament planning and arrange for lessons.

Directions: Leave I-5 at the Kuebler exit, go west to Commercial Street, turn south and drive 1 mile.

COTTONWOOD LAKES GOLF
3225 River Rd. S.
Salem, OR
(503) 364-3673

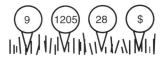

Built in 1991, this year-round course is open 8:00 a.m. to dusk during the week, and 7:00 a.m. to dusk on weekends. It's flat, easy to walk, and offers a pleasant close-in country escape. You'll find lots of water and plenty of trees to keep your game sharp. Two sets of tees are available, and reservations are not taken.

This is another bargain course; you'll pay $6.00 per 9 holes. Juniors, age 17 and under, pay $4.00 per 9 holes and seniors, 60 and older, can play for $5.00. During the winter you can play all day for $10.00. Clubs rent for $4.00 and handcarts $1.00. They have a driving range where you can get balls for $2.50 to $7.50 per bucket. Both individual and group lessons are available.

Directions: Leave South Commercial on Owen, which soon becomes River Road, and follow for 2 miles.

CREEKSIDE GOLF CLUB
6250 Clubhouse Dr. S.E.
Salem, OR
(503) 363-4653

This semi-private course has over 100 bunkers, water on 12 holes, and mature trees. The 16th hole requires golfers to shoot the ball through a narrow opening in a stand of Douglas fir. Designed by Peter Jacobsen and Jim Hardy, it opened in late 1993. The terrain is gently rolling and five sets of tees are available. Total distance from the ladies' tees is 5,265 yards. They open at 6:00 a.m. on weekends and 7:00 a.m. during the week. Non-members can get reservations five days in advance.

Friday thru Sunday, and holidays, green fees are $20.00 for 9 holes or $34.00 for 18. The rest of the week it's $18.00 and $28.00. Juniors, 17 and younger, play for $12.50 and $24.00, and seniors, 60 and older, pay $15.00 and $28.00. Clubs rent for $10.00 and $15.00, handcarts $2.00, and motorized carts $12.00 and $20.00. They have a snack bar offering cold beer, plus a full-service pro shop and driving range. Lessons are available.

Directions: Leave I-5 at the Kuebler exit, head west to Sunnyside, and go south 1 mile to the course.

McNARY GOLF CLUB
6255 River Rd. N.
Salem, OR
(503) 393-4653

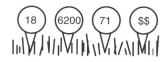

McNary is flat with elevated greens. A semi-private course, it has been in existence since 1962. You'll find several lakes, a creek, and a growing number of sand traps to keep your aim sharp. It also offers a nice view of Mt. Hood when the skies are clear. Open year round, reservations are given one week in advance. The women's par is 71 for a total distance of 5,600 yards.

You'll pay $13.00 for 9 holes, $25.00 for 18, all week long. Seniors can play before 11:00 a.m. on Mondays and Wednesdays for $11.00 and $20.00. Clubs rent for $5.00, handcarts $2.00, and motorized carts $10.00 per 9 holes.

Facilities include a restaurant and lounge with a liquor license, banquet facilities that will seat 200, a full-service pro shop, and practice greens. Help with lessons, and tournament planning, are available.

Directions: McNary is 5 miles north of Salem, 1 mile west of I-5.

MEADOWLAWN GOLF COURSE
3898 Meadowlawn Loop S.E.
Salem, OR
(503) 363-7391

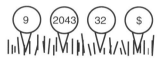

Meadowlawn was once a dairy farm and is not as easy as it looks. The terrain is flat with elevated greens, and the course is fast in the summer. Tee times are given only for weekend play.

Green fees are $9.00 per 9 holes all week long. You can rent clubs for $5.00, handcarts $2.00, and motorized carts $9.00 for 9 holes or $17.00 for 18.

Facilities include a full-service pro shop and a snack bar. Beer and wine is available, and you can arrange for lessons and get help with tournament planning.

Directions: Take the Market Street exit off I-5 and head down Lancaster. Go past State Street and after the road curves turn at the second light and follow the signs.

SALEM GOLF CLUB
2025 Golf Course Rd. S.
Salem, OR
(503) 363-6652

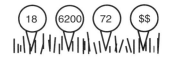

The Salem Golf Club course opened in 1928, and is the oldest in the city. This gently rolling course is easy to walk, has lots of trees and many large pines. Three sets of tees give it variety. The slope is 118 and the ratings 69.6 for men, 72.9 for women. Reservations are taken two days ahead for weekday play, and beginning on Monday for the following weekend. The course is open year round.

Green fees are $15.00 for 9 holes, or $30.00 for 18, all week long. Juniors can play for $10.00 and $20.00. Clubs rent for $10.00, handcarts $1.00, and motorized carts $25.00. Credit cards are welcome. They have a restaurant and lounge with a liquor license and banquet room, plus a snack bar, full-service pro shop, and driving range. Lessons, and help with tournament planning, are available.

Directions: Located 2 miles from downtown Salem via South River Road.

STAYTON

SANTIAM GOLF CLUB
Highway 22
Stayton, OR
(503) 769-3485

Built in 1958, the Santiam Golf Club course is flat and open year round. The greens are kept in excellent shape and hazards include trees, sand bunkers, a creek and lake. The slope is 123 and the ratings 69.9 for men, 72.2 for women. There are three tees for every hole.

Green fees are $13.00 for 9 holes and $22.00 for 18, all week long. Clubs rent for $4.00 and motorized carts $11.00 for 9 holes or $20.00 for 18. They have a restaurant and lounge with a liquor license, plus banquet facilities, a driving range, and full-service pro shop. At the driving range you'll pay $1.50 to $3.00 for a bucket of balls. They can also help you with tournament planning and arrange for lessons.

Directions: Take exit #253 off I-5 and go 12 miles east on Highway 22.

INDEPENDENCE

OAK KNOLL GOLF COURSE
6335 Highway 22
Independence, OR
(503) 378-0344

There has been a golf course at this location since 1926. Oak Knoll offers a flat to rolling terrain, has three ponds, and a nice view of the Coast Mountains. The slope is 111 and the ratings 67.1 for men, 69.2 for women. Open 7:00 a.m. to dusk year round, reservations are recommended on weekends. The women's total yardage is 5,239.

Green fees are $12.00 for 9 holes and $20.00 for 18. Juniors, age 18 and younger, can play during the week for $10.00 and $18.00. Seniors can play before 3:00 p.m. Monday thru Friday for $10.00 and $18.00.

Couples will find special rates on Tuesdays and Fridays, $17.00 for 9 holes or $34.00 for 18. Clubs rent for $5.00, handcarts $2.00, and power carts are $10.00 per 9 holes. Credit cards are welcome.

You'll find a restaurant and lounge with a liquor license, help with tournament planning, and a driving range at Oak Knoll. They offer group and private lessons. At the driving range they have both covered mats and grass tees. You get a small bucket of balls for $1.50, medium for $2.00, or a large one for $4.00. The range is open from 7:00 a.m. to dusk.

Directions: To find the Oak Knoll Golf Course, leave I-5 at the Highway 22/Ocean Beaches exit. This will take you through Salem, then you will head west 7 miles.

LYONS

ELKHORN VALLEY GOLF CLUB
Box 32295 North Fork Rd.
Lyons, OR
(503) 897-3368

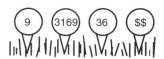

It took Don Cutler 11 years to build this course, but when it opened in 1976 most area golfers agreed it was worth the wait! Situated in a beautiful mountain valley, it offers a view of eight mountain peaks. The slope is 136 and the ratings 71.4 for men, 63.6 for women. You'll find four tees for every hole. This is one of the best 9-hole courses in the United States. The 6th hole requires you to get your ball across a canyon for a par three; a second canyon, plus plenty of water, make it very challenging.

The terrain is flat and easy to walk, and the course is open March thru October. Reservations are recommended. To get a weekend tee time you often have to call weeks in advance. The total yardage from the ladies' tees is 2,445.

Green fees are $15.00 for 9 holes or $25.00 for 18. Juniors, those 16 and under, can play for $10.00 and $18.00. Clubs rent for $5.00, handcarts $2.00, and motorized carts $10.00 per 9 holes. Credit cards are welcome. You'll find cold snacks, sandwiches, beer and wine in the pro shop.

Directions: To find Elkhorn Valley, from Lyons, take North Fork Road east 11 miles.

ALBANY

GOLF CLUB OF OREGON
905 N.W. Spring Hill Dr.
Albany, OR
(541) 928-8338

Located on a gently rolling river delta, this year-round course is a good place to improve your accuracy. You'll find several elevated greens and a well-maintained course with greens that hold all year. The original 9 was built in 1929, the second 9 added in

1951. The slope ranges from 104 to 109 and the ratings from 66.6 to 68.5. Reservations are available 7 days in advance. The par from the women's tees is 71 for a total distance of 5,076 yards.

Green fees are $11.00 for 9 holes or $20.00 for 18. Seniors, age 62 and over, can play Monday thru Friday for $9.00 and $17.00. Juniors, those in high school and younger, can also play for reduced rates. You can rent clubs for $4.00 and $6.00, handcarts $2.00 and $3.00, and motorized carts for $10.00 per 9 holes.

Facilities include a restaurant where beer and wine is served, plus a full-service pro shop. They offer help with tournament planning and can arrange golf lessons.

Directions: Located north of Highway 20, across the Willamette River from downtown Albany.

LEBANON

PINEWAY GOLF COURSE
30949 Pineway Rd.
Lebanon, OR
(541) 258-8815

Pineway is slightly hilly with elevated greens. Nestled in the side of a hill, it offers a particularly beautiful setting with a wonderful view of the Cascade Mountains. It is open year round, and reservations are advised as they are sometimes booked for tournaments.

Green fees remain the same seven days a week, $10.00 for 9 holes or $18.00 for 18. Clubs rent for $3.50, and motorized carts are $10.00 for 9 holes or $16.00 for 18.

Facilities include a driving range, and a pro shop where you can arrange for lessons and get help with tournament planning. Pineway's restaurant/lounge has a liquor license and offers a great view of the course. You can get a bucket of balls at the driving range for $2.25 to $3.00.

Directions: Located 3.5 miles east of town on Highway 20.

CORVALLIS

GOLF CITY
2115 Highway 20
Corvallis, OR
(541) 753-6213

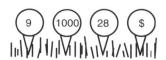

Golf City is flat, and a great place for beginners. Its 8th hole is one of the shortest known par fours around, measuring just 85 yards. The other 8 holes are all par threes on this year-round course. Reservations are not available.

Green fees are $4.50 during the week, $5.00 on weekends. Monday thru Friday juniors and seniors can play before 3:00 p.m. for $3.50. Facilities include a snack bar with a liquor license, a full-service pro shop, and an 18-hole miniature golf course.

Directions: Take Highway 20 north of Corvallis 2.5 miles.

MARYSVILLE GOLF COURSE
2020 S.W. Allen St.
Corvallis, OR
(541) 753-3421

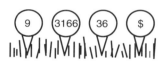

Marysville is a family owned course that was built in 1958. It is relatively flat, offers easy walking, and has no sand traps. You'll find it open year round. The women's tees have a total distance of 2,666 yards for a par of 36.

Green fees at Marysville are $8.00 on weekdays, $9.00 on weekends and holidays. Annual rates are available. Clubs and handcarts each rent for $2.00. Facilities include a minimal pro shop where you'll find light snacks and cold beer.

Directions: Take Highway 99 south of Corvallis .5 mile.

TRYSTING TREE GOLF CLUB
34028 Electric Rd.
Corvallis, OR
(541) 752-3332

This year-round course opened in 1987. Hazards include lots of water and plenty of mounds. With four sets of tees the distance ranges from 5,516 to 7,014 yards. During the spring and summer you can get on the course at 7:00 a.m. and they close at dusk; the rest of the year they do not open until 8:00 a.m. Reservations are taken one week in advance.

Green fees are $14.00 for 9 holes or $23.00 for 18 all week long. Juniors, under age 17, pay just $5.00 most afternoons, and full-time students attending college in Oregon play for $8.00 and $12.00. Clubs rent for $7.50, handcarts $2.00, and motorized carts $12.00 for 9 holes or $22.00 for 18.

Facilities include a snack bar where you'll find cold beer and wine, a full-service pro shop, and driving range. At the range you'll pay $1.25 for 22 balls. Lessons, and help with tournament planning, are available.

Directions: Take Highway 34 west of I-5 about 9 miles.

LEABURG

McKENZIE RIVER GOLF COURSE
41723 Madrone
Leaburg, OR
(541) 896-3454

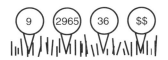

This year-round course is situated along the McKenzie River. The terrain is flat with only one hill, making it easy to walk. Two sets of tees provide variety when playing 18 holes. Reservations are taken one week in advance throughout the summer.

A 9-hole game will cost you $11.00, seven days a week. On weekends and holidays you'll pay $19.00 for 18 holes, on weekdays it'll cost you $18.00. Juniors pay just $5.00 per 9 holes on weekdays when accompanied by a playing adult. Clubs rent for $5.00, handcarts $1.50, and motorized carts $9.00 per 9 holes. Facilities include a pro shop and a snack bar where you can get cold beer. Help with tournament planning is available.

Directions: Located 10 miles northeast of Springfield via Highway 126, .5 mile beyond milepost #117.

BLUE RIVER

TOKATEE GOLF CLUB
54947 McKenzie Hwy.
Blue River, OR
(541) 822-3220 or (800) 452-6376

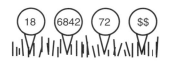

Golf Digest ranks Tokatee among America's top public courses, and its location is one of the prettiest in Oregon. The snow-capped peaks of Three Sisters present a beautiful backdrop for this lake-dotted course. It was designed by Ted Robinson and opened in 1966. The terrain is generally flat with some rolling hills, and you'll find three tees per hole. Reservations are advised, and within Oregon the call is toll free. They open about mid-February and close in mid-November.

Green fees are $16.00 for 9 holes or $30.00 for 18, but you can buy 10-play cards for $100.00 and $180.00. Juniors, those under 18, can play for $5.00, and college students receive special rates off-season. Club rental is $7.50 for a half set and $12.50 for a full set; handcarts are $3.00, and motorized carts $14.00 and $23.00. Facilities include a restaurant offering beer and wine, plus a banquet room, full-service pro shop and driving range. Lessons and help with tournament planning are available. At the driving range you'll find grass tees and can get a bucket of balls for $2.00. Credit cards are accepted for green fees.

Directions: Located in Blue River, 47.5 miles east of Eugene, on Highway 126.

EUGENE

FIDDLER'S GREEN GOLF COURSE
91292 Highway 99N
Eugene, OR
(541) 689-8464

Fiddler's Green is one of Oregon's finest par three courses and offers level, easy walking. Designed by John Zoller Sr., it opened in 1963. A year-round course, green fees are $6.00 for 9 holes or

$10.50 for 18. Seniors can play for $4.50 and $7.50. You can rent clubs for $2.50 and handcarts are $1.50. Credit cards are welcome.

Facilities include a lighted driving range that offers both covered and open turf. It has mat tees and you get a large bucket of balls for $3.00. You'll also find an indoor video lesson studio with four cameras to help you monitor your performance, personalized instruction, one of the largest on-course pro shops in North America, plus a snack bar where beer and wine is available. Children are not permitted on the course or driving range unless they are golfing.

Directions: Fiddler's Green is located on Highway 99N, 2 miles north of the airport.

LAURELWOOD GOLF COURSE
2700 Columbia
Eugene, OR
(541) 687-5321

The Laurelwood course opened in 1929 as Eugene's first country club, and sits in the heart of the city. The 1st hole is considered one of the top 10 holes in Oregon, and is 540 yards for a par of five. It has rolling hills, sloped greens, mature trees, and is rated 67.9 for men, 69.1 for women. Open year round, tee times are advisable Friday thru Sunday as well as holidays, from April thru October. Call 484-GOLF for reservations. The total yardage from the women's tees is 2,460.

Weekday green fees are $8.00 for 9 holes or $13.00 for 18. On weekends it's $9.00 and $14.00. Non-holiday weekday mornings juniors and seniors can play for $6.00 and $11.00. Clubs are $4.00 and $7.00, handcarts $2.00 and $3.00, and motorized carts $9.00 and $17.00. Facilities include a full-service pro shop where you can get a cold beer, plus a driving range with mat tees. At the range you get a bucket of balls for $2.00 to $4.25 depending on the size of the bucket. They can provide help with tournament planning, as well as golf lessons, club repair and custom clubs.

Directions: Leave I-5 northbound at the 30th Avenue exit and turn right onto Hilyard. Go right again on 24th and follow the signs. From I-5 southbound take the Eugene exit, follow the signs to Franklin Blvd., turn right onto Agate, and left onto 24th.

OAKWAY GOLF COURSE
2000 Cal Young Rd.
Eugene, OR
(541) 484-1927

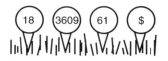

Designed by John Zoller, Oakway was built in 1983 and is open year round, weather permitting. Its terrain is slightly rolling, and the greens well kept, with some water, elevated tees and lots of sand traps. The slope is 82 for men, 90 for women, and the ratings 58 and 60. Reservations are not taken. The total distance from the ladies' tees is 3,117 yards.

Green fees at this executive 18 are $9.00 for 9 holes and $16.00 for 18. Juniors, age 17 and under, play for $5.00 and $9.00. On weekdays seniors can play 9 holes for $7.00 or 18 for $12.00. Clubs rent for $5.00, handcarts $2.00, and motorized carts are $9.00 and $16.00. You'll find a restaurant where beer and wine is served, plus a full-service pro shop, two mat practice cages, a large putting green and practice area. They can also help with tournament planning and arrange lessons.

Directions: Leave I-5 at I-105, head west to the Coburg Road exit, at the intersection turn right onto Oakway Road, follow this road to its end and turn left.

RIVERIDGE GOLF COURSE
3800 N. Delta Hwy.
Eugene, OR
(541) 345-9160

Riveridge is set along the Willamette River, and although fairly flat does have some hills. Hours are 7:00 a.m. to 8:00 p.m. year round. Designed by Ric Jeffries, it was opened in 1988. With four sets of tees, the slope is 112 to 116, and the ratings range from 67.7 to 68.8. Tee times are suggested, but not required.

Green fees are $13.00 for 9 holes or $22.00 for 18. Seniors play for $8.00 and $15.00. Juniors receive seasonal specials allowing them to play 9 holes for $5.00; call for information. Clubs can be rented for $6.00 and $10.00, handcarts will cost you $2.00, and motorized carts are $12.00 for 9 holes or $20.00 for 18.

Facilities include a driving range, plus a snack bar where beer and wine is available and a full-service pro shop. Lessons are offered and you can get help with tournament planning. At the driving range you'll find 27 covered stalls and 10 uncovered. You can get a small bucket of balls for $2.50, or a large one for $4.00.

Directions: Take Delta Highway 1 mile north of Beltline.

CRESWELL

EMERALD VALLEY GOLF CLUB
83301 Dale Kuni Rd.
Creswell, OR
(541) 895-2174

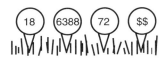

Three of the par fours at Emerald Valley have a reputation for being among the most difficult holes in Oregon. The slope is 126 and the ratings 73.0 for men, 74.7 for women. Although the course is open year round, it is occasionally closed for tournaments so you might want to call ahead.

Reservations are taken one week in advance. Emerald Valley was built in 1964, and the fairways are level to gently rolling with three sets of tees. The total yardage from the women's tees is 6,371 for a par of 73.

On weekends it will cost you $17.00 for 9 holes or $27.00 for 18; it's $14.00 and $24.00 during the week. Golfers 62 and older can play 9 holes before noon on weekdays for $10.00, or 18 for $19.00. Juniors get to play anytime Monday thru Friday for $6.00 and $11.00, and everybody gets a bargain during twilight hours. Clubs are $8.00 for 9 holes or $14.00 for 18, handcarts $2.00 and $3.00, and motorized carts $12.00 and $20.00.

Facilities include a restaurant/lounge with a liquor license and a driving range. A bucket of balls is $2.00 to $3.50 at the range, and you'll find both grass and mat tees. Lessons are available, as well as help with tournament planning, ask at the pro shop. Credit cards can be used to pay green fees.

Directions: Leave I-5 at the Creswell exit, go east on Cloverdale Road to Dale Kuni Road and the course.

OAKRIDGE

CIRCLE BAR GOLF COURSE
48447 Westoak Rd.
Oakridge, OR
(541) 782-3541

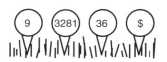

This year-round course has a flat terrain with a few good hills and only closes for snow storms. It sits in a valley, surrounded by hills, at an elevation of 1200 foot. Circle Bar opened in the early 1950s, has a slope of 119, and ratings of 70.8 for men, 73.0 for women. You'll find three tees per hole; the ladies' tees have a par of 37 for a total distance of 2,985 yards. Summer hours are 8:00 a.m. to 6:00 p.m., the balance of the year it's 9:00 a.m. to 5:00 p.m. Reservations are taken for summer weekends.

Weekday green fees are $7.00 for 9 holes or $12.00 for 18. On weekends you'll pay $9.00 and $15.00. Local juniors should call for reduced rates. The pro shop is limited and open March thru October, as well as most weekends. Clubs and handcarts can each be rented for $2.00 and $3.00, and motorized carts are $7.00 and $12.00. During the summer season they offer banquet facilities, help with tournament planning, and a snack bar where you'll find cold beer and wine.

Directions: Located in Oakridge, just follow the signs.

COTTAGE GROVE

HIDDEN VALLEY
Woodson Street
Cottage Grove, OR
(541) 942-3046

The Hidden Valley course is pretty flat with small hills on four holes. Each fairway has two sets of tees so you can play 18 with variety. Open year round, dawn to dusk, call ahead for tee times. The women's par is 36.

Weekday green fees are $8.00 for 9 holes or $14.00 for 18. On weekends and holidays it's $9.00 and $16.00. Ten-game punch cards are available for $60.00 and can be used any day of the week; senior punch cards are $50.00 but can only be used on weekdays. Juniors can play 9 holes during the week for $4.00 and on weekends for $5.00. Clubs rent for $3.00, handcarts $2.00, and motorized carts $11.00 for 9 holes or $16.00 for 18.

Facilities include a restaurant and lounge with a liquor license and banquet facilities. You can arrange for lessons at the full-service pro shop.

Directions: Leave I-5 at exit #174 and follow the signs. From Highway 99 heading south you turn right at the first signal onto Woodson. The course is behind the Elks Lodge.

MIDDLEFIELD VILLAGE COURSE
91 Village Dr.
Cottage Grove, OR
(541) 942-8730

When you play the softly rolling fairways at Middlefield, you'll encounter a sporty course lined with trees. Beginning and average players will like this course because it's not too long; better golfers will enjoy its interesting layout. Situated along the Row River, and open year round, it was designed by Bunny Mason. Weekdays you'll need to call 24 hours ahead for reservations; call on Tuesdays for weekend tee times.

Weekend green fees are $14.00 for 9 holes and $22.00 for 18, the rest of the week it's $11.00 and $19.00. Seniors pay $9.00 and $15.00 during the week, $11.00 and $17.00 on weekends. A 20-game punch card brings the cost of 9 holes down to $6.25 for seniors and $8.75 for others on non-holiday weekdays. Annual memberships are also available and allow unlimited play throughout the year. Clubs rent for $6.00 and $10.00, handcarts $2.00 and $4.00, and motorized carts $12.00 and $20.00.

Facilities include a full-service pro shop, driving range, and a deli where you can get cold beer. They also have an on-site golf school and offer both individual and group lessons. At the driving range grass tees are available during golf season; in the winter you practice from covered astroturf. You get 30 balls for $2.00.

Directions: Leave I-5 on exit #174 and go east 2 blocks, turn left and follow the signs.

SUTHERLIN

SUTHERLIN KNOLLS GOLF COURSE
1919 Recreation Ln.
Sutherlin, OR
(541) 459-4422

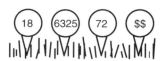

Sutherlin Knolls is in a beautiful country setting. It has rolling hills, wooded areas, and wildlife. It's a challenging older course with many new features and continual upgrades. They are open year round from daylight to dusk, and reservations are advised. The women's par is 75 for a total yardage of 5,636.

Green fees are $10.00 for 9 holes or $18.00 for 18 all week long. You can rent clubs for $3.50, handcarts $2.00, and motorized carts are $10.00 for 9 holes or $18.00 for 18. Facilities include a restaurant and lounge with a liquor license, plus a banquet room, pro shop, and driving range. The range charges $1.00 to $3.00 for a bucket of balls, depending on how many you need.

Directions: Leave I-5 at exit #36 and head west on 138th.

ROSEBURG

STEWART PARK GOLF COURSE
1005 Stewart Parkway
Roseburg, OR
(541) 672-4592

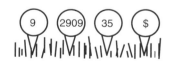

The Stewart Park course has rolling hills, bent grass greens, and a variety of vegetation and wildlife. It is open year round, from dawn to dusk. From the men's tees the slope is 112 with a rating of 68.7; the women's tees have a slope of 118 and a rating of 73.5. Par for women is 37 over a distance of 2,835 yards. Reservations are taken 7 days in advance.

During the week green fees are $7.50 for 9 holes or $13.00 for 18. On weekends you'll pay $9.00 and $13.00. Seniors, age 62 and over, can play 9 holes on weekdays for $6.75 or 18 for $11.75. Juniors, age 17 and younger, can play 9 holes for $5.00. Credit cards are accepted for green fees. Facilities include a restaurant where beer and wine is available, plus a full-service pro shop, and driving range. The range offers both mat and grass tees and charges $1.50 for 30 balls. Lessons, and help with tournament planning, are available.

Directions: Leave I-5 at the Stewart Parkway exit and head west.

GRANTS PASS

APPLEGATE GOLF
7350 New Hope Rd.
Grants Pass, OR
(541) 955-0480

This new course was designed by John T. Briggs and opened late in 1994. The slope is 104 with a rating of 65.8 for men, 114 and 69.8 for women. You'll find water on 8 holes, a flat terrain, plenty of natural trees, and a dogleg on the 6th hole with a par four. Open year round dawn to dusk, tee times are required for weekend play. Early golfers often spot deer and Osprey.

Summer green fees are $10.00 for 9 holes or $15.00 for 18. Winter rates are $7.00 and $12.00. Juniors always play for half price, and golfers age 50 and up play on Tuesdays for $8.00. On Thursdays anyone can play all day for $10.00. Clubs rent for $5.00 and handcarts are $1.00. Motorized carts are not available. Facilities include a snack bar where you'll find beer and wine, plus a lounge and pro shop. Lessons, and help with tournament planning, are available.

Directions: Leave I-5 on Highway 238 and head south 7 miles to Murphy, then follow New Hope Road 1.2 miles to the course.

COLONIAL VALLEY GOLF COURSE
75 Nelson Way
Grants Pass, OR
(541) 479-5568

The Colonial Valley course is open year round, weather permitting. You'll find a few hills, but it's an easy course to walk. The terrain includes large oaks and pines, plus a couple of ponds to help keep your game interesting. Reservations are not taken, and they are closed to the public on Tuesday and Wednesday mornings until 10:00 a.m. Par from the ladies' tees is 31.

Green fees are $7.00 for 9 holes or $11.00 for 18 all week long. Special rates are in effect on Saturdays, between 9:00 a.m. and 2:00 p.m., when everyone plays for $.50 per hole. Clubs rent for $3.00 and $5.00; handcarts are $1.00. Facilities include a small pro shop, banquet facilities, and a lounge where beer and wine is served. They can also help with tournament planning.

Directions: Take I-5 north of Grants Pass 2.5 miles to the Merlin exit and go east .5 mile.

DUTCHER CREEK GOLF COURSE
4611 Upper River Rd.
Grants Pass, OR
(541) 474-2188

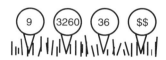

Dutcher Creek is a new links-style course. Open dawn to dusk, year round, it has a nice mountain view and a creek running through the course. Water comes into play on 7 holes. The slope is 118 with a rating of 71.2 for men, 108 and 68.6 for women. Four sets of tees are available. Reservations are given one week in advance. The total yardage from the ladies' tees is 2,700.

Green fees are $12.00 for 9 holes or $19.00 for 18, seven days a week. Seniors, 55 and older, play for $8.00 and $17.00; golfers younger than 18 pay $6.00 and $12.00. Clubs rent for $5.00, handcarts $2.00, and motorized carts $9.00 and $18.00. Facilities include a snack bar offering beer and wine, plus a discount pro shop and driving range. At the range you'll pay $1.00 to $3.00 for balls. Lessons, and help with tournament planning, are available.

Directions: Leave downtown on "G" Street, which soon becomes Upper River Road, for a total distance of 4 miles.

GRANTS PASS GOLF CLUB
230 Espey Rd.
Grants Pass, OR
(541) 476-0849

This course has a flat front 9 with lots of water, and a hilly forested back 9. A semi-private course, they are closed to the public before noon Friday thru Tuesday, prior to 1:00 p.m. on Wednesday, and before 1:30 p.m. Thursday. You'll need reservations two days in advance. The front 9 was built in 1946, the back 9 in 1973, and the 12th hole is their signature hole. The women's par is 73 for a total of 5,867 yards.

Green fees are $18.00 for 9 holes or $30.00 for 18. Clubs can be rented for $5.00 and motorized carts are $12.00 for 9 holes or $20.00 for 18. Their restaurant has a liquor license, and facilities include a driving range and full-service pro shop. Lessons can be arranged, and they offer help with tournament planning. At the driving range you'll pay $2.50 to $3.50 for a bucket of balls.

Directions: Take Highway 238 south of town 3.5 miles.

PARADISE RANCH INN GOLF COURSE
7000 Monument Dr.
Grants Pass, OR
(541) 479-4333

The Paradise Ranch Inn's course only has 3 holes; they're played three times each for a 9-hole game. Two sets of tees are available. Open year round from 7:30 a.m. to dusk, the terrain is hilly with ponds and trees. Clubs are loaned at no cost, so it's a good place to introduce a young player to the game.

Whether you're staying at the inn or not, it costs just $4.00 per 9 holes. Facilities available include overnight accommodations, a nice restaurant and lounge with a liquor license, and banquet facilities.

Directions: Leave I-5 at Merlin exit #61, head under the freeway, turn right onto Monument Drive and go 2 miles.

RED MOUNTAIN GOLF COURSE
324 N. Schoolhouse Creek Rd.
Grants Pass, OR
(541) 479-2297

The Red Mountain course is located just north of Grants Pass, in the Hugo Hills. This challenging executive 9 is open year round, sunrise to sunset. Designed by Robert and Dave Snook, the course opened in 1988. You'll find a scenic setting with rolling hills, lots of trees and water. Walk-ons are welcome.

Green fees are $6.00 for 9 holes, $10.00 for 18, or $14.00 to play all day. Juniors, 12 and under, play for $4.00 and $7.00. Seniors, 55 and over, pay $5.00 and $9.00, or $13.00 for all day. Rental clubs are $5.00, handcarts $1.00, and motorized carts $6.00 per 9 holes. Credit cards are welcome. They have a nice clubhouse where you will find cold beer and wine, plus limited banquet facilities, a snack bar and small pro shop. Driving nets are provided, as is help with tournament planning.

Directions: Leave I-5 at Merlin exit #61, head under the freeway, turn right onto Monument Drive and after 4 miles turn right on Potts Way for an additional mile.

EAGLE POINT

STONERIDGE GOLF CLUB
Antelope Road
Eagle Point, OR
(541) 830-4653

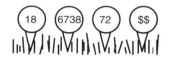

18   6738   72 $$

Opened in 1995, Stoneridge is a year-round course with a slope of 132 from the back tees for a rating of 72.5. You'll find a lot of variety here with some par threes sporting as many as 8 separate tee boxes. The terrain has some hills and offers good views. Designed by Jim Cochran, reservations are given one week in advance. From the ladies' tees the total distance is 4,986 yards.

Weekend green fees are $14.00 for 9 holes or $24.00 for 18. During the week you'll pay $12.00 or $20.00. Foursomes showing up on Mondays save 25%, and on Tuesdays golfers older than 55 save $2.00 on 9 holes or $3.00 on 18. Credit cards are accepted for green fees. Clubs rent for $4.00 and $7.00, handcarts $2.00, and motorized carts $9.00 per 9 holes.

Facilities include a snack bar where you'll find cold beer, plus a covered outdoor banquet area, driving range and full-service pro shop. At the range you'll find both mat and grass tees and pay $3.00 to $5.00 for a bucket of balls. Help with tournament planning, and lessons, are available.

Directions: Located along Highway 140, about 3 miles east of Highway 62.

GOLD HILL

LAUREL HILL GOLF COURSE
9450 Old Stage Rd.
Gold Hill, OR
(541) 855-7965

Laurel Hill was designed by Harvey Granger and opened in 1977. It operates year round and provides a challenging game that is played across a relatively flat terrain with lots of trees. The slope is 102 and the ratings 61.5 for men, 62.3 for women. Two sets of tees are available. Located in a valley, and surrounded by mountains, it's an easy-to-walk scenic course.

Weekday green fees are $6.00 for 9 holes or $11.00 for 18. On weekends you'll pay $7.00 and $12.00. If you're under 19, or over 61, you save $1.00 off the regular fees. Clubs are available for $2.50 and handcarts $1.00. They have a limited pro shop with a snack bar that offers beer and wine.

Directions: Take exit #40 off I-5; the course is just a short distance west of the freeway.

CAVE JUNCTION

ILLINOIS VALLEY GOLF CLUB
25320 Redwood Hwy.
Cave Junction, OR
(541) 592-3151

You'll find two tees on each fairway making this flat 9-hole course an interesting 18. The slope for men is 117 for a rating of 69.1, for women it's 120 and 71.1. Creeks run through the course and the pond seems to attract a lot of balls. Located in the beautiful Illinois Valley, it is open year round, dawn to dusk. Designed by Bob Baldock & Son, it opened in 1976. Reservations are taken on weekends only. A number of major tournaments are held here so it's a good idea to check the schedule during the summer.

Green fees are $10.00 for 9 holes, $15.00 for 18, all week long. Golfers over 60 save $1.00 off green fees; juniors, 17 and under, play for $3.00 and $4.50. Clubs rent for $5.00, handcarts $1.00 and $2.00, and motorized carts $9.00 and $16.00. You can get help with tournament planning and arrange for lessons at the pro shop. They have a driving range, plus a snack bar where you can get beer and wine. At the range you'll find grass tees and pay $1.00 to $5.00 for a bucket of balls.

Directions: Take Highway 199 .5 mile north of Cave Junction.

MEDFORD

BEAR CREEK GOLF COURSE
2355 S. Pacific Hwy.
Medford, OR
(541) 773-1822

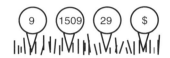

Bear Creek is a sporty little course. The slope is 84 and the ratings 56.6 for men, 56.0 for women. Open year round, it harbors both a lake and a creek which will help to keep your game sharp. A flat course, it's nestled in a valley and has a beautiful view of snow-capped mountains. Reservations are generally not needed. The par from the ladies' tees is 30.

Green fees are $6.00 during the week, $7.00 on weekends and holidays. Seniors can play for $5.50 on Fridays; golfers 16 and younger pay just $5.00 on Thursdays. Clubs can be rented for $2.50 and handcarts are $1.25. Motorized carts are not available. Facilities include a deli where you'll find cold beer and wine, plus a full-service pro shop, covered driving range, putting greens, and an 18-hole miniature golf course. Lessons are available.

Directions: Leave I-5 South on the Barnett exit and take Pacific Highway south 1 mile.

CEDAR LINKS GOLF CLUB
3155 Cedar Links Dr.
Medford, OR
(541) 773-4373

You'll find a rolling terrain at Cedar Links, plus a great view of the Rogue Valley and surrounding mountains. Its slope is 110 and the ratings 67.9 for men, 68.7 for women. The 5th hole is tough, with large oaks, water and an elevated green, and there are another half-dozen water hazards along the course. Open every day but Christmas, reservations are taken one week in advance. The women's tees have a distance of 5,160 yards for a par of 71.

Green fees are the same all week long. You'll pay $12.00 for 9 holes or $20.00 for 18. Credit cards are welcome. Clubs are available at $5.00 and $7.00, handcarts $2.00 and $3.00, and motorized carts $10.00 and $18.00. Facilities include a restaurant with a liquor license, plus banquet rooms, a full-service pro shop and driving range. The driving range has mat tees and charges $2.00 to $3.00 for bucket of balls. Lessons, and help with tournament planning, are available.

Directions: Follow Cedar Links Drive.

QUAIL POINT GOLF COURSE
Shannon Road
Medford, OR
(541) 857-7000

This year-round course was designed by Bob Foster, and opened in 1993. Winter hours are 8:00 a.m. to dusk; the rest of the year they open at 7:00 a.m. A hilly course, you'll find lots of trees, plenty of water, and four sets of tees. Reservations are advised for weekend play. The total yardage from the ladies' tees is 2,557.

Green fees are $12.00 for 9 holes or $20.00 for 18 all week long. Clubs rent for $5.00, handcarts $2.00, and motorized carts $10.00 and $18.00. Facilities include a driving range, pro shop, and snack machines. At the driving range balls cost $2.00 to $4.00. Lessons can be arranged.

Directions: Leave I-5 on Barnett and head east, take a right on Black Oak, go right on Mira Mar, and again on Shannon.

STEWART MEADOWS GOLF COURSE
1301 S. Holly St.
Medford, OR
(541) 770-6554

Stewart Meadows is flat and easy to walk with lots of mounds. A year-round course, it was designed by Chuck Magnum and opened in 1993. Winter hours are 7:30 a.m. to dusk; they open at 6:30 a.m. the balance of the year. Reservations are taken 7 days in advance. From the ladies' tees the total yardage is 2,800.

Green fees are the same all week long, $10.00 for 9 holes or $18.00 for 18. On Thursdays, golfers older than 55 can play for $5.00 per 9 holes. Juniors, age 17 and younger, play for $5.00 on all non-holiday weekdays. They do not rent clubs, but handcarts are $1.00 per 9 holes and motorized carts $10.00 and $18.00.

Facilities include a restaurant and lounge where you can get cold beer and wine, plus a full-service pro shop. Lessons are available, and they will soon be opening a lighted driving range.

Directions: To find Stewart Meadows Golf Course, leave I-5 on Barnett and turn right. After about .5 mile turn left on Holly and go 2 blocks to the course.

ASHLAND

OAK KNOLL GOLF COURSE
3070 Highway 66
Ashland, OR
(541) 482-4311

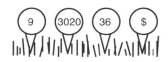

There has been a course here since the 1920s. Oak Knoll provides beautiful mountain views and is open year round. The terrain is hilly, two of the holes are very hilly, and the fairways are lined with trees. The slope is 119 and the ratings 69.1 for men, 70.5 for women. A second set of tees is available for playing 18 holes. Tee times are necessary, and available one week in advance. The total yardage from the women's tees is 2,656 for a par of 38.

During the week you can play 9 holes for $9.50 or 18 for $14.00. Winter rates are $8.00 and $12.00. Juniors, those under age 17, can play 9 holes for $7.00. Clubs rent for $5.00 and $9.00, handcarts $2.00 and $3.00, and motorized carts $11.00 and $18.00.

They have a restaurant and lounge with a liquor license and banquet facilities, plus a full-service pro shop and practice putting green. Lessons, and help with tournament planning, are available. Credit cards are welcome.

Directions: This course is located less than a mile off I-5; take Highway 66 toward Klamath Falls.

CENTRAL OREGON

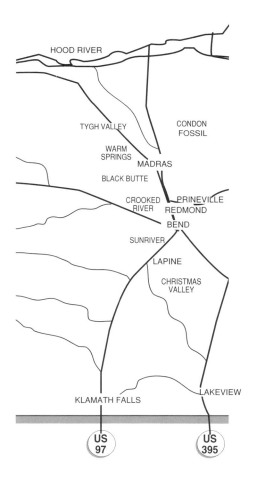

Central Oregon
Table of Contents

HOOD RIVER

HOOD RIVER GOLF
1850 Country Club Rd.
Hood River, OR
(541) 386-3009

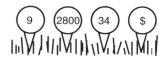

Hood River is one of the prettiest courses in the state. From the fairways you'll find outstanding views of Mt. Adams, Mt. Hood, and the Hood River Valley. This course first opened in 1922 and only closes during heavy snows. The terrain is varied, with some hills, and you'll find four sets of tees. Call ahead for tee times.

Green fees are $8.00 for 9 holes or $15.00 for 18. Juniors play for $5.00 and $10.00, and on Mondays and Fridays seniors play for that same discount rate. Clubs rent for $4.00, handcarts $2.00, and motorized carts are $8.00 for 9 holes or $15.00 for 18.

Facilities include a restaurant and lounge with a liquor license and banquet facilities, plus a full-service pro shop and driving range. You can arrange for lessons and get help with tournament planning. At the driving range you'll pay $2.50 for 150 balls or $4.75 for 300.

Directions: Take I-84 to exit #62, head toward West Hood River, turn right on Country Club Road and go 4.5 miles.

INDIAN CREEK GOLF COURSE
3605 Brookside Dr.
Hood River, OR
(541) 386-7770

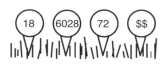

There's a view of Mt. Hood or Adams from every hole at Indian Creek. The greens are smooth and true rolling, and the fairways lined with trees and water. Open year round, the slope is 124 with a rating of 70.2. Reservations are taken one week in advance. The total distance from the women's tees is 5,342 yards.

Weekday green fees are $11.00 for 9 holes or $20.00 for 18. On weekends they're $12.00 and $24.00. Seniors can play on Mondays and Wednesdays for $7.00 and $14.00; juniors get that rate 7 days a week. Clubs rent for $4.00 and $7.00, handcarts $2.00, and motorized carts $12.00 and $22.00.

Facilities include a full-service pro shop, driving range, and a snack bar where you'll find cold beer. They provide help with tournament planning and offer lessons. At the driving range you'll pay $2.00 to $4.00 for a bucket of balls.

Directions: To find the Indian Creek Golf Course, take exit #62 off I-84, head east on Cascade, turn right onto 13th Street, and right on Brookside.

TYGH VALLEY

PINE HOLLOW GOLF COURSE
8-A South County Rd.
Tygh Valley, OR
(541) 544-2035

Pine Hollow's terrain is semi-hilly, and two sets of tees allow you to play 18 holes with variety. Its 2nd hole is often referred to as one of the most difficult in the state because of its narrow tree-lined dogleg. Designed by Earl Davis Jr. and Associates, it opened in 1989. The slope is 95 with a rating of 61.6.

On Tuesday nights the course is reserved for men; Wednesdays after 10:00 a.m. only the ladies can play. Reservations can be made up to one month in advance. The course is open April thru October, dawn to dusk.

Green fees at Pine Hollow are $7.00 for 9 holes or $14.00 for 18, all week long. On Mondays, juniors age 12 and under play for free when golfing with an adult. On Thursdays they have special rates for couples. Clubs rent for $2.50, handcarts $2.50, and motorized carts $7.50 per 9 holes. Credit cards are welcome.

Facilities include a lounge and snack bar where you can get cold beer and wine, a limited pro shop, driving net and practice putting green. They can also provide help with tournament planning.

Directions: To reach Pine Hollow Golf Course, take Highway 197 west of Tygh Valley for 8 miles.

CONDON

CONDON MUNICIPAL GOLF COURSE
North Lincoln
Condon, OR
(541) 384-4266

The Condon Municipal Golf Course is open year round. Its terrain is slightly rolling but easy to walk, and the course is challenging with narrow fairways.

Facilities are at a minimum here, and green fees are paid on the honor system. Current rates will be posted, but it generally costs about $5.00 to play all day.

Directions: Located at the north end of town.

FOSSIL

KINZUA HILLS GOLF CLUB
Hoover
Fossil, OR
(541) 763-3287

Although this course has only 6 holes, you can use the two sets of tees to play 18 with some variety. Built in 1929, volunteers have somehow managed to keep the course alive although most of the people and businesses around it have disappeared. The terrain is hilly with a creek running through it, and some of the greens are not visible from the tees. You can generally play from early May until mid-September.

Kinzua Hills operates on the honor system, so bring correct change. You can play 6 holes for $5.00, 9 for $8.00, or 18 for $10.00. Annual membership is available to county families for $100.00; those living outside the county pay $65.00. When the clubhouse is open you can rent clubs, handcarts and motorized carts. They also have a limited pro shop, and can help with tournament planning.

Directions: Located 9 miles east of Fossil; head towards Kinzua.

WARM SPRINGS

KAH-NEE-TA RESORT GOLF COURSE
Kah-Nee-Ta Resort
Warm Springs, OR
(541) 553-1112 ext. 371

Kah-Nee-Ta is a great place to hide from the rain since it sees sunshine about 300 days out of the year. A year-round course, it has lush greens surrounded by sand and water, large fairways, and a river running alongside. The front 9 was designed by William Bell, the back 9 by Bunny Mason. From the ladies' tees the total distance is 5,418 yards for a par of 73.

Green fees are $18.00 for 9 holes or $27.50 for 18. If you're under 17, or over 55, you can play for $14.50 and $24.00. Clubs rent for $8.00 and motorized carts are $12.00 for 9 holes or $22.00 for 18. At the driving range you get a small bucket of balls for $2.00 or a large one for $4.00.

Facilities include a practice area, full-service pro shop, banquet facilities, and a restaurant and lounge with a liquor license. At the pro shop you can get help with tournament planning and arrange for lessons. The resort offers a luxurious hotel that overlooks the golf course, mineral baths and pool, nearby fishing, horseback riding, tennis, bicycling and camping.

Directions: Take Highway 26 east toward Warm Springs, turn at the Kah-Nee-Ta junction and go 11 miles.

MADRAS

NINE PEAKS GOLF COURSE
1152 N.W. Golf Course Dr.
Madras, OR
(541) 475-3511

True to its name, this Madras course offers a clear view of nine mountain peaks. The slope is 103 and the ratings 68.4 for men, 67.3 for women. From the ladies' tees the total yardage is 5,745. The terrain is flat with some ponds, and you'll find three tees at each hole. Open year round, except when snow impedes the game, you can play between dawn and dusk. The front 9 at Nine Peaks was built in 1956, the back 9 in 1992. Tee times are given 24 hours in advance for weekend play.

During the week you can play 18 holes for $16.00, on weekends it'll cost you $18.00. You can rent a set of clubs for $5.00, handcarts are $1.00, and motorized carts $9.00 per 9 holes. Credit cards are accepted for green fees. You can arrange for lessons and get help with tournament planning at the full-service pro shop. A snack bar offers sandwiches, beer and wine.

Directions: Located .5 mile north of Madras, at the junction of Highways 26 and 97.

BLACK BUTTE

BLACK BUTTE RANCH COURSE
Black Butte Ranch
Black Butte, OR
(541) 595-6689 or (800) 452-7455

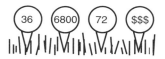

You'll find two 18-hole golf courses at Black Butte. Big Meadow is easiest to walk; Glaze Meadows is a bit hilly. Both have been carved out of the forest and have a beautiful view of snow-capped mountains. Weather permitting, they are open April thru October.

Green fees are $29.00 for 9 holes or $49.00 for 18 all week long. Twilight rates are available Sunday thru Thursday for a $5.00 savings per 9 holes. Juniors, 17 and under, play for half price after 2:00 p.m. if accompanied by a golfing adult. Clubs rent for $10.00 and $15.00, handcarts $2.00 and $4.00, and motorized carts $17.00 and $28.00.

Each course has its own driving range and a pro shop where lessons can be arranged. Facilities include a restaurant and lounge with a liquor license, plus meeting rooms and overnight accommodations. If you plan to stay at Black Butte Ranch ask about their golf packages.

Directions: The ranch is located 9 miles northwest of Sisters, at the foot of Black Butte.

CROOKED RIVER

CROOKED RIVER RANCH COURSE
5195 Club House Rd.
Crooked River, OR
(541) 923-6343

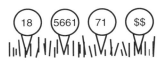

The Crooked River course provides a challenge for golfers of all levels. From the 3rd tee you have a terrific view of the 300 foot deep Crooked River Gorge and on the 5th hole you play across it, along a curve in the river. The slope is 107 and the ratings 66.3 for men, 67.2 for women. A year-round course, it has rolling hills with juniper, sagebrush and rocks lining the fairways. The second 9 was added in 1994 and designed by Jim Ramey. Reservations are available one week in advance.

Green fees are $14.00 for 9 holes, $22.00 for 18. Golfers under 19, or over 60, should call for seasonal junior and senior discounts. Motorized carts are available February thru November, when the pro shop is open, and cost $14.00 for 9 holes or $22.00 for 18. Clubs are $6.00 and $10.00, handcarts $2.00, and credit cards are welcome. The women's total yardage is 5,000.

Amenities include a lounge where beer and wine is available, plus a restaurant, banquet facilities, pro shop, RV park and tennis courts. At the pro shop you can get help with tournament planning and arrange for lessons. On the driving range you'll pay $2.00 for a small bucket of balls, $3.00 and $5.00 for larger buckets.

Directions: Take Highway 97 north of Redmond 5 miles to Lower Bridge Road West. Signs will direct you from there.

PRINEVILLE

MEADOW LAKES GOLF COURSE
300 Meadow Lakes Dr.
Prineville, OR
(541) 447-7113

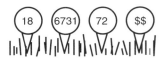

Built in 1993, Meadow Lakes was designed by William Robinson. This is a links-style course with water on all 18 holes. You also get a nice view of the Ochoco Mountains. The slope is 131 for men with a rating of 73.1; for women it's 121 and 69.1. The total distance from the ladies' tees is 5,155 yards. Open year round, dawn to dusk, you can get reservations up to a year in advance.

Green fees for 9 holes are $15.00 all week long. On weekends 18 holes are $29.00, it's $18.00 during the week. Juniors can play 9 holes during the week for $8.00 or 18 for $12.00, on weekends it's $9.00 and $14.00. Credit cards are welcome. Clubs rent for $7.00 and $12.00, handcarts $2.00 and $3.00, and motorized carts $12.00 and $22.00. They have a restaurant/lounge with a liquor license, plus a banquet room, snack bar, full-service pro shop and driving range. The range has grass tees and you get 35 balls for $2.00. Lessons, and help with tournament planning, are available.

Directions: Take Highway 26 north and east of Bend.

REDMOND

EAGLE CREST RESORT
1522 Cline Falls Rd.
Redmond, OR
(541) 923-5002

Eagle Crest has two 18-hole courses, the resort course and the ridge course. Reservations are available one week in advance, and hours are 7:00 a.m. to dusk. Green fees are $23.00 for 9 holes or $38.00 for 18. Juniors play for free after 3:00 p.m. Clubs rent for $7.50 and $12.00, handcarts $1.00 and $2.00, and motorized carts $16.00 and $25.00. Credit cards are welcome.

The resort course was designed by Bunny Mason and built in 1986. Its slope is 123 and the ratings 71.5 for men, 69.8 for women. The total yardage from the ladies' tees is 5,395. Open year round, you'll find three tees per hole.

The ridge course was designed by John Thronson and opened in 1993. It also has a slope of 123; the ratings are 70.8 for men and 66.6 for women. From the men's tees the distance is 6,497 yards, it's 4,792 from the ladies' tees. You'll find water on four holes, fast greens, good drainage, and four tees per hole. Ridge is only open from March to November.

Facilities include a restaurant with a liquor license, plus a snack bar where you'll find cold beer, a full-service pro shop and driving range. The range has grass tees and you get a bucket of balls for $2.00 to $5.00. Tournament planning assistance and lessons are available.

Directions: Eagle Crest Resort is located 4 miles west of Highway 126 on Cline Falls Road.

JUNIPER GOLF CLUB
139 S.E. Sisters Ave.
Redmond, OR
(541) 548-3121

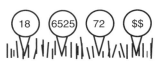

Juniper is open year round, weather permitting. Its original 9 holes were built in 1952 and it was expanded to 18 holes in 1987. The terrain is fairly flat and easy to walk, with four ponds to keep it challenging. The view is impressive and includes several snow-capped mountains. Juniper's slope is 124 for men and 115 for women. From the ladies' tees the total yardage is 5,598. Although this is a semi-private course, they are only closed to the public on Wednesday mornings and Thursday afternoons.

During the week green fees are $12.00 for 9 holes, $20.00 for 18. On weekends and holidays you'll pay $15.00 and $25.00. Junior golfers can play for half price on weekdays. Clubs are available for $6.00 and $10.00, handcarts $1.00 per 9 holes, and motorized carts $12.00 and $20.00. Facilities include a driving range, pro shop, restaurant, and lounge. Lessons are available, and they have a banquet room that holds 180 people.

Directions: Located east of Highway 97, at the south end of town.

THE GREENS AT REDMOND
2475 S.W. Greens Blvd.
Redmond, OR
(541) 923-0694

Robert Muir Graves designed this executive course. It opened in 1995 and has three sets of tees. The 6th hole is a real challenge with both water and a dogleg to overcome for a par four. Open dawn to dusk, year round, reservations are not taken.

Green fees are the same all week long, $9.00 for 9 holes or $13.00 for 18. Clubs rent for $3.50 and $5.00, handcarts $2.00 and $3.00, and motorized carts $9.00 and $13.00. Facilities include a snack bar serving cold beer and wine, plus a full-service pro shop where you can get help with tournament planning.

Directions: Located right in Redmond and well marked.

BEND

AUBURY GLEN GOLF COURSE
2500 N.W. Aubury Glen Dr.
Bend, OR
(541) 385-6011

Aubury Glen is a semi-private course that's open to the public February thru October from 7:00 a.m. to dusk. You'll find four sets of tees; the shortest has a distance of 5,389 yards.

Green fees at Aubury Glen are $75.00 per player; that includes a motorized cart. A full set of clubs rents for $15.00. At the driving range you get 30 balls for $2.00. Lessons are available.

Directions: Take Highway 97 to the center of town and turn onto Greenwood. Follow this to Newport Avenue, head west to Mt. Washington Drive, and turn right to the course.

MOUNTAIN HIGH GOLF COURSE
60650 China Hat Rd.
Bend, OR
(541) 382-1111

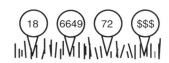

Mountain High is open April thru October. Built in 1987, most golfers find the 5th hole's island green quite challenging. This level tree-lined course offers three sets of tees, and you get a great mountain view. Hours are 7:00 a.m. to dusk, and reservations are taken one week in advance.

Green fees are $20.00 for 9 holes or $36.00 for 18 all week long. Credit cards are welcome. Clubs rent for $5.00 and $10.00, handcarts $2.00, and motorized carts $10.00 per 9 holes.

Facilities include a snack bar where you can get a cold beer, plus a driving range and a pro shop offering help with tournament planning. At the driving range you get 30 balls for $2.00. Lessons are available.

Directions: Leave Bend heading south on Highway 97 and turn east on China Hat Road. The course is .5 mile.

ORION GREENS GOLF COURSE
61525 Fargo Ln.
Bend, OR
(541) 388-3999

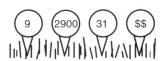

This is a real pretty executive 9-hole course located south of town. Open year round, weather permitting, it offers an easy-to-walk rolling terrain. You'll find lots of trees, some water and a nice view of the mountains. The slope is 98 and the ratings 58.3 for men, 62.0 for women. Built in 1981, it was designed by Orion Reid and Steve Perrigan. Three sets of tees are provided. The total distance from the women's tees is 2,100 yards. Tee times are recommended.

You'll pay $12.00 for 9 holes or $20.00 for 18 all week long. Weekday punch cards are available allowing seniors, 60 and over, to play 9 holes for $7.50 and others to play for $8.00. You can rent clubs for $6.00 and $10.00, handcarts $1.00 per 9 holes, and motorized carts $10.00 and $19.00. Facilities include a putting green, chipping and pitching area, plus a restaurant and lounge with a liquor license and banquet facilities. Help with tournament planning and lessons are available at the pro shop.

Directions: Take Highway 97 to Reed Market Road, turn left for 1.5 miles, then right onto Fargo Lane.

RIVER'S EDGE GOLF COURSE
400 Pro Shop Dr.
Bend, OR
(541) 389-2828

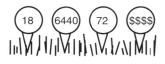

Located between the Deschutes River and Awbrey Butte, River's Edge was designed by Robert Muir Graves and opened in 1988. The second 9 was finished in 1992. It has a number of small hills, valleys, and some excellent views. You'll find a waterfall feeding a lake in front of the 5th hole and a 100 foot drop in elevation on the

15th. The slope is 135 and the ratings 71.6 for men, 71.8 for women. Four tees are available on each hole. Weather permitting, it is open year round. They take reservations 7 days in advance. The women's par is 73 for a total distance of 5,381 yards.

Green fees are $32.00 all week long. Golfers under 18 can generally play for $10.00. You can rent clubs for $15.00, pull carts $3.00, and motorized carts $25.00. Credit cards are welcome. Snacks, beer and wine are available at the pro shop. Lessons can be arranged and they will help you with tournament planning. They also have a driving range with grass and mat tees.

Directions: Take Mt. Washington Drive off Highway 97 and follow the signs.

WIDGI CREEK GOLF CLUB
18707 Century Dr.
Bend, OR
(541) 382-4449

This Robert Muir Graves course opened in 1990. It has undulating greens, narrow fairways, lots of trees, lakes and bunkers to challenge your game, plus four tees per hole. The slope is 134 for men with a rating of 73.4; for women it's 112 and 64.8. From the ladies' tees the total distance is 5,070 yards.

This semi-private course is open to the public from 10:00 a.m. to 4:00 p.m. Widgi Creek is closed November thru February. The rest of the year reservations are available two weeks in advance.

Green fees are $40.00 for 9 holes or $60.00 for 18 all week long. Golfers 17 and under can play 18 holes for $27.00 when space is available. Credit cards are accepted for green fees. Clubs rent for $10.00 and $18.00, handcarts $2.00 and $3.00, and motorized carts $13.00 per person.

Facilities include a restaurant/lounge with a liquor license, plus a banquet room, snack bar, full-service pro shop, large practice green, and driving range. At the range you'll find grass tees and get a bucket of balls for $2.50 to $5.00. Lessons, and help with tournament planning, are available.

Directions: Take the Cascade Lakes Highway toward Mt. Bachelor; the course is just a 5 minute drive out of Bend.

SUNRIVER

SUNRIVER GOLF COURSE
Sunriver Resort
Sunriver, OR
(541) 593-1221

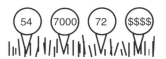

Sunriver has three 18-hole golf courses. The South Meadows course was designed by Fred Federspiel and has numerous pine trees, lots of water, sand and meadows. The North Woodlands Course was designed by Robert Trent Jones II and features multiple tees, white sand and several lakes. Crosswater Club opened in 1995, was designed by Robert Cupp, and is reserved for lodge guests. All three courses are well-maintained and offer fast true greens. Reservations are necessary.

Lodge guests pay $39.00 for 18 holes on South Meadows, $49.00 for North Woodlands, and $95.00 for Crosswater. Crosswater's rates include a motorized cart as well as time on the driving range. Non-guests will pay $49.00 for South Meadows and $59.00 for North Woodlands. Motorized carts rent for $25.00, handcarts $5.00, and clubs $12.00 for a half set or $20.00 for a full set. At the driving range you'll find grass tees and pay $3.00 to $5.00 for a bucket of balls.

Facilities at Sunriver include a full-service pro shop, banquet rooms, a great restaurant and lounge with a full liquor license, deluxe accommodations, and many recreational activities. Lessons, and help with tournament planning, are available. Credit cards are welcome.

Directions: Located behind Sunriver Lodge.

LAPINE

QUAIL RUN GOLF COURSE
16725 Northridge Dr.
LaPine, OR
(541) 536-1303

The fairways at Quail Run are carved out of the woods, and each one is separated by acres of trees. Several fairways offer terrific mountain views which include Mt. Bachelor. The course was designed by Jim Ramey and opened in 1991. It has four tees per hole, a rolling terrain, water hazards, and white sand bunkers that present a challenge to golfers of all levels. The slope is 126 with a rating of 72.2 for men, it's 116 and 69.6 for women. From the women's tees the total distance is 2,707 yards. Open February thru December, weather permitting, tee times are advised.

You can play 9 holes at Quail Run for $16.00 or 18 for $27.00. Juniors, age 14 and younger, play for $10.00 and $18.00. Clubs are available for $5.00 and $8.00, handcarts $2.00 and $3.00, and motorized carts $12.00 for 9 holes or $20.00 for 18. Amenities include a restaurant offering cold beer and wine, plus a driving range and full-service pro shop. Lessons, and tournament planning assistance, are available. At the driving range you'll find grass tees and get a bucket of balls for $2.50 to $4.50.

Directions: Take Highway 97 south of Sunriver 9 miles to the East Lake/Paulina junction and head 2 miles west.

CHRISTMAS VALLEY

CHRISTMAS VALLEY GOLF COURSE
#1 Christmas Tree Ln.
Christmas Valley, OR
(541) 576-2216

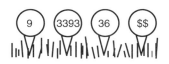

The terrain at Christmas Valley is flat with raised greens and tee boxes. Managed by the local parks and recreation department, they are open year round from dawn to dusk. Reservations are not necessary. The women's tees have a par of 38 for a total distance of 3,070 yards.

A family can purchase a seasonal pass at Christmas Valley for $90.00. Others pay $10.00 for 9 holes or $15.00 for 18. At the Christmas Valley Lodge you can rent clubs for $10.00 for 9 holes or $18.00 for 18. Handcarts are $2.00, and at times you'll also find motorized carts for rent. Facilities include a restaurant and lounge with a liquor license.

Directions: The course is easy to reach from downtown Christmas Valley, just follow the signs to Christmas Tree Lane.

LAKEVIEW

LAKERIDGE GOLF & COUNTRY CLUB
Highway 140
Lakeview, OR
(503) 947-3855

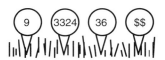

Weather permitting, Lakeridge is open year round. This is a long, flat course with a pond on the 9th hole. In recent years they have added several new sandtraps. Tee times are not necessary, but you might want to call ahead to see if any tournaments are in process, especially during late June and early July. The women's par is 37 for a total distance of 2,898 yards.

Green fees are $10.00 for 9 holes or $15.00 for 18. Clubs rent for $5.00, and motorized carts are $10.00 for 9 holes or $15.00 for 18. They have a full-service pro shop, driving range, and a restaurant with banquet facilities and a liquor license. At the driving range you can get a bucket of balls for $1.00 to $3.00 depending on how many you need. They can also help you with golf lessons as well as tournament planning.

Directions: Located 4 miles west of Lakeview on Highway 140.

KLAMATH FALLS

HARBOR LINKS GOLF COURSE
601 Harbor Isles Blvd.
Klamath Falls, OR
(541) 882-0609

You'll find lots of water at the Harbor Links course. Built in 1985, it's open year round and they take reservations one week in advance. The course is very walkable and has links-type construction.

On weekends and holidays green fees are $15.00 for 9 holes or $22.00 for 18. On weekdays you'll pay $12.00 and $20.00. Unless the course is crowded, golfers 17 and under pay just $5.00 per 9 holes. Seniors receive a discount of $1.00 per 9 holes. Rental clubs are $7.00 for 9 or $10.00 for 18 holes, handcarts $3.00 and $4.00, and motorized carts $12.00 and $20.00.

Facilities include a restaurant and lounge with a liquor license, plus a full-service pro shop and driving range. Lessons, and help with tournament planning, are available. The range has mat tees and you can get a bucket of balls for $2.00 to $4.00.

Directions: Located north of the yacht club, along Klamath Lake.

ROUND LAKE GOLF COURSE
4000 Round Lake Rd.
Klamath Falls, OR
(541) 884-2520

This scenic executive course is surrounded by pine trees and mountains. Open from the middle of March through the middle of November, reservations are generally not needed.

Green fees at Round Lake are extremely reasonable. Any day of the week you can play 9 holes for $6.00 or 18 for $10.00. Rental clubs are $3.50 for a starter set or $5.50 for a complete set. Handcarts are $1.00. They do not offer motorized carts, but have a limited pro shop where you will find some snacks.

Directions: Head west 4.4 miles on Highway 66 to Round Lake Road, turn right and go 3.6 miles to Round Lake Estates and the course.

SHIELD CREST GOLF COURSE
3151 Shield Crest Dr.
Klamath Falls, OR
(541) 884-1493

Shield Crest offers terrific views of Mt. Shasta from almost anywhere on the course. Open year round, it was built in 1989, and operates from sunrise to sunset. You'll find only a few hills on this fairly flat course, and three tees at every hole. The women's par is 74 for a total distance of 6,318 yards. Reservations are available up to 72 hours in advance.

Weekday green fees are $10.00 for 9 holes or $20.00 for 18. On weekends and holidays it's $12.00 and $22.00. Juniors and seniors can play 18 holes Monday thru Thursday for $16.00.

Rental clubs are $4.00 and $7.00, and motorized carts $10.00 and $18.00. They have a restaurant and lounge where liquor is served, plus a driving range and full-service pro shop. Lessons, and help with tournament planning, are available. At the driving range you'll find grass tees, and pay $1.50 for 30 balls.

Directions: Located 2 miles east of Highway 140's Lakeview Junction.

EASTERN OREGON

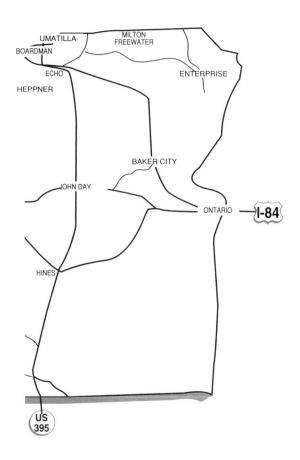

Eastern Oregon
Table of Contents

UMATILLA

UMATILLA GOLF COURSE
705 Willamette
Umatilla, OR
(541) 922-3006

This moderately flat course was built in the 1940s and is open year round. It has a view of the Columbia River and operates from daylight to dark. Although the Umatilla Golf Course may look easy, it's not. The greens are good and the roughs natural. You'll want to call ahead for reservations during the summer to avoid arriving during a tournament. Par from the ladies' tees is 74 for a distance of 5,940 yards.

Weekday green fees are $8.00 for 9 holes or $15.00 for 18. On weekends they charge $9.00 and $17.00. Clubs rent for $5.00 and $8.00 and motorized carts are $10.00 per 9 holes. They have a full-service pro shop and can help with lessons and tournament planning.

Directions: Located 1 mile east of town, right off Highway 730, in McNary Addition.

MILTON-FREEWATER

MILTON-FREEWATER GOLF COURSE
W301 Catherine Street
Milton-Freewater, OR
(541) 938-7284

This executive course offers a flat bottom 9 and a hilly upper 9, with a 125 foot difference in elevation. From the upper 9 you have a 270 degree view of Walla Walla Valley and the Blue Mountains. The slope is 80 for men and 83 for women, and the ratings 55.4 and 58.1. Open 362 days a year, weather permitting, the first 9 holes were built in 1973 and the second opened in 1986. The women's tees have a par of 61 for a total distance of 3,314 yards. Reservations are recommended on weekends and holidays.

During the week green fees are $7.00 for 9 holes or $11.00 for 18. It'll cost you $8.00 and $12.00 on weekends and holidays. Monday thru Friday juniors pay $5.00 and $8.00; seniors pay $6.00 and $10.00. You can rent clubs for $3.00, handcarts $1.50, and motorized carts are $12.00 for 9 holes or $18.00 for 18.

Facilities include a restaurant and lounge where liquor is served, plus a full-service pro shop and practice area. Lessons, and help with tournament planning, are available.

Directions: This course is located right in Milton-Freewater, and is well marked.

BOARDMAN

WILSON'S WILLOW RUN GOLF
Wilson Road
Boardman, OR
(541) 481-4381

Willow Run is an interesting course with lots of water. Open year round, it's closed on Mondays except for holiday weekends. This course is easy to walk and sometimes quite windy.

Facilities include a small pro shop where you'll find snacks and cold drinks, plus a clubhouse that is open March thru November. When the clubhouse is closed golfers are on the honor system, so have the exact amount ready to drop in the slot.

During the week green fees are $5.00 for 9 holes or $8.00 for 18. On weekends and holidays it's $6.00 or $10.00. High school students can purchase an annual pass allowing them to play for reduced rates.

During the primary golf season clubs rent for $2.00 and $4.00, handcarts $1.00 and $2.00, and motorized carts $7.50 for 9 holes or $12.50 for 18. Clubs, handcarts, and motorized carts are not available December thru February.

Directions: Wilson's Willow Run Golf Course is located 4 miles southwest of Boardman, on Wilson Road.

ECHO

ECHO HILLS GOLF COURSE
Golf Course Road
Echo, OR
(541) 376-8244

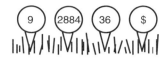

On a clear day you can see both Mt. Adams and Mt. Rainier from the Echo Hills course. The terrain is hilly, with sagebrush-filled roughs, and trees separate the fairways. Open year round, the slope is 113 and the ratings 68.1 for men, 68.8 for women. The women's tees have a par of 37 for a total distance of 2,607 yards. Tee times are required only on weekends.

On weekends and holidays you can play 9 holes for $8.00 or 18 for $16.00. Weekday green fees are $6.00 and $12.00, but juniors get to play for $5.00 and $10.00. Seniors get a $1.00 discount per 9 holes on Mondays. Clubs can be rented for $5.00, handcarts $2.00 and $3.00, and motorized carts are $10.00 per 9 holes. Facilities include a driving range, pro shop, and a snack bar that serves beer and wine. At the driving range you'll find both mat and grass tees and can get 45 balls for $2.00 or 85 for $3.50. Tournament planning assistance is available.

Directions: Located 2 miles off I-84 via exit #188. After heading south, turn left at the school and again 4 blocks later where you'll see signs directing the way.

ENTERPRISE

ALPINE MEADOWS GOLF COURSE
Golf Course Road
Enterprise, OR
(541) 426-3246

Open April thru October, reservations are not needed at Alpine Meadows. The terrain is flat and easy to walk with two sets of tees. This is a beautiful course with a brook running across three fairways and a view of the Wallowa Mountains. It was built in the 1930s and is surrounded by low rolling hills.

Green fees are $9.00 for 9 holes or $15.00 for 18, all week long. Juniors and seniors can purchase an annual pass for discounted play. Clubs rent for $7.00, handcarts $2.00, and motorized carts $10.00. Facilities include a pro shop, restaurant and lounge with a liquor license, and banquet facilities. Lessons, and help with tournament planning, are available.

Directions: Located just off Highway 82, on the west end of town.

HEPPNER

WILLOW CREEK COUNTRY CLUB
Golf Course Road
Heppner, OR
(541) 676-5437

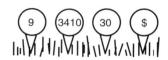

This year-round course has a gently rolling terrain and narrow fairways. A creek comes into play on five holes. Willow Creek began with just one hole, gradually grew to three holes, and now sports nine. Two sets of tees allow for playing 18. Reservations are not available.

Fees are a real bargain at Willow Creek, 9 holes for $5.00 or 18 for $8.00, all week long. The only rental equipment is handcarts which you can rent for $2.00. They have a limited pro shop, open March thru October, and can help you with tournament planning.

Directions: Located 1 mile north of town.

BAKER CITY

BAKER GOLF COURSE
2801 Indiana Ave.
Baker City, OR
(541) 523-2358

This course is flat with relatively few obstacles; a creek comes into play on three holes. The surroundings are pleasant, with the

Elk Horn and Eagle Mountains in the background. Built in 1936, it is open year round except during heavy snows. Tee times are given one day in advance. Several tournaments are held here, at least one a month from May thru September, so call ahead. The women's par is 38 for a total of 2,706 yards.

Green fees are $9.00 for 9 holes or $15.00 for 18. On weekdays golfers younger than 15 can play for $5.00 and $8.00. Rental clubs will cost you $5.00, handcarts $1.00, and motorized carts $9.00 per 9 holes.

Facilities include a lounge with a liquor license, plus banquet facilities and a full-service pro shop where you can get help with tournament planning and arrange for lessons.

Directions: Take Highway 7 out of Baker City and follow the signs.

JOHN DAY

JOHN DAY GOLF COURSE
Highway 26
John Day, OR
(541) 575-0170

The John Day Golf Course is open year round except when snow prevents play. Located 3,200 feet above sea level, this hilly course offers a beautiful view of Rudio Canyon and the Blue Mountains. It opens at 9:00 a.m. on weekends and 10:00 a.m. the rest of the week; they close at dusk. Reservations are not needed, but you might want to call about their tournament schedule; they host four major ones during the season. Two sets of tees are available. The women's par is 37.

All week long green fees are $12.00 for 9 holes or $18.00 for 18. You can rent clubs for $5.00, handcarts $1.00, and motorized carts are $10.00 for 9 holes or $18.00 for 18. They have a limited pro shop where you can get help with tournament planning, and a driving range. At the range you'll pay $1.00 for a small bucket of balls or $2.00 for a large one.

Directions: Located 3 miles west of John Day on Highway 26.

ONTARIO

SHADOW BUTTE GOLF COURSE
Highway 201
Ontario, OR
(541) 889-9022

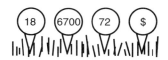

The Shadow Butte Golf Course is situated in the shadow of Malheur Butte. It opened in 1965, and was once the longest course in the state. You'll find excellent greens, very few hills, and a terrain that is easy to walk. The slope is 111 and the ratings 69.7 for men, 72.4 for women. Par from the ladies' tees is 74 for a total distance of 5,800 yards. Shadow Butte is open February 15th thru November 30th.

Green fees are $9.00 for 9 holes or $11.00 for 18, all week long. On Mondays you can play all day for $9.00. Juniors and seniors get a $1.00 discount Tuesday thru Thursday, except on holidays. Clubs rent for $3.00 and $5.00, handcarts $3.00, and motorized carts $7.50 per 9 holes. Facilities include a restaurant with a liquor license, plus a driving range and pro shop. Lessons are available. At the driving range you'll find grass tees and get a bucket of balls for $2.00 to $3.00.

Directions: Located 1 mile west of town on Highway 201.

HINES

VALLEY GOLF CLUB
Highway 20
Hines, OR
(541) 573-6251

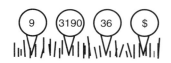

Valley Golf is open year round, weather permitting. The course is flat and easy to walk. Although reservations are not needed, you'll want to check their tournament schedule the first weekend in July and over Labor Day weekend before heading out. The women's par is 38.

Green fees remain the same all week long at this reversible 9-hole course. You'll pay $9.00 for 9 holes or $15.00 for 18. Clubs can be rented for $2.00 and handcarts $1.00. Gas carts are $10.00 for 9 holes or $18.00 for 18. Lessons are available, and facilities include a pro shop and snack machines.

Directions: Located on Highway 20, in Hines.

SECTION TWO

WASHINGTON'S
PUBLIC GOLF COURSES

AN INTRODUCTION
TO WASHINGTON'S COURSES

Washington has nearly two hundred public and semi-private golf courses that have regular public hours. Nine of these locations offer 27 holes, the rest 9 or 18. All of the multi-course sites are found in and near the I-5 Corridor.

Those 27-hole courses include Burlington's Avalon Golf Club, Marysville's Battle Creek Golf Course, Port Ludlow Golf, Seattle's Jackson Park Golf Course, Kent's Riverbend Golf Complex, the Meadow Park Golf Course in Tacoma, Orting's High Cedars Golf Club, Newaukum Valley Golf in Chehalis, and the Mint Valley Golf Course in Longview.

New courses have opened in Lacey, Ridgefield and Stevenson. Lacey's Meriwood Golf Course opened in 1995, and was designed by Bill Overdorf. The Tri Mountain Golf Course in Ridgefield was designed by William G. Robinson and built in 1994. Stevenson's Skamania Lodge Golf Course opened in 1993. It was designed by Bunny Mason.

Changes were made to several Washington courses. This includes the addition of a third 9 holes at Port Ludlow and a major renovation of the Maplewood Golf Course in Renton. The following courses were expanded from 9 to 18 holes: The Highland Golf Course in Cosmopolis, Maple Valley's Elk Run Golf Course, the Alta Lake Golf Club in Pateros, Clarkston's Quail Ridge Golf Course, and Sunnyside's Lower Valley Golf Club.

Washington golfers often see wildlife on the course. At the Leavenworth Golf Club an occasional bear is spotted, elk and deer visit Cathlamet's Skyline Golf Course, and deer and coyote are regularly sighted at Stanwood's Kayak Point and Woodinville's Wellington Hills. Deer also visit Port Townsend's Chevy Chase Golf Club, the Gig Harbor Golf Club course, and Olympia's Scott

Lake Golf Course. At the Carnation Golf Club you may see bald eagles as well as deer.

Golf courses in the Evergreen State also offer beautiful views. You can see Mount St. Helens from the Riverside Country Club in Chehalis, Mt. Rainier from Allyn's Lakeland Village, Auburn's Jade Greens, Olympia's Capitol City Golf and Yelm's Nisqually Valley Golf Course, and Mt. Adams from Toppenish's Mt. Adams Country Club, the Goldendale Country Club and White Salmon's Husum Hills Golf Course. The San Juan Islands will dazzle you at the San Juan Golf Club, the Columbia River Gorge at North Bonneville's Beacon Rock Golf Course, and 55-mile-long Lake Chelan at the Lake Chelan Golf Course.

This book makes it simple to locate every course in a particular area. The state has been divided into the four regions shown below. Each of those regions has its own section which opens with a map, followed by a regional table of contents where cities, and page numbers, appear in the same north to south order as you see them on the region map.

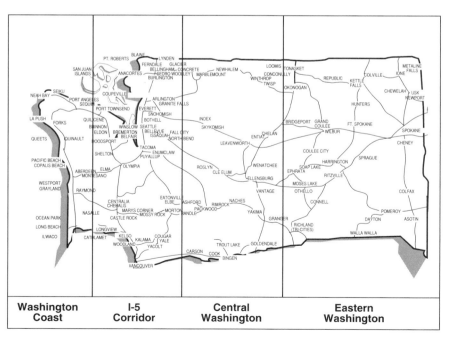

| Washington Coast | I-5 Corridor | Central Washington | Eastern Washington |

With 184 Washington golf courses to choose from, everyone will find a variety of places perfect for their level of ability as well as budget. Why not join the exclusive group who can honestly say, they have golfed them all!

Note: Unless otherwise noted, fees quoted in this section do not include Washington state sales tax.

THE WASHINGTON COAST

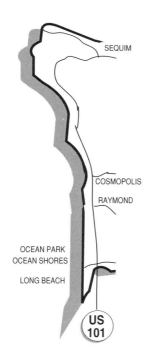

SEQUIM

COSMOPOLIS

RAYMOND

OCEAN PARK
OCEAN SHORES

LONG BEACH

US
101

Washington Coast
Table of Contents

SEQUIM

DUNGENESS GOLF CLUB
1965 Woodcock Rd.
Sequim, WA
(360) 683-6344

The Straits of Juan de Fuca are visible from Dungeness' 7th tee, and the course includes a sand bunker on the 3rd hole that's shaped like a crab. This is a great winter course and is relatively flat and easy to walk. Reservations are advised. Built in 1969, the women's total distance is 5,400 yards.

Green fees April thru September are $20.00 Monday thru Thursday, and $24.00 Friday thru Sunday as well as holidays. The rest of the year it's $16.00 during the week, $18.00 on weekends. Twilight rates are available. Clubs rent for $7.00 and $10.00, and motorized carts are $21.00.

Facilities include a restaurant/lounge with a liquor license, plus a driving range, banquet area and full-service pro shop. At the range you can get a bucket of balls for $2.50 to $4.50. Help with tournament planning, and lessons, are available.

Directions: To reach the Dungeness Golf and Country Club, head south on Sequim Avenue to Woodcock Road, turn left, and drive 3 miles.

SUNLAND GOLF & COUNTRY CLUB
109 Hilltop Dr.
Sequim, WA
(360) 683-6800

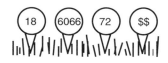

This semi-private course is open to the general public after 2:00 p.m. on Mondays, Wednesdays and Thursdays, after 2:30 p.m. on Fridays, and if tee times are secured 48 hours in advance on weekends. The course has a fairly flat terrain and a fantastic view of both the Olympic Mountains and the Strait of Juan de Fuca. They have two sets of tees. The distance from the women's tees is 5,567 yards for a par 73.

During the week, green fees are $12.00 for 9 holes or $22.00 for 18. On weekends and holidays it'll cost you $14.00 or $28.00. You can rent clubs for $6.00 and $10.00, handcarts $2.00 and $3.00, and motorized carts $12.00 and $22.00.

They have a full-service pro shop, driving range, and a snack bar that offers cold beer. Help with tournament planning, and lessons, are available. At the driving range you can get a small bucket of balls for $1.75.

Directions: To locate the Sunland Golf and Country Club course, leave Highway 101 on Sequim-Dungeness Way, and head north for 3 miles.

COSMOPOLIS

HIGHLAND GOLF COURSE
2200 First St.
Cosmopolis, WA
(360) 533-2455

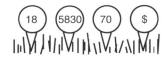

Open year round, Highland was built in 1929; a second 9 holes were added in 1994. This course is wooded, hilly, and offers three tees per hole. The slope is 106 and the ratings 66.5 for men, 68.1 for women. Reservations are recommended. The women's par is 71 for a total distance of 5,165 yards.

Weekend green fees are 10.00 for 9 holes or $15.00 for 18. On weekdays it'll cost you $8.00 and $13.00. Juniors can play before 3:00 p.m. on weekdays for special rates, as can seniors all day Monday thru Friday. Clubs rent for $5.00, handcarts $1.50, and power carts $20.00 for 18 holes.

Facilities include a snack bar that serves beer, plus a driving range, and a full-service pro shop where you can get help with tournament planning and schedule lessons. Credit cards are welcome. At the driving range you'll find a covered area offering both mat and grass tees.

Directions: The Highland Golf Course is located right in Cosmopolis. Simply leave Highway 101 south of Aberdeen, and drive to First Street.

RAYMOND

WILLAPA HARBOR GOLF COURSE
Fowler Street
Raymond, WA
(360) 942-2392

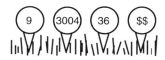

The South Fork River winds its way through this course, in fact it snakes through twice on one hole. The fairways are flat with gentle slopes, and the 5th hole is ranked among the best par fours in the Pacific Northwest. Built in 1926, it's open year round and offers four tees per hole. The slope is 119 and the ratings 68.8 for men, 72.7 for women. Tee times can be reserved two weeks in advance May to October. The total distance for women is 2,878 yards.

You can play 9 holes for $10.00, or 18 holes for $16.00, all week long. Juniors pay $6.00 per 9 holes Monday thru Friday, except holidays. Clubs are $3.50 and $5.00, handcarts $1.50 and $2.50, and motorized carts $12.00 and $20.00.

Facilities include a snack bar where you can get a cold beer, plus a full-service pro shop and driving range. At the range you'll pay $1.50 per 30 balls. Help with tournament planning, and lessons, are available. Credit cards are welcome. This golf course also offers an RV campground.

Directions: At Raymond, leave Highway 101 on Fowler Street and follow to the course.

OCEAN PARK

SURFSIDE GOLF COURSE
31508 "J" Place
Ocean Park, WA
(360) 665-4148

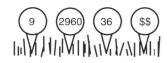

Surfside was built in 1968 and remains open year round from 7:00 a.m. to dusk. Tee times are recommended at all times. This is a fairly level course right on the ocean. Two sets of tees allow you to play 18 holes with a total length of 6,065 yards. The distance from the ladies' tees is 5,605 yards for 18 holes, or 2,788 for 9.

Green fees remain the same seven days a week, $10.00 for 9 holes or $17.00 for 18. Seniors can play on non-holiday weekdays for $8.00 and $14.00. Clubs rent for $2.50 and $3.50, handcarts $1.50 per 9 holes, and motorized carts $12.00 and $20.00.

You'll find a full-service pro shop offering help with tournament planning and lessons, plus a driving range and a snack bar that sells beer. The driving range is for irons, and a bucket of balls will cost you $2.00 to $3.50.

Directions: The Surfside Golf Course is located north of Ocean Park; simply follow the signs.

OCEAN SHORES

OCEAN SHORES GOLF COURSE
Canal Drive
Ocean Shores, WA
(360) 289-3357

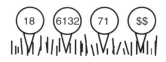

The Ocean Shores Golf Course is open year round and offers tough, fast greens. The fairways are fairly flat and lined with trees. The women's par is 72 for a distance of 5,263 yards.

Green fees are $15.00 for 9 holes or $23.00 for 18 all week long. Winter rates are $10.00 and $15.00. Seniors pay $10.00 and $15.00 in the summer, $8.00 and $12.00 in the winter. Juniors can play for $10.00 in the summer, or $8.00 in the winter, whether they play 9 or 18 holes.

Clubs rent for $10.00 and $15.00, motorized carts are $14.00 and $22.00. You can get help with tournament planning, and arrange lessons, at the full-service pro shop.

Directions: Ocean Shores Golf Course is located on Canal Drive, right in Ocean Shores.

LONG BEACH

PENINSULA GOLF COURSE
9604 Pacific Way
Long Beach, WA
(360) 642-2828

Built in 1947, this Scottish-type course is fairly flat with a few slight hills. It's a good test of skills for most golfers. Two sets of tees are available adding challenge to an 18-hole game. Open year round, from 8:00 a.m. to 7:00 p.m., reservations are generally needed on the weekend.

You'll pay $9.00 for 9 holes, or $13.00 for 18, all week long. You can rent clubs for a flat $2.00, handcarts are $1.00, and motorized carts $9.00 and $15.00.

They have a snack bar, putting green, and limited pro shop. The staff can help with tournament planning, and they offer group golf lessons at very good rates.

Directions: Located just north of the Long Beach city limits.

WASHINGTON'S I-5 CORRIDOR

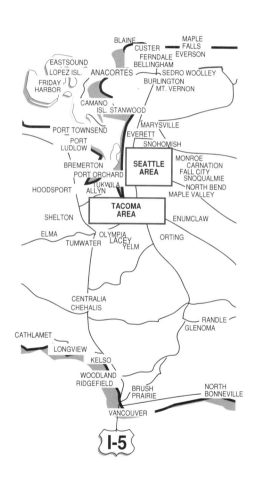

Washington's I-5 Corridor
Table of Contents

BLAINE

SEA LINKS GOLF COURSE
7878 Birch Bay Dr.
Blaine, WA
(360) 371-7933

Sea Links was built on the site of the old Birch Bay Golf Resort. Designed by John Robbins, it opened in 1984. This executive course is basically open, with rolling hills, 5 ponds, 33 sand traps, bent grass greens, and homes lining several fairways. It is a fairly dry course. Tee times are available seven days in advance, and the course is open year round. Summer hours are 7:00 a.m. to dark, winter hours 9:00 a.m. to 5:00 p.m.

During the week, green fees are $9.00 for 9 holes or $11.00 for 18. On weekends you'll pay $11.00 whether you play 9 or 18 holes. Juniors and seniors can play for $7.00 Monday thru Friday. Handcarts rent for $2.00, clubs $7.00, and motorized carts $10.00 per 9 holes.

Sea Links offers a restaurant and lounge with a liquor license, plus a full-service pro shop and banquet facilities. Lessons are available.

Directions: Leave I-5 at exit #270 and head west to Harborview where you'll turn left onto Birch Bay Drive.

SEMI-AH-MOO GOLF COURSE
8720 Semi-ah-moo Parkway
Blaine, WA
(360) 371-7005

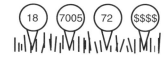

This challenging year-round course was designed by Arnold Palmer, and opened in 1986. The terrain is fairly flat with undulating fairways and offers four sets of tees. Tee times are necessary, and they give preference to members and inn guests. You can call three days in advance for midweek reservations. In spring and summer you can golf as early as 6:30 a.m.; the rest of the year the course opens at 8:00 a.m. Call ahead to check their tournament schedule.

Green fees for 18 holes are $70.00 Friday thru Sunday, and $66.00 the rest of the week. If you don't start till after 2:00 p.m.

you can play at reduced rates. Winter rates are $35.00 for 18 holes. To rent clubs it'll cost you a flat $22.00, handcarts are $4.00, and motorized carts $14.00 per seat.

Semi-ah-moo offers overnight accommodations, a nice restaurant and lounge with a liquor license, banquet facilities, a full-service pro shop, and driving range. At the range you'll find both mat and grass tees, and a bucket of balls will cost you $2.75 to $4.50. Lessons, and help with tournament planning, are available.

Directions: Leave I-5 South at exit #274, or I-5 North on exit #270, and head west. Signs will direct you from either exit.

CUSTER

DAKOTA CREEK GOLF CLUB
3258 Haynie Rd.
Custer, WA
(360) 366-3131

This tough little course has grass tees, some hills, and a second set of tees for 18-hole play. Open year round, weather permitting, reservations are available one week in advance.

Weekday green fees are $7.00 for 9 holes or $11.00 for 18. On weekends you'll pay $9.00 and $15.00. Seniors receive a $1.00 discount per 9 holes during the week. Clubs rent for $4.00, handcarts $2.00, and motorized carts $8.00 per 9 holes. You'll find a limited pro shop and help with tournament planning. Other improvements are underway.

Directions: Leave I-5 at exit #270, follow Birch Bay-Lynden Road to Valley View Road, proceed to Haynie Road, and turn right.

GRANDVIEW GOLF COURSE
7738 Portal Way
Custer, WA
(360) 366-3947

The Grandview course has lots of water hazards, a flat terrain, and a delightful view of Mt. Baker. The slope is 114 for men with a rating of 69.4, it's 107 and 66.4 for women. Built in 1968, it is open year round. You can play between 6:00 a.m. and dusk in the spring and summer; they open up at 9:00 a.m. in the winter, and 8:00 a.m. in the fall. Reservations for weekend play are taken one week in advance.

During the week you'll pay $13.00 for 9 holes or $18.00 for 18. If you're under 17, or over 62, you can play for $12.00 and $15.00. On weekends everyone pays $14.00 and $20.00. They also offer good twilight rates. Clubs rent for $5.00, handcarts $3.00, and motorized carts $15.00 and $22.00. You'll find a snack bar offering cold beer and wine, and a limited pro shop where you can get help with tournament planning.

Directions: Take the Birch-Bay Road exit #270 off I-5, head 1 mile south to Portal Way, and then west to the course.

MAPLE FALLS

PEACEFUL VALLEY GOLF COURSE
8225 Kendall Rd.
Maple Falls, WA
(360) 599-2416

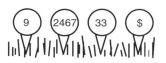

Built on an 80-acre meadow, this course is flat, has no water hazards, and two sets of tees. The terrain is quite open with a few bunkers. Open year round, weather permitting, you can golf at Peaceful Valley between dawn and dusk. Reservations are taken one week in advance.

Green fees are $8.00 for 9 holes or $11.00 for 18 during the week, $10.00 and $13.00 on weekends. Tuesdays, Wednesdays and Thursdays after 2:00 p.m. you can play 18 holes for the price of 9. Handcarts rent for $2.00, clubs $5.00, and motorized carts $10.00 per 9 holes. Facilities include a snack bar and a limited pro shop.

Directions: Leave I-5 at the Mt. Baker Highway, just after milepost marker #23, on the Kendall-Sumas Road. Turn left, go 2.5 miles, turn left again, and then right to the course.

EVERSON

EVERGREEN GOLF COURSE
413 Main St.
Everson, WA
(360) 966-5417

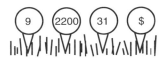

Evergreen Golf Course is open March thru October, from dawn to dusk. The terrain is fairly flat and easy to walk. This course has tight out of bounds, plenty of trees, and a creek you have to cross three to four times during your game.

On weekends, green fees at Evergreen are about $8.00 for 9 holes; the rest of the week it'll cost you around $7.00. Clubs rent for $2.00, as do handcarts. Facilities include a snack bar where you'll find cold beer and wine, and a limited pro shop.

Directions: Located right in town, on Main Street.

RASPBERRY RIDGE GOLF COURSE
6827 Hannegan Rd.
Everson, WA
(360) 354-3029

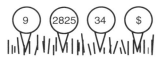

Raspberry Ridge is a year-round course with a fairly flat terrain, and is easy to walk. You'll find three sets of tees, large greens, fairly wide fairways, and a terrific view of Mt. Baker. Winter hours are 8:00 a.m. to 5:00 p.m. During the spring and summer they open at 6:30 a.m. on weekends, 7:00 a.m. on weekdays, and stay open until dark. Tee times are available one week in advance. The total distance from the women's tees is 2,335 yards.

Green fees are the same seven days a week, $9.50 for 9 holes or $15.00 for 18. On weekdays, juniors and seniors play for $8.50 and $13.00. Clubs rent for $4.50, handcarts $2.00, and motorized carts $9.00 and $15.00.

Facilities include a limited pro shop, and a restaurant where beer and wine is served. At the pro shop you can get help with tournament planning.

Directions: Leave I-5 at exit #256-A and follow Highway 539 north 7 miles to Highway 544. After traveling east 2 miles, turn right onto Hannegan Road and follow to the course.

FERNDALE

RIVERSIDE GOLF COURSE
5799 Riverside Dr.
Ferndale, WA
(360) 384-4116

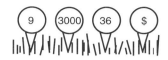

Riverside was built just after the turn of the century, and is open year round. The course is level with small rolling ridges, and has three sets of tees. The women's tees have a total distance of 2,860 yards for a par of 37.

Weekday green fees are $8.00 for 9 holes or $12.00 for 18. On weekends they're $9.00 and $13.00. If you're under 15, or over 60, you'll save $2.00 off 9 holes and $4.00 off 18. Clubs are $4.00 and $6.00, handcarts $2.00 and $3.00, and motorized carts $14.00 and $20.00. Facilities include a pro shop, plus a snack bar that offers cold beer. Help with tournament planning is available.

Directions: To reach the course take exit #262 off I-5.

BELLINGHAM

LAKE PADDEN GOLF COURSE
4882 Samish Way
Bellingham, WA
(360) 738-7400

The Lake Padden course was built in 1970. Cut out of a forest, each hole is separated by thick stands of cedar. The terrain is moderately rolling, the slope 124, and the rating 72.0. Open year round, summer hours are 6:00 a.m. to dusk, but in the winter they don't open until 8:00 a.m. They are closed to the public on Labor Day. Reservations are taken one week in advance, and the total yardage from the women's tees is 5,505.

Seven days a week local residents pay $15.00, and non-residents $20.00, at Lake Padden. On weekdays, golfers younger than 18, and those 62 or older, play for reduced rates. You can rent clubs for $10.00, handcarts $2.50, and motorized carts $22.00. They have a limited pro shop, restaurant, lounge, snack bar, driving range, and banquet facilities. Beer and wine are available. The range has a 300 yard grass tee and offers balls for $3.00 to $5.00. Lessons, and help with tournament planning, are available.

Directions: Leave I-5 North at exit #246 and follow Samish Way north. Leave I-5 South on exit #252, and take Samish Way south.

SUDDEN VALLEY GOLF CLUB
2145 Lake Whatcom Blvd.
Bellingham, WA
(360) 734-6435

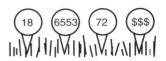

This course overlooks beautiful Lake Whatcom. Designed by Ted Robinson, it was built in 1970. The front 9 is great for long hitters, but you'll need plenty of accuracy to avoid the lakes and creek. The back 9 is wooded, hilly, and where you'll find the signature "cliff" hole. Open year round, the slope is 129 and the ratings 72.4 for men and 72.5 for women. From the ladies' tees the distance is 5,627 yards. Tee times are given one week in advance.

July thru September weekday green fees are $25.00; on weekends it'll cost you $34.00. Lower rates are charged off season, and juniors also play for discounted rates; call for current fees. Credit cards are accepted for green fees. You can rent clubs for $14.00, handcarts $3.00, and motorized carts $23.00. Facilities include a lounge and restaurant with a liquor license, plus banquet and meeting rooms, a driving range and pro shop. Lessons are available, as is help with tournament planning. The range has grass tees and charges $2.50 to $4.50 for balls.

Directions: Take the Lakeway exit off I-5 and head east 8 miles.

EASTSOUND

ORCAS ISLAND GOLF CLUB
Golf Course Road
Eastsound, WA
(360) 376-4400

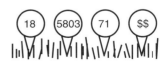

The Orcas Island Golf Club is found in the beautiful San Juan Islands. The terrain is a combination of hills and flat areas with bent greens, well designed tees, and three large ponds. It sits in an evergreen forest and the ponds attract wildfowl as well as golf balls. This was once a farm, and the original farmhouse serves as the clubhouse. Open year round, from 7:00 a.m. to 7:00 p.m., tee times are suggested at least three days in advance. The par for women is 73 for a total distance of 5,464 yards.

Green fees are $17.50 for 9 holes or $25.00 for 18. Clubs rent for $7.00, and motorized carts $15.00 and $20.00. They have a full-service pro shop and can help you with tournament planning.

Directions: Orcas Island is accessible by ferry; from the docks you simply follow Horseshoe Highway.

LOPEZ ISLAND

LOPEZ ISLAND GOLF COURSE
Airport Road
Lopez Island, WA
(360) 468-2679

Located on an island in the San Juans, golfers at Lopez Island arrive by ferry, private boat, or small plane. The Lopez Airport has a 2,900-foot runway adjacent to the course, and boaters can take a taxi from the docks. The course is open year round, April thru September, from 9:00 a.m. to 7:00 p.m. Thursday thru Monday.

Many golfers spot deer or rabbits along the narrow fairways; eagles and hawks often circle above. Opened in 1958, the terrain is easy to walk with undulating greens. Green fees are about $12.00 for 9 holes, with reduced rates for juniors. October thru March you pay on the honor system. When the pro shop is open you can rent clubs for $5.00 and handcarts for $2.00.

Facilities include a limited pro shop with a few snack machines, plus banquet facilities. They will provide help with tournament planning.

Directions: This course is 6 miles from the Lopez Island ferry landing. Simply follow Fisherman Bay Road to Airport Road and go 1.5 miles.

FRIDAY HARBOR

SAN JUAN GOLF & COUNTRY CLUB
2261 Golf Course Rd.
Friday Harbor, WA
(360) 378-2254

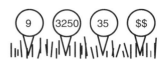

The San Juan course is relatively flat with some hills, long fairways, small greens, and plenty of water. The view is terrific and includes Griffin Bay, Mt. Baker, and other islands within the San Juans. Built in 1965, and open April thru October, this course is much tougher than it looks. The slope is 115 and the ratings 70.0 for men, 71.3 for women. Tee times are not required, and the women's par is 72 for a total distance of 5,466 yards.

You'll pay $17.50 to play 9 holes, or $25.00 for 18, seven days a week at the San Juan Golf and Country Club. Juniors are allowed to play for $10.00 when space is available. You can rent clubs for $7.50, handcarts $2.50, and motorized carts are $12.00 for 9 holes or $20.00 for 18.

Facilities include a snack bar, pro shop, and driving range. At the range a bucket of balls will cost you $2.25 to $3.25. They offer both mat and grass tees, and remain open until 5:00 pm. Lessons are available.

Directions: Located on San Juan Island, 3 miles south of Friday Harbor, off Cattle Point Road.

ANACORTES

SIMILK GOLF COURSE
1250 Christiansen Rd.
Anacortes, WA
(360) 293-3444

This year-round course is surrounded by trees, and the terrain is a combination of flat and hilly. The slope is 107 and the ratings 67.1 for men, 71.1 for women. Similk is open from dawn to dusk during the primary golfing season; in the winter they open at 8:00

a.m. Reservations are taken one day in advance. Par from the ladies' tees is 76 for a distance of 5,934 yards.

On weekends and holidays you'll pay $13.00 for 9 holes or $19.00 for 18. The rest of the week it'll cost you $11.00 and $17.00. You can rent a full set of clubs for $8.00, or a half set for $4.00. Handcarts are $2.50, and motorized carts $10.00 per 9 holes.

Facilities include a snack shop, banquet room, driving range, and a limited pro shop where you can get help with tournament planning. The driving range charges $2.50 per 40 balls.

Directions: Located 10 miles west of I-5, as you head toward Anacortes on Highway 20.

SEDRO WOOLLEY

GATEWAY GOLF COURSE
839 Fruitdale Rd.
Sedro Woolley, WA
(360) 856-0315

This year-round course's terrain is a combination of flat and hilly, and provides a nice view of the Cascade Mountains. During the winter it is open during daylight hours, in the summer from 7:00 a.m. to dusk. Three sets of tees add variety to your game, and the women's tees have a total distance of about 2,500 yards.

Weekday green fees are $9.00 for 9 holes or $13.00 for 18, with seniors saving $1.00 per 9 holes. On weekends, everybody pays $10.00 for 9 holes or $15.00 for 18. Clubs rent for $5.50 and $6.50, handcarts $2.00 and $3.00, and motorized carts $10.00 and $15.00.

Facilities include a limited pro shop where you'll find light snacks and cold beer. Lessons, and help with tournament planning, are available. They also have a putting and chipping green.

Directions: You'll find the Gateway Golf Course located 3 blocks off Highway 20, on Fruitdale Road.

BURLINGTON

AVALON GOLF CLUB
1717 Kelleher Rd.
Burlington, WA
(360) 757-1900

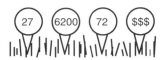

Avalon offers spectacular views of the Skagit Valley, and its gently rolling hills provide an enjoyable walk. Designed by Robert Muir Graves, it was built in 1991. Open year round, they take reservations five days in advance, or up to a year in advance if prepaid. Credit cards are welcome. Avalon's slope is 124 and the ratings 70.0 for men, 72.2 for women. The women's tees have a total distance of 5,300 yards.

June thru September green fees for 18 holes are $26.00 Monday thru Thursday, $32.00 on Friday, and $35.00 on the weekends. During May and October it's $24.00, $27.00, and $32.00. Off-season rates are $20.00 Monday thru Friday, and $26.00 on weekends. Juniors play for half the regular green fees. Motorized carts are $23.00, clubs $12.00 to $18.00, and handcarts $3.00.

Monday is senior day, and anyone over 55 can play 18 holes for $18.00, 9 holes for $10.00, and rent carts for $8.00 per rider. Everybody gets special rates after 2:00 p.m., $11.00 for 9 holes or $19.00 for 18. November thru March two golfers can play for $30.00 on Tuesdays and Thursdays.

Facilities include a restaurant where beer and wine are available, a tournament facility that seats 250, full-service pro shop, and driving range. The driving range has grass tees and offers a small bucket of balls for $3.00, a large one for $4.50. They can also help you with tournament planning and offer video golf lessons.

Directions: From I-5 North take Cook Road exit #232, turn right, take the first left onto Highway 99, follow for 2 miles, and turn right onto Kelleher Road.

From I-5 South take Bow Hill exit #236, turn left, proceed down the hill to Highway 99, turn right, and after 2 miles turn left onto Kelleher for .7 mile.

MT. VERNON

OVERLOOK GOLF COURSE
1785 Hwy. 9
Mt. Vernon, WA
(360) 422-6444

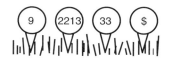

This challenging course has a great view of Big Lake and the surrounding mountains. Built in 1985, the terrain has some hills and a little water. The slope is 97 for men with a rating of 60.2, for women it's 96 and 60.3. Reservations are recommended on weekends and holidays. You can play at Overlook year round, weather permitting. Summer hours are 7:00 a.m. to dark.

Weekday green fees are $8.00 for 9 holes or $14.00 for 18. On the weekend you'll pay $10.00 or $17.00. You can rent clubs for $3.50, handcarts $2.00, and motorized carts $9.00 per 9 holes. Facilities include a pro shop where you can get help with tournament planning and arrange for lessons, plus a snack bar where you can get a cold beer.

Directions: To reach Overlook, leave I-5 at exit #227, head east on College Way for about 3.5 miles to Highway 9, turn right and go an additional 3.5 miles.

CAMANO ISLAND

CAMALOCH GOLF COURSE
326N E. Camano Dr.
Camano Island, WA
(360) 387-3084 or (800) 628-0469

Camaloch Golf Course is relatively flat with just one hill to climb. Located in the Olympic Mountain's rain shadow, the greens are smooth, consistent, and nicely bunkered. A new 9 was added in 1991. Designed by Bill Overdorf, he is also redesigning the old 9. The slope is 122 to 125 and the ratings 68.7 to 70.0 for men, 70.9 for women. Open year round, tee times are recommended. The women's tees have a distance of 5,239 yards.

During the week green fees are $16.00 Monday thru Friday, and $23.00 on weekends and holidays. On weekdays juniors and seniors can play for $15.00, and the twilight rates are $10.00 for everyone. Clubs rent for $5.00, handcarts $3.00, and motorized carts $20.00. Credit cards are welcome.

Facilities include a snack bar offering cold beer and wine, plus a banquet room, full-service pro shop, driving range and practice putting green. They can arrange lessons, and help you with tournament planning.

Directions: To reach the Camaloch Golf Course, leave I-5 at exit #212 and go west 11.5 miles.

STANWOOD

KAYAK POINT GOLF COURSE
15711 Marine Dr.
Stanwood, WA
(360) 652-9656

This is one of Washington's best courses. Built in 1977, the slope ranges from 121 to 144, and the ratings are 72.7 for men, 72.8 for women. Its sloping terrain, tree-lined fairways, undulating greens, and numerous bunkers provide a real challenge. Carved out of a fir and alder forest, it has views of Puget Sound and the Olympic Mountains. Raccoons, deer, and an occasional coyote wander across its fairways. The ladies tees have a total distance of 5,332 yards. Open year round, Kayak Point offers excellent winter golf. Reservations are taken one week in advance.

Monday thru Thursday, green fees are $15.00 for 9 holes or $23.00 for 18. The rest of the week they're $15.00 and $27.00. Monday thru Thursday, juniors and seniors can play all day for $15.00. Children under 12 must have adult supervision on the course. Clubs rent for $18.00, handcarts $3.00, and motorized carts $12.50 per 9 holes. Credit cards are welcome.

Facilities include a restaurant and lounge where you have a view overlooking Puget Sound, Camano Island, and the 18th green. They have a liquor license and offer banquet facilities. At the full-service pro shop you can get help with tournament planning and lessons. The driving range has grass tees, and charges $2.00 to $4.00 for balls.

Directions: The Kayak Point Golf Course is located south of Stanwood. From Seattle, take the Marysville/Tualip exit #199, turn left, and follow Marine Drive for 13 miles.

MARYSVILLE

BATTLE CREEK GOLF COURSE
6006 Meridian Ave. N.
Marysville, WA
(360) 659-7931

You'll find both an 18- hole and 9-hole course at Battle Creek. The 9-hole course is a par 27 with a total distance of 1,113 yards. The 18-hole course is situated in a scenic wetland area surrounded by fir and pine. The rolling terrain has two large ponds and a nice view of Puget Sound. Designed by Fred Jacobson, and built in 1989, the slope is 121 and the ratings 69.5 for men, 70.9 for women. The women's tees have a total distance of 5,286 yards. Both courses are open year round during daylight hours.

During the week, green fees on the par three course are $7.00 for 9 holes or 11.00 for 18; they're $8.00 and $14.00 on weekends. The 18-hole course charges $12.00 and $18.00 Monday thru Friday, $14.00 and $23.00 on weekends. Juniors and seniors can play 18 holes during the week for $15.00. Clubs rent for $6.00 to $20.00, handcarts $2.00 and $3.00, and motorized carts $12.00 and $21.00.

You'll find a restaurant with banquet facilities where beer and wine is served, plus a driving range and full-service pro shop. Lessons are available, as is assistance with tournament planning. At the range you'll pay $3.00 for 40 balls or $4.00 for 70.

Directions: Take exit #199 off I-5, head west on Marine drive 2.7 miles to Meridian Avenue, turn right and go .7 mile to the Battle Creek Golf Course.

CEDARCREST MUNICIPAL GOLF
6810 84th St. N.E.
Marysville, WA
(360) 659-3566

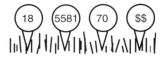

Cedarcrest is currently undergoing reconstruction and will not re-open until early in 1998. The original construction was finished in 1927. Green fees should remain reasonable at this municipal course. Current facilities include a restaurant/lounge, banquet rooms, and a pro shop.

Directions: Cedarcrest is located 2 miles northeast of Marysville on the road to Granite Falls. From I-5, take exit #199 and follow State Highway 528 east approximately 2 miles before turning left onto 67th Avenue. The course is 1.5 miles north.

PORT TOWNSEND

CHEVY CHASE GOLF CLUB
7401 Cape George Rd.
Port Townsend, WA
(360) 385-0704

This course has a great view of Discovery Bay and the Olympic Mountains, plus fairways surrounded by huge trees. A year-round course, it was constructed about 1925. You enter through a hand-split cedar fence that was built by the original settler in the 1800s. Golfers often encounter rabbits and deer. The terrain is relatively flat, the slope 115, and the ratings 69.4 for men and 75.6 for women. The total distance from the women's tees is 2,797 yards.

In season, green fees are $13.00 for 9 holes or $19.00 for 18. Senior rates on weekends are $12.00 and $16.00, midweek it's $10.00 and $14.00. Weekend rates for juniors are $6.00 and $9.00; it's $5.00 and $8.00 the balance of the week. The twilight special begins at 4:00 p.m., when you'll pay $9.00 on weekdays or $10.00 on weekends. Winter midweek rates are $12.00 and $17.00.

Rental clubs will cost you $6.00 for 9 holes or $10.00 for 18, handcarts $2.00 and $3.00, and motorized carts $14.00 and $20.00. They have a snack bar offering beer and wine, plus banquet facilities and a driving range with mat tees. At the full-service pro shop they can help you with lessons and tournament planning. Credit cards are welcome.

Directions: Take Highway 20 to Four Corners and drive west 1.5 miles.

PORT TOWNSEND GOLF CLUB
1948 Blaine St.
Port Townsend, WA
(360) 385-0752

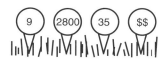

This course sits on a hill overlooking the Kaitai Lagoon, and includes a view of Port Townsend Bay and the Olympic Mountains. Built in 1925, it is open year round. Winter hours are 8:00 a.m. to dusk, but in the summer they open up at 6:00 a.m. Reservations are taken one week in advance for summer weekends.

Green fees are $10.00 for 9 holes or $15.00 for 18 all week long. Juniors can play for $5.00 per 9 holes on Mondays and Fridays; seniors pay $6.00 per 9 holes. After 2:00 p.m. on Saturdays, anyone can play for a flat $8.00. Clubs rent for $4.00 and $6.00, handcarts $2.00 and $3.00, and motorized carts $10.00 and $18.00. They have a restaurant, lounge, and banquet area with a liquor license, plus a driving range and full-service pro shop. Lessons, and help with tournament planning, are available. At the driving range you can get a bucket of balls for $3.00 to $5.00.

Directions: Coming into town on Highway 20, take a left at the first stoplight, then go right at the stop sign.

PORT LUDLOW

PORT LUDLOW GOLF COURSE
751 Highland Dr.
Port Ludlow, WA
(360) 437-0272

Designed by Robert Muir Graves, the Port Ludlow Golf Course first opened in 1975. In 1993 they added a third nine holes. The terrain is very hilly, and it has tree-lined fairways, elevated tees, and plenty of sand. Surrounded by forest, it also has a number of creeks and ponds, and is extremely challenging. The slope is 124 for men and 126 for women, and the ratings 70.3 and 72.9. Hours are 7:00 a.m. to 7:00 p.m. April thru October, and 8:00 a.m. to 4:00 p.m. November thru March. Reservations are available one week in advance.

May thru September you'll pay $50.00 during the week, and $55.00 on weekends. In April and October it's $40.00 and $45.00, and November thru March 30.00 and $35.00. Twilight rates begin at 3:00 p.m., and are $27.50 to $30.00 depending on the time of year. Motorized carts rent for $13.00 and $26.00, handcarts $3.00, and clubs $18.00.

Port Ludlow has deluxe resort accommodations, a marina, restaurant and lounge, snack bar, full-service pro shop, and a driving range. They offer help with tournament planning and lessons. At the driving range you'll find mat tees during the winter, grass tees in the summer, and can get 40 balls for $2.50.

Directions: Located just west of the Hood Canal Bridge.

EVERETT

HARBOUR POINTE GOLF CLUB
11817 Harbour Pointe Blvd.
Mukilteo, WA
(206) 355-6060

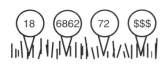

Harbour Pointe offers a terrific view of Puget Sound from the 11th hole, and is open year round, from sun-up to sun-down. Reservations are taken five days in advance. You'll find a flat terrain, a challenging layout, and four sets of tees. The total distance from the women's tees is 5,321 yards.

Monday thru Thursday green fees are $22.00 for 9 holes or $40.00 for 18. On Mondays and Tuesdays, juniors, 17 and under, play for $25.00, and seniors for $30.00. Friday thru Sunday everybody pays $25.00 for 9 holes or $45.00 for 18. Clubs rent for $12.00 and $20.00, handcarts $2.00 and $3.00, and motorized carts $15.00 and $26.00.

Facilities include a restaurant and lounge with a liquor license, plus a full-service pro shop and driving range. Lessons are available, and you can get help with tournament planning. At the range you'll pay $3.00 for 30 balls or $5.00 for 60.

Directions: Located southwest of Everett. Take Highway 525 to Mukilteo, and after about a mile turn left onto Harbour Pointe Blvd. for 1.5 miles.

LEGION MEMORIAL GOLF COURSE
144 W. Marine View Dr.
Everett, WA
(206) 259-4653

This year-round course is open from dawn to dusk, and has a fairly flat terrain. Weekday reservations are taken one day in advance; weekend reservations are taken on Mondays for the following weekend. The women's tees have a total distance of 5,681 yards for a par of 73.

You'll pay $13.75 to play 9 holes or $16.50 for 18, seven days a week. Everett residents receive a $4.50 discount. You can rent clubs for $7.00, handcarts $3.00, and motorized carts are $10.00 for 9 holes or $20.00 for 18.

The Legion Memorial Golf Course offers banquet facilities, and a restaurant where beer and wine is served. The full-service pro shop can provide help with tournament planning and lessons.

Directions: Take exit #195 off I-5 at Everett; the course is just 2 miles off the highway.

WALTER E. HALL MEMORIAL GOLF
1226 S.W. Casino Rd.
Everett, WA
(206) 353-4653

Hall Memorial is a reasonably dry winter course. It's a good place to build your iron skills and practice putting. You'll find several dog legs, 6 ponds, 5 creeks, and large undulating greens. The women's par is 73 for a total distance of 5,676 yards. They open at dawn every day but Christmas. Weekday reservations are taken one week in advance, and they begin taking weekend reservations the preceding Monday.

145

Green fees are $13.75 for 9 holes or $16.50 for 18, all week long. You can rent a full set of clubs for $10.00 or a half set for $7.00. Handcarts are $3.00 and motorized carts $10.00 and $20.00. You'll find pitching and chipping areas with four greens as well as a spot to practice with your medium to long irons.

Facilities include a restaurant serving beer and wine, plus a banquet area and full-service pro shop. Lessons, and assistance with tournament planning, are available.

Directions: Located 1 mile west of Highway 99 via Casino Road.

SNOHOMISH

ECHO FALLS COUNTRY CLUB
20414 121st Ave. S.E.
Snohomish, WA
(360) 668-3030

This public country club is open year round, and the 18th hole features an island green with a par three. The slope is 126 and the ratings 68.0 for men, 64.6 for women. You'll find good views of the Cascade and Olympic Mountains, tree-lined fairways, plenty of bunkers and water hazards, plus four tees per hole. Reservations are taken five days in advance. The total distance from the women's tees is 4,265 yards for a par of 71.

Friday, Saturday, Sunday and holidays, it costs $37.50 to play at Echo Falls. The balance of the week it's $27.50, but golfers under 17, or over 60, can play for $20.00. Rates are lower off-season, as well as after twilight. Credit cards are welcome for green fees. Clubs rent for $20.00, handcarts $3.00, and motorized carts $10.00 per 9 holes.

Facilities include a restaurant and lounge that serves beer and wine, plus a banquet area, driving range, and a full-service pro shop where you can get help with tournament planning and arrange lessons. At the driving range you get 30 balls for $2.50 or 70 for $5.00.

Directions: Leave I-405 on Highway 522, go east 7 miles, turn right at the light onto Echo Lake Road, and follow the signs.

KENWANDA GOLF COURSE
14030 Kenwanda Dr.
Snohomish, WA
(360) 668-1166

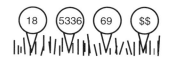

Kenwanda is a year-round course that offers golfers a challenging, but fun game. The slope for men is 119 for a rating of 65.3; for ladies it's 126 and 70.4. Built in 1962, and open year round, this is a great winter course. The terrain is hilly with a view of the Snohomish Valley, has small greens, and interconnecting fairways. You'll find doglegs, blind holes, trees, bunkers, water, and plenty of slopes. Par from the ladies' tees is 72. Reservations are taken up to seven days in advance.

Green fees remain the same at the Kenwanda Golf Course, all week long. You'll pay $11.00 for 9 holes, $18.00 for 18 holes, or $25.00 to golf all day. Clubs rent for $8.50, handcarts $2.50, and motorized carts $20.00. Facilities include a coffee shop where you can get beer and wine, plus a full-service pro shop. Help with tournament planning is available.

Directions: Located 4 miles south of Snohomish, east of Highway 9.

LOBO COUNTRY CLUB
8324 121st St. S.E.
Snohomish, WA
(360) 568-1638

Lobo is a lovely little par three course that is open year round, from dawn to dusk, weather permitting. The setting is nice, with a creek running through the course, and it's flat and easy to walk. Improvements are currently underway, and when they're completed, fees may rise.

Green fees are currently $6.00 for 9 holes or $10.00 for 18, including taxes. On weekdays seniors save $1.00 on 9 holes. Clubs rent for $3.00 and handcarts $2.00. Motorized carts are only rented to golfers with disabilities; the charge is $8.00 for 9 holes or $12.00 for 18. They can provide help with tournament planning, and arrange for lessons. Snack machines are found in the limited pro shop.

Directions: Leave Highway 2 and follow 123rd Street S.E. to the clubhouse.

SNOHOMISH PUBLIC GOLF COURSE

7806 147th Ave. S.E.
Snohomish, WA
(360) 568-9932

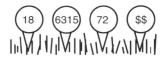

This Snohomish course has elevated greens, rolling hills, tree-lined fairways, and lots of sand traps. It's long enough to challenge the good golfer, but open enough for beginners. Three sets of tees are available. Open year round, from 6:30 a.m. to dusk, reservations are taken one week in advance. The women's tees have a distance of 5,980 yards for a par of 74.

On weekends and holidays, green fees are $14.00 for 9 holes or $22.00 for 18. The rest of the week they're $12.00 and $17.00. If you're under 17, or over 65, weekday green fees for 18 holes are $15.00. You can rent a full set of clubs for $6.00 or a half set for $4.00, handcarts are $2.00 and $3.00, and motorized carts $12.00 and $20.00. Tax is added to all fees. They have a restaurant with banquet facilities where you'll find cold beer, plus a full-service pro shop and driving range. At the range you can get 35 balls for $2.50 or 70 for $3.50. Lessons, and help with tournament planning, are available.

Directions: Leave I-5 at Everett and head east on Highway 2 to the third exit. You can follow signs from here.

SEATTLE AREA

(SEATTLE)

GREEN LAKE GOLF COURSE

5701 Greenlake Way N.
Seattle, WA
(206) 632-2280

The Green Lake Golf Course is open March thru October, from 9:00 a.m. to dusk. It's a quick little course with a flat terrain.

Green fees here are a real bargain; you'll pay $4.00 for 9 holes or $6.00 for 18 all week long. Juniors and seniors can play for $3.00 and $4.50. Clubs rent for $.25 each, and handcarts are $.50.

Motorized carts are not needed. They offer a minimal pro shop where you'll find cold pop and light snacks.

Directions: This course is located near the southern tip of Green Lake. From I-5 take the 50th Street exit, head west on 50th to Green Lake Way, turn right and go 7 blocks.

JACKSON PARK GOLF COURSE
1000 N.E. 135th St.
Seattle, WA
(206) 363-4747

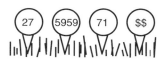

Jackson Park has both an 18-hole championship, and a 9-hole par three course. The longer course is fairly hilly, and provides an interesting challenge. Its slope ranges from 111 to 118, and the ratings are 67.4 for men, 71.8 for women. The total distance from the women's tees is 5,697 yards for a par of 74. Built in 1930, walk-ins are welcome, but they also take reservations one week in advance. The course is closed on Christmas Day.

Green fees on the 18-hole course are $15.00, whether you're playing 9 or 18 holes. During the week, seniors can play for $10.50, juniors and students for $10.00. Clubs rent for $11.00, handcarts $2.00 and $3.00, and motorized carts $13.00 and $18.00. Seniors get a discount on motorized carts on Mondays and Fridays. Credit cards are okay for green fees.

Green fees on the 9-hole course are $6.50, and you can rent clubs for $4.50. Facilities include a restaurant where beer and wine are served, plus a snack bar and full-service pro shop. Lessons, and help with tournament planning, are available. Children under 8 are not allowed on either course.

Directions: Leave I-5 North at exit #175, turn left on 145th, right on 15th, and right on 135th. From I-5 South it's exit #174, right on 130th, and left on 10th.

JEFFERSON PARK GOLF COURSE
4101 Beacon Ave.
Seattle, WA
(206) 762-4513

This Seattle course was built in 1928, and although the front 9 is flat, the back 9 is hilly. A challenging course, it's open year round and easy to walk. There are only a few sand traps and no water. Winter hours are 8:00 a.m. to 4:00 p.m. Summer hours are 6:00 a.m. to 9:00 p.m. on weekdays, 7:00 a.m. to 9:00 p.m. on weekends. Reservations are available one week in advance. The distance from the women's tees is 5,524 yards for a par of 73.

If you live in King County, green fees are $15.00 whether you play 9 or 18 holes. If you're from out of the area it'll cost you $19.50. County golfers younger than 17, or over 65, can play 18 holes for $10.50 Monday thru Friday. Clubs rent for $6.00 and $12.00, handcarts $3.00, and motorized carts $13.00 and $18.00.

Facilities include a restaurant and lounge where beer and wine is served, plus a driving range and full-service pro shop. They offer help with tournament planning and lessons. The driving range charges $3.00 to $4.75 for a bucket of balls.

Directions: Take the Columbia Way exit off I-5, turn left right after the first light onto Columbia Way, turn right at the second light and you'll find the course just up the street.

TYEE VALLEY GOLF CLUB
2401 S. 192nd St.
Seattle, WA
(206) 878-3540

Tyee Valley is a year-round course. They open at 7:00 a.m. during the winter, 5:30 a.m. on summer weekends, and 6:00 a.m. the balance of the year. You'll find lots of water and trees, plus some hills, sand, and a shallow stream. The stream has been planted with salmon which are usually visible. The women's tees have a total distance of 5,663 yards for a par of 73.

Green fees are $12.50 for 9 holes or $18.00 for 18 during the week, and $19.00 for 18 holes on weekends. During the summer, before 1:00 p.m., you can only play 18 holes. If you're under 17, or over 62, and arrive before 10:00 a.m. on weekdays, you can play 9 holes for $10.50; after 10:00 a.m. it'll cost you $12.50. A full set of clubs rents for $10.00 and a starter set $5.00, handcarts are $2.00 and $3.00, and motorized carts $10.00 and $18.00. If you bring your own cart the trail fee is $5.50.

They have a restaurant with banquet facilities that serves beer and wine, plus a full-service pro shop. Lessons are available, as is help with tournament planning.

Directions: Located just south of the airport. Take the 151st Street exit off I-5 northbound to Pacific Highway South, turn right, then turn left at 192nd and follow to the course.

WEST SEATTLE GOLF CLUB
4470 35th Ave. S.W.
Seattle, WA
(206) 935-5187

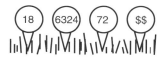

The terrain on this course is slightly hilly, and it offers a good view of downtown Seattle. Open year round, winter hours are 8:00 a.m. to 4:00 p.m.; in the summer they open at 5:00 a.m. on weekends and 6:00 a.m. on weekdays. Reservations are taken one week in advance. The women's tees have a total distance of 6,107 yards for a par of 73.

If you live outside King County, green fees are $19.50 whether you play 9 or 18 holes. County residents pay just $15.00, if they're under 17 it's only $10.00, and seniors, handicapped golfers and college students pay $10.50. Sundown rates are $12.00 for residents and $15.75 for others. You can rent a full set of clubs for $11.00 or a half set for $6.00, handcarts are $3.00, and motorized carts $13.00 and $18.00. They have a restaurant, lounge, and banquet facilities where beer is served, plus a full-service pro shop. Lessons, and help with tournament planning, are available.

Directions: Leave I-5 at exit #163 and follow the West Seattle Freeway west 2.5 miles to the first light, turn left and go 2 blocks to the course.

(BAINBRIDGE ISLAND)

MEADOWMEER GOLF CLUB
8530 Renny Ln. N.E.
Bainbridge Island, WA
(206) 842-2218

This is a narrow, challenging course with well-placed bunkers, excellent greens, a rolling terrain, and a great view of the Olympic Mountains. The slope for men is 117 with a rating of 67.0, for women it's 121 and 69.5. Open every day but Christmas, Meadowmere is one of the most playable winter courses in the state. Built in 1972, they take reservations one week in advance. The women's par is 37 for a total distance of 2,567 yards.

Weekend and holiday green fees are $14.00 for 9 holes or $18.00 for 18. The rest of the week they charge $11.00 and $15.00, but juniors and seniors get to play all day for $10.00. Major credit cards are accepted for green fees. Clubs rent for $6.00 and $10.00, handcarts $2.00 and $3.00, and motorized carts $13.00 and $21.50.

Facilities include a snack bar serving beer and wine, plus a banquet area and full-service pro shop. Lessons, and tournament planning help, are available.

Directions: From the Seattle Ferry take Highway 305 for 3.5 miles to Koura Road and the course.

(BELLEVUE)

BELLEVUE GOLF COURSE
5500 140th Ave. N.E.
Bellevue, WA
(206) 451-7250

Tee times at Bellevue are needed on weekends, on weekdays they're not taken. During the summer months this course can get pretty busy. The women's tees have a total distance of 5,081 yards. Facilities include a restaurant where beer and wine is served, plus a pro shop where you can arrange for lessons, and a driving range.

Green fees are $18.00 seven days a week whether you play 9 or 18 holes. During the week juniors and seniors play for $12.00. You can rent a half set of clubs for $10.00 or a full set for $12.50, handcarts are $3.00, and motorized carts $21.00. Twilight rates begin four hours before sundown; you can play for $13.50 and rent a cart for $14.00. At the driving range you get a basket of balls for $3.50 to $5.00.

Directions: Leave I-405 north at the Redmond exit #18 and head east to 140th Avenue, turn right and go 1.5 miles.

CROSSROADS PARK GOLF COURSE
16000 N.E. Tenth
Bellevue, WA
(206) 453-4875

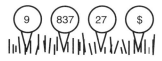

Crossroads is a good course for irons. You'll find easy walking with some hills, grass tees, and trees along the fairways at this small par three course. Open March thru October, Crossroads' hours are 9:00 a.m. to dusk. Reservations are not taken.

This is a nice, inexpensive place to play; 9 holes will cost you $5.00 all week long. If you're under 17, or over 55, you can play for $4.00. Clubs rent for $1.00. They have a limited pro shop where you'll find snack machines, help with tournament planning, and golf lessons.

Directions: You'll find this par three course located behind the Crossroads Shopping Center.

(BOTHELL)

WAYNE GOLF CLUB
16721 96th N.E.
Bothell, WA
(206) 486-4714

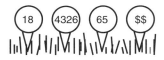

The front 9 at the Wayne Golf Club has been here since 1924. This 18-hole course is hilly, and the Sammamish River winds through its fairways. Open year round, dawn to dusk, reservations are taken one week in advance.

Weekday green fees are $12.00 for 9 holes or $15.00 for 18. Weekend fees are $18.00 before noon and $13.00 after. Seniors can play during the week for $11.00 and $13.50; juniors pay $10.50 and $13.00. Clubs rent for $6.00 and $10.00, handcarts $1.50 and $2.00, and motorized carts $12.00 and $18.00. They have a limited pro shop where you'll find help with tournament planning, plus a restaurant with a liquor license.

Directions: Leave Highway 522 on Bothell Way, and turn right, at 96th turn left and follow to the course.

WELLINGTON HILLS GOLF COURSE
7026 Wellington Heights Dr.
Woodinville, WA
(206) 485-5589

Wellington Hills' terrain is pretty hilly, and offers a fantastic view of the Olympic Mountains. Owned by the University of Washington, this year-round course sits in a country setting surrounded by trees. An occasional coyote or deer will wander across the fairways. Weekend and holiday tee times are available two days in advance. Wellington was recently saved from being bulldozed, and has new operators. Improvements are underway.

Green fees are $9.00 for 9 holes or $12.00 for 18 during the week, and $10.00 and $14.00 on weekends. Monday thru Saturday seniors can play 9 holes for $7.00, as can juniors younger than 12. Annual passes and punch cards offer savings to all golfers. Clubs rent for $5.50, handcarts $2.00, and motorized carts $11.00 and $20.00. They have a restaurant where beer and wine is served, plus a limited pro shop. Tournament planning assistance is available.

Directions: The Wellington Hills Golf Course is located in Woodinville, 3 miles east of Bothell. Take Highway 9 north to 240th and head east to the course.

(CLINTON)

ISLAND GREENS
3890 E. French Rd.
Clinton, WA
(360) 579-6042

Wildlife abounds on this challenging little par three; deer, heron and ducks are often sighted. The course emerged from a farm, and the owner has made every effort to keep the land as natural as possible. Island Greens is a beautiful place to play April thru June when over 250 rhododendrons are in bloom. You'll also find natural ponds, wetlands, and huge evergreens. Open from dawn to dusk, you'll find three sets of tees on each hole. The back tees demand exacting shots.

Green fees are $5.00 per 9 holes, and you can get a weekday coupon book for further savings. An attendant is there most weekends; the rest of the time fees are on the honor system so be sure to bring exact change. When an attendant is there clubs are available for $2.00 and handcarts $1.00.

Directions: Located on south Whidbey Island. From Everett, take the Mukilteo ferry, drive 2 miles to Cultus Bay Road, turn left, drive an additional 2 miles to French Road, turn right and follow a short distance to the course.

(KENT)

RIVERBEND GOLF COMPLEX
2019 W. Meeker St.
Kent, WA
(206) 833-8463

(27) (6603) (72) ($$)

Riverbend has an outstanding view of Mt. Rainier. Covering 130 acres, the complex includes three lakes, lots of trees, and dozens of bunkers. The Green River cuts right through this flat course. It's dry in the winter, and only closed on Christmas Day. The women's tees have a total distance of 5,485 yards. Besides the 18-hole course, you'll also find a short par three.

Green fees on the 18-hole course are $19.00 during the week and $23.00 on weekends. Juniors and seniors play for $15.00. Clubs rent for $12.00 and motorized carts $20.00. At the par three course the total distance is 1,253 yards and the cost $6.00 per 9 holes. Juniors and seniors can play this course during the week for $5.00.

The driving range has 38 lighted stalls, 28 are covered, and they can provide rental clubs. You get a small bucket of balls for $2.00 or a large one for $4.00. The complex also includes a miniature golf course, full-service pro shop, and a snack bar where cold beer and wine is available. Both individual and group lessons are offered, and they can help with tournament planning.

Directions: Leave I-5 at the Kent/Des Moines exit and head east to Meeker Street where you will turn left.

(LYNNWOOD)

LYNNWOOD MUNICIPAL GOLF
19100 44th Ave. W.
Lynnwood, WA
(206) 672-4653

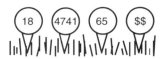

Lynnwood has tree-lined fairways with lots of bunkers and ponds. Designed by John Steidel, and opened in 1991, its terrain is flat and includes two sets of tees. The slope is 107 and the ratings 62.9 for men, 63.5 for women. Open year round, between daylight and dusk, reservations are taken five days ahead for weekends and seven days in advance for weekdays.

Green fees are $13.00 for 9 holes or $18.00 for 18. Juniors, age 17 under, as well as seniors, 62 and over, receive a $2.00 discount on weekdays. Credit cards are welcome. You can rent a half set of clubs for $10.00 or a full set for $15.00. Handcarts are $3.00 and motorized carts $10.00 per 9 holes.

Facilities include a restaurant, banquet room, pro shop and a driving range. At the driving range a bucket of balls will cost you $2.50. Lessons, and help with tournament planning, are available.

Directions: Located behind Edmonds Community College.

(MOUNTLAKE TERRACE)

BALLINGER PARK GOLF COURSE
23000 Lakeview Dr.
Mountlake Terrace, WA
(206) 775-6467

Located on the north shore of Lake Ballinger, this course has a flat terrain with a creek running across the fairway. Built in 1958, it is open year round. Reservations are recommended one week in advance during the busy season.

Weekend green fees for 9 holes at Ballinger Park are $9.00. During the week it's $8.50, with seniors playing for $7.50, and students for $7.00. Unless they're over-crowded, the fee for an additional 9 holes is just $6.00. Twilight rates are $5.50, and season punch cards are available. Rates are slightly lower in the winter. Clubs rent for $5.50 and handcarts $1.85. No motorized carts are available. Facilities include a restaurant where beer and wine is served, plus banquet rooms and a full-service pro shop.

Directions: From I-5 northbound, take exit #177 and turn left on 236th Street, keeping to the left after crossing over the freeway. From I-5 southbound, take the 220th Street exit, turn right, then at 66th Avenue West turn left, and when the road ends turn right.

(RENTON)

MAPLEWOOD GOLF COURSE
4050 Maple Valley Hwy.
Renton, WA
(206) 277-4444

This course was built in 1927 and has just undergone a major renovation. Maplewood is open year round, from sunrise until dark. The slope is 111 and the ratings 66 for men, 72 for women. Reservations are taken one week in advance. Two sets of tees are available for variety, and the total distance from the second set is 5,132 yards.

Weekend green fees for 18 holes are $20.00, on weekdays it'll cost you $18.00. It's $13.00 for 9 holes all week long. Credit cards are accepted for green fees. Golfers 62 and older, or younger than 18, can play 9 holes during the week for $10.00 or 18 for $13.00. You can rent clubs for $4.00, handcarts $2.00 and $3.00, and motorized carts $10.00 and $18.00.

You'll find a restaurant, lounge, and banquet facilities with a liquor license. They also have a full-service pro shop, new driving range, and can help you with tournament planning. Lessons are available. The 30-station driving range offers mat tees. You'll find the driving range open from sunrise to 9:00 p.m., except Sunday when it closes at 7:00 p.m.

Directions: Take exit #4 off I-405 and go east on the Maple Valley Highway for 2 miles.

MONROE

BLUE BOY WEST GOLF COURSE
27927 Florence Acres Rd.
Monroe, WA
(360) 793-2378

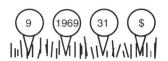

Blue Boy West sits in a mountain setting on an old horse farm. You'll find lots of traps, four ponds, and rolling hills. They are open year round, during daylight hours, and recommend that you call ahead for tee times.

Weekday green fees are $8.00 for 9 holes or $14.00 for 18, and juniors and seniors can play for $7.00 and $12.00. On weekends, everybody pays $10.00 and $17.00. Clubs rent for $5.00, handcarts $3.00, and motorized carts $8.00 and $16.00. Facilities include a restaurant, banquet area, and a full-service pro shop. Ask at the pro shop for help with tournament planning.

Directions: Located 6 miles northeast of Monroe. Leave Highway 2 on Old Owen Road and stay left at the Y; you'll find yourself on Florence Acres Road which leads to the course.

MONROE GOLF COURSE
22110 Old Owen Rd.
Monroe, WA
(360) 794-8498

This year-round course is easy to walk, with just one hill. The slope is 105 and the ratings 62.5 for men, 66.9 for women. Its greens are well established and the course is scenic, with old-growth timber and grass bunkers. Built in 1928, it is open sunup to sundown, but closes for snow. Reservations are not taken.

Weekend green fees are $14.00 for 9 holes or $20.00 for 18. During the week you'll pay $10.00 and $15.00. Juniors, age 16 and under, can play during the week, and after 4:00 p.m. on weekends, for $5.00 and $10.00. Clubs rent for $5.00, handcarts $3.00, and motorized carts $8.50 per 9 holes. Seniors receive discounts on motorized carts. Facilities include a restaurant and a full-service pro shop. Help with tournament planning is available.

Directions: Located 1 mile northeast of Monroe, on the Old Stevens Pass Highway.

CARNATION

CARNATION GOLF CLUB

1810 W. Snoqualmie River Rd.
Carnation, WA
(206) 583-0314 or 333-4151

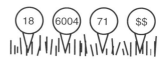

The Carnation Golf Club course sits in a beautiful valley and is surrounded by the Snoqualmie River. It has mountain views in all directions and golfers often see deer and bald eagles. Designed by Bob Tachell, it opened in 1965. The slope is 113 and the ratings 67.6 for men, 65.1 for women. Open year round, from dawn to dusk, the terrain is flat and easy to walk with some water. Reservations are taken, but must be guaranteed by credit card for Friday thru Sunday tee times.

Monday thru Thursday green fees are $14.00 for 9 holes, $22.00 for 18. Friday thru Sunday you can only play 18 holes and it will cost you $24.00. A reduced rate of $12.00 is in effect daily after 4:00 p.m., and real early Monday thru Friday. If you're under 17, or over 60, you can play 9 holes for $10.00 or 18 for $16.00 Monday thru Friday.

Clubs rent for $10.00, handcarts $2.00, and motorized carts $22.00. They have a restaurant and banquet decks where you'll find cold beer and wine. Tournament planning help, and lessons, are available at the full-service pro shop. The driving range is huge, offers grass tees, and you can get a large bucket of balls for $4.00. They also have a practice bunker and greens.

Directions: Follow Snoqualmie River Road for 2 miles.

FALL CITY

SNOQUALMIE FALLS GOLF COURSE

Highway 202
Fall City, WA
(206) 222-5244

This is a great course for seniors, and open year round. It is surrounded by forests and has a beautiful view of Mt. Si. During the winter they are open dawn to dusk; the rest of the year they open at 6:00 a.m. during the week and 5:00 a.m. on weekends. Tee times are given six days in advance. If you're calling from Seattle or Bellevue you can call toll free by dialing 392-1276. The women's tees have a total distance of 5,175 yards.

Weekend green fees are $15.00 for 9 holes or $23.00 for 18. The rest of the week it's $13.00 and $21.00, and juniors and seniors can play for $10.00 and $16.00. Clubs rent for $5.00, handcarts $3.00, and motorized carts $12.00 and $22.00.

Facilities include a restaurant that sells beer and wine, plus a driving range and full-service pro shop. Lessons, and help with tournament planning, are available. At the driving range you get 50 balls for $3.00.

Directions: The Snoqualmie Falls Golf Course is located .5 mile east of Fall City on Highway 202.

TALL CHIEF GOLF COURSE
1313 W. Snoqualmie River Rd.
Fall City, WA
(206) 222-5911

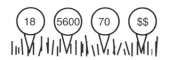

The Tall Chief course has a beautiful view of the snow-capped Cascade Mountains. It is open year round, offers a flat front 9, and a hilly, challenging back 9. The greens are well kept with traps on 12 of them. Trees line the course, and wildlife sometimes wanders through. The women's par is 71 for a total distance of 5,200 yards. Built in 1964, reservations are taken six days in advance.

During the week, green fees are $13.00 for 9 holes or $20.00 for 18. On weekends you'll pay $14.00 and $23.00. Juniors and seniors can play 9 holes during the week for $11.00 or 18 for $16.00. Handcarts rent for $3.00, clubs $5.00, and power carts $12.00 and $20.00.

Facilities include a restaurant serving beer and wine, plus a banquet area and pro shop. Lessons, and help with tournament planning, are available.

Directions: Tall Chief is located 3 miles west of town, just off Highway 202.

SNOQUALMIE

MT. SI GOLF COURSE
9010 Boalch Ave. S.E.
Snoqualmie, WA
(206) 888-1541

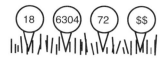

This gently rolling course is situated near the base of Mt. Si, which provides a breathtaking backdrop for the lush green fairways. The slope is 116 for men and 113 for women, the ratings 72.6 and 67.4. Open year round, except Christmas Day, they operate from daylight to dusk. You can call one week ahead for tee times October to March, and farther in advance the balance of the year. Two sets of tees are available.

During the summer, weekend green fees are $16.00 for 9 holes or $25.00 for 18. On weekdays it's $14.00 and $21.00. October thru February, if you play before 11:00 a.m. on weekends, it'll cost you $14.00 or $21.00; the rest of the season it's $11.00 and $16.00. You can rent a full set of clubs for $15.00 or a half set for $9.00, handcarts are $2.00 and $3.00, and motorized carts $14.00 and $22.00. Credit cards are accepted for green fees.

You'll find a nice restaurant and banquet facilities with a liquor license, plus a snack bar, full-service pro shop and driving range. They can help you with tournament planning and lessons. At the driving range, you'll find grass tees and pay $2.50 to $6.50 for a bucket of balls.

Directions: Leave I-90 at exit #27, go 1 mile to the Snoqualmie Falls exit, and follow the signs.

BREMERTON

GOLD MOUNTAIN GOLF COURSE
W. Belfair Valley Road
Gorst, WA
(360) 674-2363

Gold Mountain is open year round, dawn to dusk. The terrain varies from flat to rolling hills, with plenty of trees, some water, and lots of sand bunkers. It has a wonderful view of the Olympic Mountains, and reservations are taken six days in advance. They have a practice putting green and two chipping greens. The total distance from the ladies' tees is 5,428 yards for a par of 75.

Weekdays green fees are $13.00 for 9 holes or $19.00 for 18. If you're under 17 you can play 18 holes for $7.50; golfers 62 and over pay $16.00 for 18 holes. Everybody pays the same on weekends, $16.00 for 9 holes or $23.00 for 18. Twilight rates are $13.00 on weekdays, $16.00 on weekends. Clubs rent for $8.00, handcarts $3.00, and motorized carts $12.00 and $20.00.

Gold Mountain has a large pro shop, a restaurant and lounge with a liquor license, banquet facilities that will seat 200, and a driving range. They can help with tournament planning, and arrange for lessons. At the driving range you can get 15 balls for $2.00, 25 for $3.00, or 35 for $4.00.

Directions: The Gold Mountain Golf Course is located in the town of Gorst. From Bremerton, simply follow Highway 3 southwest for 3 miles.

ROLLING HILLS GOLF CLUB
2485 N.E. McWilliams Rd.
Bremerton, WA
(360) 479-1212

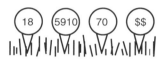

Rolling Hills sports a view of snow-capped mountains and is closed only on Christmas Day. The terrain is rolling, and you'll find water hazards at a few of the holes. This is a pleasant course to walk and offers two sets of tees. It was designed by Don Hogan and opened in 1972. The slope is 115 with a rating of 67.9 for men, it's 117 and 71.0 for women. Reservations are taken one week in advance. The total yardage from the ladies' tees is 5,465.

On weekends you'll pay $13.88 for 9 holes or $19.43 for 18, including taxes. Weekday green fees are $12.03 and $17.58, but if you're under 18, or over 62, you can play 18 holes for $13.88. Credit cards are accepted for green fees. Clubs rent for a flat $6.00, handcarts $2.00, and motorized carts are $12.95 for 9 holes or $18.50 for 18.

They have a nice restaurant, lounge, and banquet facilities with a liquor license, plus a full-service pro shop and a covered driving range. At the range you'll find mat tees and can get a bucket of balls for $1.50 to $4.00. Lessons, and help with tournament planning, are available.

Directions: Located right in Bremerton, just follow the signs.

PORT ORCHARD

CLOVER VALLEY GOLF COURSE
5180 Country Club Way S.E.
Port Orchard, WA
(360) 871-2236

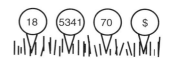

The Clover Valley course offers a challenging, fun game in a beautiful setting. It has a relatively flat terrain with only a few hills, and water comes into play on five holes. The course is open year round, and tee times are recommended. The women's tees have a total distance of 4,824 yards.

Weekday green fees are $9.00 for 9 holes or $12.50 for 18; on weekends they're $11.00 and $16.00. Juniors play for $6.00 on weekdays and $7.50 on weekends and holidays. Seniors pay $7.00 and $10.00 on weekdays, and $8.50 and $13.00 on weekends and holidays. Clubs rent for $4.00, handcarts $3.00, and power carts $10.00 and $18.00.

Facilities include a restaurant with a liquor license, plus a banquet area, driving range and pro shop. Lessons, and help with tournament planning, are available. At the driving range you'll pay $2.25 to $4.00 for a bucket of balls.

Directions: Take Highway 160 off Highway 16, turn right onto Sedgwick Road, right on Long Lake Road, and follow the signs.

HORSESHOE LAKE GOLF COURSE
15932 Sidney Rd. S.W.
Port Orchard, WA
(206) 857-3326

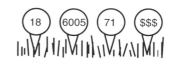

You'll find a terrific view of the Olympic Mountains at Horseshoe Lake. Designed by Jim Richardson, the course was completed in

1992, and is open year round. The slope is 115 and the rating 68.0. You'll find easy-to-walk sculpted fairways on the front 9, along with three lakes and lots of evergreens. The back 9 is hilly, and crosses the canyon twice. Reservations are taken one week in advance. The total yardage from the women's tees is 5,035.

Green fees are $29.00 on weekends and holidays, $24.00 during the week. Motorized carts are mandatory on the back nine and included in the price; they are $5.00 per person on the front 9. November thru March you can play 18 holes on weekdays for $23.00, cart included. Weekday rates for juniors, 17 and under, is $10.00 for 9 holes or $14.00 for 18, and carts are not required. Seniors, 62 and over, can play on weekdays for $11.00 and $21.00, including the cart on the back 9. Winter rates are $20.00 for 18 holes, including a cart. Handcarts can be rented for $3.00.

Facilities include a restaurant and lounge with a liquor license, plus a banquet area, snack bar, full-service pro shop and driving range. At the range you'll pay $2.00 for a small bucket of balls, $4.00 for a bigger one, and $10.00 will get you a gigantic super-sized bucket. Lessons, and help with tournament planning, are available.

Directions: Located 8 miles west of the Tacoma Narrows Bridge; take the Purdy exit, head west on Highway 302, turn right at 94th Avenue, and follow the signs.

McCORMICK WOODS GOLF COURSE
5155 McCormick Woods Dr. S.W.
Port Orchard, WA
(360) 895-0130 & (800) 323-0130

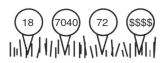

This year- round course was built in 1986, and carved out of old-growth timber. Designed by Jack Frye, the front 9 is fairly flat but the back 9 is rolling with some elevated holes. The slope is 135 and the ratings 74.1 for men, 73.6 for women. Each hole has five separate tees, offering all levels of golfers a terrific challenge. Water comes into play on 8 holes, sand on 14, and the fairways are tree lined and well separated. The course has a great view of Mt. Rainier and golfers often encounter wildlife. The women's tees have a total distance of 5,299 yards.

Reservations are taken five days ahead for local players; those coming from Eastern Washington, or out of state, can get tee times 30 days in advance. No children under eight years of age are allowed on the course. You'll find a pro shop, snack bar, chipping and putting greens, practice bunkers, and a driving range on site. The range is open during daylight hours, has grass tees, and charges $2.50 for 40 balls. Lessons are available.

Green fees are $20.00 for 9 holes and $35.00 for 18 Monday thru Thursday. You'll pay $45.00 Friday, Saturday, Sunday and holidays. Seniors, age 60 and over, can play 18 holes for $25.00 Monday thru Thursday. They also have special rates for twilight, evening, and off-season golfers that save you up to $20.00 on 18 holes. Clubs rent for $12.00 and $20.00, handcarts $2.00 and $3.00, and motorized carts $12.00 and $20.00.

Directions: To find Port Orchard's McCormick Woods Golf Course, leave Highway 16 at the Old Clifton/Tremont exit, turn left, and drive 1.8 miles.

VILLAGE GREENS GOLF CLUB
2298 Fircrest Dr. S.E.
Port Orchard, WA
(360) 871-1222

This Kitsap County course is kept in excellent condition and open every day but Christmas, from daylight to dark. Its rolling terrain stays dry throughout the winter and provides a great view of Mt. Rainier. The slope is 87.0 and the rating 57.1. Two sets of tees are available, par from the second set is 62.

Green fees are $8.00 for 9 holes and $10.00 for 18 all week long. If you're in the military, or 65 or older, you can play for $7.00 and $9.00. Juniors, 17 and younger, pay just $6.00 for 9 holes. Clubs rent for $5.00, handcarts $2.00, and motorized carts $10.00 and $15.00.

Golf lessons, and help with tournament planning, are available at the pro shop. They also have a covered, lighted driving range, which closes one hour before dark. At the range, you can get a bucket of balls for $3.00 to $4.00.

Directions: To reach the Village Greens Golf Club, take the second Port Orchard exit off Highway 16, follow this road past four stop lights, and turn right at the first stop sign.

TUKWILA

FOSTER GOLF LINKS
13500 Interurban S.
Tukwila, WA
(206) 242-4221

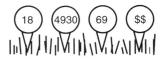

The Duwamish River winds right thru the Foster Golf Links. Built in 1925, and operated by the city parks department, it is open year round. The course is fairly flat, with a few gentle rises, and is challenging, yet easy. It's a good spot for beginners, and those looking for a quick game. The slope is 94 and the rating 62.3. From the ladies' tees par is 71 for a total distance of 4,952 yards.

Green fees are $13.00 for 9 holes, or $17.00 for 18 holes, all week long. On weekdays, golfers 17 and under, as well as those 62 and older, can play for $11.00 and $13.50. You can rent clubs for $4.50 and $6.50, handcarts $1.00 and $2.00, and motorized carts $11.00 and $18.00. Facilities include a restaurant and lounge, plus a full-service pro shop. Children under six are not allowed on the course; those six thru nine must be accompanied by an adult.

Directions: Leave I-5 at the Marginal/Tukwila exit, and head right .5 mile to the course.

HOODSPORT

LAKE CUSHMAN GOLF CLUB
N. 210 W. Fairway Dr.
Hoodsport, WA
(360) 877-5505

Lake Cushman is open year round, unless the rain is really pounding. You can get reservations two weeks in advance during the summer, and in the winter this course operates on the honor system. The terrain is very walkable, with lots of trees and a nice view of the mountains. A second set of tees adds enjoyment to playing 18 holes. The women's tees have a total distance of 2,682 yards for a par of 37.

Weekday green fees are $11.00 for 9 holes or $16.00 for 18. On weekends and holidays you'll pay $15.00 and $19.00. Tuesday is bargain day; you can play 9 holes for $6.00. Clubs rent for $4.00, handcarts $2.50, and motorized carts $12.00 and $20.00.

Facilities include a covered driving range, full-service pro shop, and a snack bar where you'll find sandwiches and cold beer. Tournament planning help is available. The driving range has mat tees, and you can get balls for $1.50 to $3.00, depending on the size of the bucket.

Directions: Leave downtown Hoodsport on Highway 101, turn left onto Fairway, and drive 3 miles west.

ALLYN

LAKELAND VILLAGE
E. 200 Old Ranch Rd.
Allyn, WA
(360) 275-6100

The view from Lakeland's 5th tee includes Mt. Rainier, the Olympic Mountains, and Hood Canal. Designed by Bunny Mason, it was built in 1972. The course is fairly flat and open year round from sunrise to sunset. A semi-private course, Lakeland is only closed to the public on Tuesdays and Wednesdays before 2:00 p.m. The slope is 117 and the ratings 68.5 for men, 69.6 for women. The total distance for women is 4,925 yards for a par of 72. Reservations are available seven days in advance.

During the week green fees are $18.00, on weekends they're $22.00. Seniors can play on Mondays for $14.00. Clubs rent for $5.00, handcarts $3.00, and motorized carts $21.00. Facilities include a restaurant where beer and wine are served, plus a pro shop and driving range. At the driving range you'll find grass tees, and pay $2.00 to $4.00 for a bucket of balls. The range is open dawn to dusk. Lessons, and help with tournament planning, are available.

Directions: Located on Highway 3, just before you get to Allyn.

NORTH BEND

CASCADE GOLF COURSE

14303 436th Ave. S.E.
North Bend, WA
(206) 888-0227

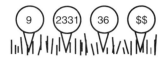

The Cascade Golf Course is surrounded by mountains and offers dry play year round. Built in 1950, the terrain is flat and easy to walk. The slope for men is 93 and the rating 62.8; for women it's 107 and 67.3. Open from daylight to dusk, tee times are recommended May thru October.

Monday thru Friday green fees are $12.00 for 9 holes or $18.00 for 18. Juniors and seniors play for $9.00 and $15.00. On weekends, everybody pays $14.00 and $20.00. You can save 30% by purchasing a 10-game pass. Motorized carts are $10.00 and $18.00, clubs rent for $5.00 and $6.00, and handcarts $2.00 and $3.00. Facilities include a restaurant where beer is served, and a full-service pro shop where you can get help with tournament planning.

Directions: Located just off I-90 via exit #32.

MAPLE VALLEY

ELK RUN GOLF COURSE

22500 S.E. 275th Place
Maple Valley, WA
(206) 432-8800

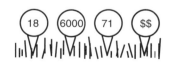

This is a very dry winter course with a beautiful view of Mt. Rainier. The terrain is flat with some hills, it has grass tees, and large greens. Elk Run's second 9 was designed by Pete Peterson and added in 1994; the original 9 was designed by Jack Frye and built in 1989. The slope is 108 and the ratings 63.4 for men, 65.0 for women. It is open year round and takes reservations one week in advance. The women's par is 72 for a distance of 5,800 yards.

Monday thru Friday green fees are $14.00 for 9 holes and $22.00 for 18. On weekends they charge $16.00 and $25.00. Monday thru Thursday seniors, age 55 and up, can play for $12.00 and $18.00. Clubs rent for $7.00, handcarts $2.00, and motorized carts are $12.00 and $18.00, with discounted rates available Monday thru Thursday. Credit cards are welcome.

Facilities include a restaurant that serves beer and wine, plus a banquet room, snack bar, full-service pro shop, and driving range. Lessons, and help with tournament planning, are available. At the driving range you'll find mat tees and can get 35 balls for $2.50 or 70 for $4.00. The range is open 7:00 a.m. to 7:00 p.m. during the winter, but doesn't close until 10:00 p.m. in the summer.

Directions: From I-405 take exit #4 southbound, exit #4A northbound, to Highway 169. Turn right on Kent-Langley Road and follow 1 mile to 228th where you'll turn left to the course.

LAKE WILDERNESS GOLF COURSE
25400 Witte Rd. S.E.
Maple Valley, WA
(206) 432-9405

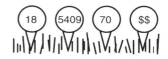

Lake Wilderness underwent reconstruction in 1992. It's narrow and demanding, with lots of water, wetlands, sand and trees. The terrain is semi-hilly and offers a great view of Mt. Rainier. It has a slope of 118 and the ratings are 66.1 for men, 66.6 for women. The total distance from the ladies' tees is 4,657 yards. Open year round, reservations are taken 7 days in advance, 30 days ahead if prepaid. Credit cards are welcome.

Weekday green fees are $18.00; on weekends you'll pay $22.00. Monday thru Friday golfers under 18, or over 55, can play for $15.00. Twilight rates begin about five hours before sunset, and anyone can play 18 holes for $15.00. Winter rates are in effect from October thru mid-February; they are $15.00 and $17.00. Clubs are $10.00 for 18 holes, handcarts $3.00, and motorized carts $10.00 per 9 holes.

Lake Wilderness has a restaurant and lounge with a liquor license, plus banquet facilities to seat 300, a snack bar and full-service pro shop. Lessons, and help with tournament planning, are available.

Directions: Take Highway 169 off I-405 and drive 15 miles to Witte Road. You can follow the signs from there.

TACOMA AREA

(TACOMA)

ALLENMORE PUBLIC GOLF CLUB
2125 S. Cedar
Tacoma, WA
(206) 627-7211

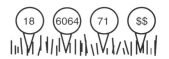

This course was built around 1916 by Sam Allen. The second 9 was added in 1935. Allenmore has a large lake at its center, as well as two smaller lakes on the 12th and 16th fairways. It is open year round. Hours are 6:00 a.m. to dusk in the summer, and daylight to dusk the balance of the year. Reservations are taken one week in advance for weekend play. The women's par is 75.

Green fees are $14.50 for 9 holes or $20.00 for 18, all week long. If you're under 17, or over 62, you can play 9 holes for $10.00 or 18 for $14.50. Clubs rent for $5.00, handcarts $2.00 and $3.00, and motorized carts $10.00 and $20.00. Facilities include a restaurant and lounge with banquet facilities and a liquor license, plus a driving range and full-service pro shop. You can get help with tournament planning and arrange for lessons. The driving range is 150 yards long, and you get 35 balls for $2.00

Directions: Leave I-5 at the Bremerton exit, and follow Sprague Street to 19th, where you turn left to the course.

BROOKDALE GOLF COURSE
1802 Brookdale Rd. E.
Tacoma, WA
(206) 537-4400

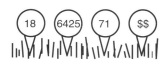

Built in 1931, Brookdale was designed by Christopher Mahan and is open year round. It offers a fairly flat terrain and is fun for all levels of golfers. The slope is 112 and the rating 69.6. From the ladies' tees the par is 74 for a total distance of 5,847 yards. During the summer months you can get on the course at 6:00 a.m., the rest of the year you'll have to wait until 7:00 a.m. Reservations are taken one week in advance.

To play 9 holes you'll pay $14.00, it's $20.00 for 18 holes. Seniors, over age 62, can play during the week for $9.00 and $14.00, juniors for $7.00 and $12.00. Clubs rent for $6.00, handcarts $3.00, and motorized carts $10.00 and $17.00. Credit cards are welcome. Facilities include a restaurant and lounge where you'll find beer and wine, plus a driving range and full-service pro shop. Lessons, and help with tournament planning, are available. The range has a 24-stall automatic warm-up center that is completely enclosed.

Directions: Leave I-5 on Highway 512, turn right toward Parkland, and after about a mile turn left onto 131st. The course is just a short distance from here.

FORT STEILACOOM GOLF COURSE
8202 87th Ave. S.W.
Tacoma, WA
(206) 588-0613

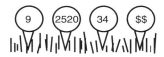

Fort Steilacoom is a good course for beginners, or those looking to tune up their game. The slope is 98 for men and 105 for women, the ratings 62.8 and 66.8. Two tees are available at each hole, adding a little variety to an 18 hole game. This course is only closed on Christmas Day, and tee times are given seven days in advance.

This course has lower rates for Pierce County residents. They pay $9.00 for 9 holes or $14.00 for 18. Out-of-area golfers pay $11.75 and $18.75. Local juniors and seniors can play on weekdays for $6.75 and $10.50. Clubs, handcarts, and motorized carts are available for rental. They have a pro shop, snack bar, and can provide help with tournament planning, or arrange for lessons. Credit cards are welcome.

Directions: Leave I-5 at exit #129, take 74th west 2 miles, turn left onto S. Tacoma Way for 3 miles, turn right on Steilacoom Boulevard for 3 miles, turn right on 87th Avenue S.W., and go about .5 mile to the course.

HIGHLANDS GOLF CLUB
1400 Highland Parkway N.
Tacoma, WA
(206)759-3622

Tacoma's Highlands Golf & Racquet Club is nestled among the houses in the city's Westgate area. Opened in 1969, the course is level, includes two water holes, and plenty of traps. It takes about 75 minutes to play, and is only closed on Christmas Day.

Green fees for 9 holes are $7.50, it's $12.00 for 18. Golfers 17 and younger, as well as those 60 and over, can play during the week for $6.50 and $10.00. Clubs rent for $4.50 and handcarts $2.00. Motorized carts are not available. You'll find a pro shop, tennis courts, and a clubhouse that is available for private tournaments.

Directions: Leave I-5 on Highway 16, take the 6th Avenue exit, turn right onto Westgate Boulevard, left to Highland Parkway North, and left again after one block.

MEADOW PARK GOLF COURSE
7108 Lakewood Dr. W.
Tacoma, WA
(206) 473-3033

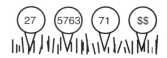

You'll find a sporty 9-hole, and a challenging 18-hole course at Meadow Park. Both are fairly level with some hills, and open year round. During the summer you can start your game at 5:30 a.m.; in the winter they don't open until 7:00 a.m. Three sets of tees are available, and the total distance from the women's tees is 5,262 yards for a par of 73.

Monday thru Thursday, green fees are $14.00 for 9 holes or $20.00 for 18 on the longer course. Seniors play for $12.00 and $18.00, and juniors $10.00 and $13.00. The rest of the week, and on holidays, everyone pays $15.00 and $23.00. The short course charges $8.00 per 9 holes all week long. Monday thru Thursday, seniors can play that course for $7.00, and juniors for $6.00.

No matter which course you're playing, clubs rent for a flat $5.00 and handcarts $2.00. Motorized carts are $10.00 and $18.00 during the week, $12.00 and $20.00 on weekends and holidays. Amenities include a restaurant, lounge and banquet facilities with a liquor license, plus a full-service pro shop and driving range. Lessons, and help with tournament planning, are available. At the driving range you'll pay $3.50 to $6.00 for balls.

Directions: Take the 74th Street exit off I-5 at Tacoma; the course is just 1 block to the left.

NORTH SHORE GOLF CLUB
4101 North Shore Blvd. N.E.
Tacoma, WA
(206) 927-1375

North Shore is a dry winter course with a nice view of Mt. Rainier. The front 9 is fairly flat, but the back 9 has a couple of hills. It's well maintained, with grass tees and large greens. Open year round, from dawn to dark, reservations are taken one week in advance.

Friday thru Sunday, green fees are $30.00 whether you play 9 or 18 holes, or $18.00 during twilight. On Mondays and Tuesdays you'll pay $13.50 and $20.00, on Wednesdays and Thursdays $14.00 and $22.00. You can rent clubs for $9.00 and $12.00, handcarts are $3.00, and motorized carts $20.00. You'll find a covered, lighted driving range and teaching studio, plus a well-stocked pro shop, a restaurant offering beer and wine, as well as banquet rooms. At the driving range you get 35 balls per token; tokens sell for $2.50, 3 for $6.00, or 6 for $10.00.

Directions: Leave I-5 at exit #142-B, go west 5 miles, turn left onto Nassua, go .5 mile and follow the signs.

UNIVERSITY GOLF CLUB
754 124th St. S.
Tacoma, WA
(206) 535-7393

This course is on the Pacific Lutheran University campus. Open year round, you can begin playing at 6:30 a.m. in the summer and 7:30 a.m. in winter. The terrain is flat and easy to walk with excellent greens. It is surrounded by tall evergreens, and is a dry winter course.

Green fees remain the same seven days a week, 9 holes for $9.00 or 18 for $14.00. Monday thru Friday, golfers under 16, or over 62, can play for $7.00 and $11.00. Clubs rent for a flat $5.00, handcarts $2.00, and motorized carts $7.00 per 9 holes. Facilities include a coffee shop and full-service pro shop. Lessons, and help with tournament planning, are available.

Directions: Take exit #127 off I-5, follow Highway 512 east to Highway 7, go south 1 mile to 125th Street, follow to Yakima Avenue, drive west and turn onto 124th Street.

(AUBURN)

AUBURN GOLF CLUB
29630 Green River Rd. S.E.
Auburn, WA
(206) 833-2350

The Auburn Golf Club's front 9 is flat, the back 9 is hilly, and you'll find water throughout the course. It's open 8:00 a.m. to sundown in the winter, in the summer they open at 7:00 a.m. on weekdays and 5:15 a.m. on weekends. Tee times are given out one week in advance during spring and summer. The women's par is 73 for a total distance of 5,571 yards.

All week long green fees remain the same, $13.00 for 9 holes or $17.00 for 18. During the summer, before noon, seniors can play for $9.75 and $12.75. Juniors pay $6.50 for 9 holes or $8.50 for 18. You can rent clubs for $5.00, handcarts $2.00 and $3.00, and motorized carts $12.00 and $20.00.

Facilities include a limited pro shop where you can arrange for lessons and get help with tournament planning, plus a snack shop, restaurant, and lounge. Beer and wine are available.

Directions: Located east of town along the Green River.

JADE GREENS GOLF COURSE
18330 S.E. Lake Holm Rd.
Auburn, WA
(206) 931-8562

The Jade Greens course surrounds 30 acres of natural wetlands. As you play, you'll enjoy nice views of Mt. Rainier, the Cascade Mountains, and the wetlands. Open year round, this course was completed in 1989 and takes reservations one week in advance. The slope is 110 and the ratings 65.0 for men, 65.8 for women.

You'll find two tees per hole, and an extra hole on #1 and #9, to add variety to an 18-hole game. When playing 18, the men's par is 69 for a total distance of 5,099 yards; the women's tees have a distance of 2,232 yards for a par of 35 when playing 9 holes, 4,501 and 71 for 18 holes.

Weekday green fees are $11.00 for 9 holes or $16.00 for 18. Juniors and seniors can play during the week for $7.00 and $11.00. On weekends everybody pays $13.00 and $18.00. Credit cards are welcome. Clubs are $10.00 for 18 holes, handcarts $4.00, and motorized carts $18.00.

Facilities include a restaurant where you can get cold beer and wine, plus a pro shop and driving range. The driving range has mat tees and you get a large bucket of balls for $4.00. Golf lessons, and help with tournament planning, are available.

Directions: Leave Highway 18 at the Auburn-Black Diamond exit, turn right and drive 5 miles, turn right at the stop sign and after 1 mile turn right again onto Lake Holm Road. The entrance is .5 mile on the right.

(FEDERAL WAY)

CHRISTY'S PAR 3
37712 28th Ave. S.
Federal Way, WA
(206) 927-0644

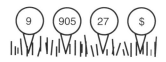

Christy's opened in 1988 and can be played year round. It's challenging, has plenty of trees, a few small hills, and stays pretty dry during the winter. Summer hours are 10:00 a.m. to 8:00 p.m., but they open up at 9:00 a.m. on the weekends. During the winter they are open 10:00 a.m. to dark, all week long.

Green fees are $6.00 for 9 holes and $11.00 for 18, seven days a week. Seniors can play for $4.50 and $9.00. Clubs are $2.00, handcarts $1.00, and they have no motorized carts.

Facilities include a full-service pro shop where you'll find cold pop, plus a covered driving range. At the range you'll pay $3.00 to $6.00 for a bucket of balls, depending on how many you need. They also rent clubs at the range. Lessons are available.

Directions: To find this par three course, leave I-5 at exit #142-B, head west .5 mile to 161st, turn left after 2.5 miles onto 28th Avenue, and follow to the course.

(GIG HARBOR)

GIG HARBOR GOLF CLUB
6909 Artondale Dr. N.W.
Gig Harbor, WA
(206) 851-2378

This semi-private, hilly course offers well-maintained greens and fairways that are narrow and challenging, with lots of trees and some water. It includes a nice view of Mt. Rainier and golfers often see deer. Open year round, reservations are taken seven days in advance for weekends and holidays. You'll find four sets of tees; the women's tees have a total distance of 2,574 yards.

Green fees are $13.00 for 9 holes or $18.00 for 18. During the week, golfers 17 and under, as well as those 55 and over, pay just $13.00 for 18 holes. Twilight play begins at 3:00 p.m., and anyone can play for $10.00. Credit cards are welcome. Clubs rent for $6.00, handcarts $3.00, and motorized carts $12.00 and $18.00.

They have a snack bar with a liquor license, banquet facilities, a pro shop, practice bunker, putting green, short game facility, and recently reconstructed their driving range. Lessons, and help with tournament planning, are available. At the driving range you'll find both mat and grass tees, and pay $2.50 to $5.00 for a bucket of balls. It is open from dawn to dusk.

Directions: Cross the Narrows Bridge, take the Gig Harbor city center exit, turn left on Wolchiet, and go 2.2 miles to Artondale Road and the course.

MADRONA LINKS GOLF COURSE
3604 22nd Ave. N.W.
Gig Harbor, WA
(206) 851-5193

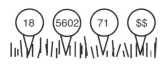

Madrona Links is open year round, dawn to dusk, and offers a flat, easy to walk terrain. It was designed by Ken Tyson and opened in 1978. The slope is 107 and the ratings 63.7 for men, 65.6 for women. You'll find four lakes, dozens of sand traps, and nicely-landscaped fairways. The Madrona trees are beautiful, and deer often wander across this country course.

Reservations are taken one week in advance. Three sets of tees provide plenty of variety. The total distance from the women's tees is 4,737 yards for a par of 73.

Weekday green fees are $14.00 for 9 holes or $19.00 for 18. On weekends it's $15.00 and $20.00. Golfers over age 62 can play 9 holes during the week for $10.00, or 18 for $15.00. Juniors, age 16 and under, pay $8.00 and $10.00 on weekdays as well as after 3:00 p.m. on weekends. Twilight rates vary depending on the time of year, and credit cards are accepted for green fees. Clubs rent for $10.00, handcarts $2.50, and motorized carts $20.00.

They have a pro shop, restaurant, lounge and banquet facilities with a liquor license, plus a driving range. The range is for irons only, has grass tees, and you get a bucket of balls for $2.00 to $3.50. Lessons, and help with tournament planning, are available.

Directions: To find the Madrona Links Golf Course, take the first exit off I-16 after crossing the Narrows Bridge, turn right onto John Road, and follow 2 miles to the course.

(PUYALLUP)

LIPOMA FIRS GOLF COURSE
18615 110th Ave. E.
Puyallup, WA
(206) 841-4396

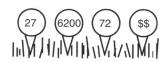

Lipoma Firs is a relatively flat, dry winter course. This former Christmas tree farm has narrow, tree-lined fairways and some very challenging holes. The slope is 116 and the ratings 69.7 for men, 70.6 for women. From the ladies' tees the total distance is 5,500 yards. As you play, you'll enjoy outstanding views of Mt. Rainier. Designed by Bill Stowe, the course opened in 1989 and operates year round, dawn to dusk. Reservations are advised one week in advance.

On weekends and holidays green fees are $14.00 for 9 holes or $21.00 for 18. The rest of the week you'll pay $10.00 or $16.00, with reduced rates for juniors and seniors. They offer reduced rates November thru February. Clubs can be rented for $8.00, handcarts $3.00, and motorized carts $18.00. Beer and wine are offered at the restaurant, and they have a banquet area. You'll also find a full-service pro shop, and driving range, plus practice greens and bunker. Lessons, and help with tournament planning, are available. At the range they offer both grass and mat tees, and you'll pay $2.50 to $4.50 for a bucket of balls.

Directions: Leave Highway 512 at the South Hill/Eatonville exit, go south 6 miles, turn left at 187th, and follow to the course.

MERIDIAN GREENS GOLF CLUB
9705 136th St. E.
Puyallup, WA
(206) 845-7504

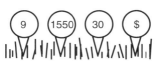

This course is wide open and provides a good place to work with your irons. The terrain is treeless, and occupies 28 acres of former pasture. Three ponds provide natural hazards, and two sets of tees are available. This year-round course is open from 7:00 a.m. to 9:00 p.m. Reservations are taken only for weekends, 24 hours in advance.

Monday thru Friday you'll pay $7.00 for 9 holes or $10.00 for 18, and juniors and seniors pay $5.00 and $8.00. On weekends, everybody pays $8.00 for 9 holes or $11.00 for 18. Clubs rent for a flat $5.00 and handcarts $2.00. You'll find a coffee shop, covered driving range, and a limited pro shop. Lessons, and help with tournament planning, are available. At the range you'll pay $4.00 for a bucket of balls.

Directions: Take Highway 512 eastbound to the South Hill exit, turn right on Meridian East, drive to 136th, and turn right to the course.

(SPANAWAY)

CLASSIC COUNTRY CLUB
4908 208th St. E.
Spanaway, WA
(206) 847-4440 or (800) 924-9557

Classic opened in 1991 and has over 60 sand bunkers, 30 grass bunkers, and a couple of lakes to challenge your game. Highly rated by Golf Digest, it offers undulating fairways and large, well-protected greens. The terrain is flat with some hills, and you'll find four tees at every hole. Open year round, sunup to sundown, it's a fairly dry winter course. Lush green fairways, and views of Mt. Rainier, also make it a scenic place to play. Reservations are taken one week in advance.

Weekday summer green fees are $30.00; you'll pay $45.00 on weekends and holidays. Join the men's or ladies' club and save $10.00 off all green fees. Winter green fees are $20.00 and $30.00; they also offer 9-hole rates. Monday thru Wednesday, when space is available, seniors, age 60 and over, and juniors, can play after 1:00 p.m. for $18.00. Twilight green fees are $15.00. Clubs rent for $20.00, handcarts $3.00 and $5.00, and motorized carts $23.00, or $15.00 after twilight.

Facilities include a restaurant that serves beer and wine, plus banquet facilities, a snack bar, chipping and putting greens, full-service pro shop, and driving range. At the range you'll find grass tees, and get buckets of balls for $3.00 to $5.00. Help with tournament planning is available. They can also help you with lessons, which can include video. Credit cards are welcome.

Directions: To find the Classic Country Club, leave I-5 at exit #127, head east on Highway 512, turn right on Pacific Avenue, stay left when the road Ys and follow Highway 7 a short distance before turning left onto 208th Street.

LAKE SPANAWAY GOLF COURSE
15602 Pacific
Spanaway, WA
(206) 531-3660

Lake Spanaway is a county course, and open year round from dawn to dusk. The terrain is fairly flat. Reservations are taken one week in advance, and you will want to call ahead to check their weekend schedule for tournaments. Three sets of tees add variety to your game. The women's tees have a par of 74 for a total distance of 5,935 yards.

Pierce County residents pay $12.25 for 9 holes or $19.00 for 18, all week long. Resident juniors and seniors can play on non-holiday weekdays for $8.75 and $13.25. Out-of-area golfers pay $16.00 and $24.50 seven days a week. Twilight rates are $19.50

for non-residents, $15.25 for residents, and $9.50 during the week for local seniors. Clubs rent for $10.00, handcarts $3.00, and motorized carts $12.00 and $20.00.

They have a restaurant and banquet facilities where beer and wine is served, plus a full-service pro shop and covered driving range. At the pro shop you can get help you with lessons, or tournament planning. The range includes a green-tee box for woods, and you get a bucket of balls for $2.50 to $4.00.

Directions: To reach the Lake Spanaway Golf Course, take exit #127 off I-5. It's located just south of Parkland.

(SUMNER)

TAPPS ISLAND GOLF COURSE
20818 Island Parkway E.
Sumner, WA
(206) 862-7011

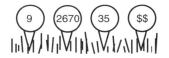

Tapps Island is short and tough. It has water, sand, trees, and slight hills, plus a beautiful view of Mt. Rainier. Two sets of flags and tees will give you a challenging 18-hole game. This year round course opens at 7:00 a.m. October thru March, and 6:00 a.m. the rest of the year. The total distance from the women's tees is 4,848 yards.

Weekday green fees are $13.00 for 9 holes or $19.00 for 18; golfers under 17, or over 55, pay $9.00 and $14.00. On weekends and holidays everyone pays $15.00 and $22.00. Clubs rent for $7.00, handcarts $3.00, and motorized carts $15.00 and $20.00.

You'll find a restaurant with banquet facilities that serves beer and wine, plus a full-service pro shop where you can get help with tournament planning, and arrange for lessons.

Directions: To reach the Tapps Island Golf Course, head east on Highway 14, going thru Bonney Lake, and turn left at 214th Avenue. When you come to the second stoplight turn left again onto Island Parkway. This will take you to the course.

(UNION)

ALDERBROOK GOLF CLUB
E. 300 Country Club Dr.
Union, WA
(360) 898-2560

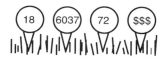

This course is open year round, weather permitting, and offers a gently rolling terrain that is easy to walk. Built in 1965, the front 9 is flat but the back 9 has some hills. You'll find a gorgeous view of the Olympic Mountains, lots of trees, and occasionally spot wildlife on the course. Reservations are available one week in advance. The women's par is 73 for an overall yardage of 5,500.

During the week, green fees are $25.00 for 18 holes, seniors play for $18.00. On weekends and holidays everyone pays $30.00. Credit cards are welcome. Rental clubs are $10.00, handcarts $3.00, and motorized carts $22.00. Facilities include a snack bar serving beer and wine, plus a a banquet room, full-service pro shop, and covered driving range. You can get help with tournament planning and lessons. At the driving range a bucket of balls will cost you $2.50 to $4.00.

Directions: Take Highway 106 8 miles to the Alderbrook Resort.

SHELTON

LAKE LIMERICK GOLF CLUB
E. 790 St. Andrew Dr.
Shelton, WA
(360) 426-6290

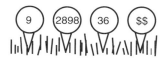

Lake Limerick's narrow fairways are lined with trees and the terrain is fairly flat. Built in 1967, the slope ranges from 114 to 120 and the ratings are 67.2 for men, 70.9 for women. You'll find four tees on each hole. Lake Limerick is open year round from 7:00 a.m. to dusk. Reservations are taken three days in advance, and the total distance from the ladies' tees is 2,658 yards.

During the week green fees for 9 holes are $10.00, 18 holes are $13.00. On weekends and holidays you'll pay $13.00 and $18.00. Clubs rent for a flat $4.00, handcarts are $2.00 and $4.00, and motorized carts $12.00 and $20.00. They have a restaurant that serves beer and wine, a banquet room, and pro shop. Tournament planning assistance and lessons are available. Credit cards are welcome.

Directions: Leave downtown Shelton heading north on Highway 3 to Mason Lake Road, turn left, and after 3 miles turn left again onto St. Andrew Drive.

SHELTON BAYSHORE GOLF CLUB
E. 3800 Hwy. 3
Shelton, WA
(360) 426-1271

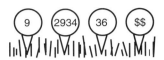

Bayshore includes an extra green on the 2nd hole for use when playing 18 holes. The greens are tight, tricky, and well-maintained. The course is flat, and enjoyable for golfers of all levels. Reservations are recommended on weekends and holidays, and the women's total distance is 2,752 yards.

Weekday green fees are $10.00 for 9 holes or $15.00 for 18. On weekends and holidays it'll cost you $11.00 and $17.00. You can rent clubs for $7.00, handcarts $3.00, and motorized carts $13.00 and $20.00.

Facilities include a snack bar and lounge with a liquor license. Lessons, and help with tournament planning, are available at the pro shop.

Directions: To find the Shelton Bayshore Golf Club, leave downtown Shelton heading north on Highway 3 for 4.5 miles.

ENUMCLAW

ENUMCLAW GOLF COURSE
45220 288th S.E.
Enumclaw, WA
(360) 825-2827

The Enumclaw course is situated in the foothills of Mt. Rainier and surrounded by trees. It's open year round and is a picturesque country course with rolling hills. You'll find lots of water on the back 9. Reservations are taken ten days in advance, and the women's par is 71.

Green fees are $12.00 for 9 holes or $17.00 for 18. Seniors can play during the week for $9.00 and $11.00; juniors pay $8.00 and $10.00. You can rent clubs for $6.00, handcarts $3.00, and motorized carts $10.00 and $20.00. Facilities include a restaurant serving beer and wine, plus a pro shop where you can arrange for lessons.

Directions: Take Highway 410 out of town, towards Chinook Pass, and you'll quickly spot the course.

ELMA

OAKSRIDGE GOLF COURSE
1052 Monte-Elma Rd.
Elma, WA
(360) 482-3511

Oaksridge is an easy-to-walk course situated in a pleasant country setting. The slope for men is 100 and the rating 65.3, it's 108 and 68.9 for women. Open year round, tee times are available for weekend and holiday play. During the winter they open up at 8:00 a.m., 7:00 a.m. in the spring and summer. The course offers two sets of tees. From the women's tees the total yardage is 5,423 for a par of 72.

Green fees are $8.00 for 9 holes or $14.00 for 18. Golfers age 17 and under, and those 60 and over, can play 9 holes during the week for $6.00 or 18 for $11.00. Clubs rent for $3.00, handcarts $2.00, and motorized carts $9.00 and $16.00.

You'll find a snack bar and a full-service pro shop. Help with tournament planning is available, as are lessons. At the driving range you'll pay $1.75 for 35 balls or $2.75 for 80.

Directions: To find the Oaksridge Golf Course, take Highway 12 to Elma and follow the signs.

OLYMPIA

CAPITOL CITY GOLF COURSE
5225 Yelm Hwy. S.E.
Olympia, WA
(360) 491-5111

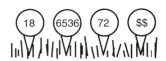

This year-round course has a great view of Mt. Rainier and is one of the most playable winter courses in the Pacific Northwest. Capitol City is flat to mildly rolling, kept in excellent condition, has more than 30 sand bunkers and large greens. Built in 1968, it is open sunrise to sunset. They take reservations one week in advance. The total distance from the women's tees is 5,510 yards.

During the week green fees are $15.00 for 18 holes, on weekends they're $20.00. Juniors play for $6.00 after 2:00 p.m., and seniors for $14.00. Clubs rent for $10.00 and handcarts $3.50.

Facilities include a restaurant and lounge where beer and wine is served, plus a full-service pro shop and driving range. Help with tournament planning, and golf lessons, are available. At the driving range you'll pay $2.00 to $3.00 for a bucket of balls.

Directions: To find Olympia's Capitol City Golf Course, leave I-5 at exit #109, follow College Street to Yelm Highway, and turn left. The course is 6 blocks.

DELPHI GOLF COURSE
6340 Neylon Dr. S.W.
Olympia, WA
(360) 357-6437

The Delphi course requires a good deal of accuracy with its small, undulating greens. Built in 1974, it was designed by Glen Correa and has three tees per hole. The terrain is mostly flat, with greens bordered by trees. Sand and water come into play throughout the game, and the 5th hole is played over water. The slope is 102 and the ratings 60.6 for men, 61.8 for women. The women's par is 34 for a total distance of 1,789 yards.

You can play year round at Delphi, unless there is snow or standing water on the course. Reservations are necessary on summer weekends. April thru September, Wednesday is Men's Day, Thursday is Ladies' Day, and Mixed Couples play on Friday evenings. They have a snack bar where you can get cold beer, offer help with tournament planning, and give lessons.

Weekday green fees are $8.50 for 9 holes or $12.50 for 18, and juniors accompanied by a parent can play for $3.00. On weekends it's $9.50 and $14.50. Seniors can play during the week, and after 2:00 p.m. on weekends, for $8.00. October thru February, and after 4:00 p.m. during the summer, anyone can play 9 holes for $8.00. Clubs rent for $5.00, handcarts $2.00, and motorized carts $12.00 and $18.00. Credit cards are welcome.

Directions: Leave Highway 101 at the Blacklake exit, head south 4 miles to Delphi Road, turn left, then right on Alpine Drive and follow .5 mile to the course.

SCOTT LAKE GOLF COURSE

11746 Scott Creek Dr. S.W.
Olympia, WA
(360) 352-4838

The Scott Lake Golf Course has lots of water hazards, fantastic greens, and a terrain that is flat and easy to walk. Built in 1964, it is inhabited by deer and geese, and a picturesque creek runs through the fairways. The slope is 94 for men and 97 for women, and the ratings 62.9 and 64.4. They are open year round beginning at 6:00 a.m., but take reservations only during the summer. The women's par is 36 for a total distance of 2,131 yards.

During the week, green fees are $8.00 for 9 holes or $12.00 for 18. On weekends it's $9.00 and $14.00. If you're under 18, or older than 61, you can play on weekdays for $6.50 and $9.00. Clubs rent for $3.00 and $5.00, handcarts $2.00, and motorized carts $9.00 and $16.00.

Facilities include a restaurant that serves beer and wine, plus a pro shop and banquet room. They offer help with tournament planning.

Directions: Leave I-5 at exit #99 to Case Road, turn right and proceed to Scott Lake.

TUMWATER

TUMWATER VALLEY GOLF COURSE
4611 Tumwater Valley Dr.
Tumwater, WA
(360) 943-9500

Tumwater Valley is situated above the artesian wells made famous by the Olympia Brewery, and offers some nice mountain views. Lakes are found on the 2nd, 16th and 17th fairways, and a stream winds through the course. It is fairly wide open, flat, and easy to walk. Open year round, they offer winter rates November thru February, and take reservations eight days in advance.

Weekday green fees are $12.00 for 9 holes or $17.00 for 18. Juniors can play for $10.00, and after 5:00 p.m. anyone can play for $8.00. On weekends, everybody pays $10.00 for 9 holes; 18 holes cost $24.00 before 2:00 p.m. and $15.00 after 2:00 p.m. You can rent a full set of clubs for $12.00 or a half set for $6.00, handcarts are $2.00, and motorized carts $14.00 and $20.00.

Facilities include a restaurant and lounge with a liquor license, plus a banquet area, driving range and pro shop. At the driving range you'll pay $3.00 to $5.00 for a bucket of balls. Lessons, and help with tournament planning, are available.

Directions: Leave I-5 South at exit #103, turn left over the highway, right at the first stop light, left at the next light, and follow this road to the course. From I-5 North begin by turning right.

LACEY

MERIWOOD GOLF COURSE
4550 Meriwood Dr.
Lacey, WA
(360) 412-0495

Each hole is different on this year-round course. Designed by Bill Overdorf, it opened in 1995. It has a rolling terrain, lots of woods, and water on several holes. The slope ranges from 116 to 128 for men, with ratings of 67.4 to 74.6. For women the slope is 123 to 140, and the ratings 72.8 to 81.2. The dress code is strict; proper golf attire is required, including a shirt with a collar. Open 7:00 a.m. to 7:00 p.m., reservations are available 30 days in advance.

Green fees Friday thru Sunday, and on holidays, are $35.00 for 18 holes; after 3:00 p.m. it drops to $23.75. It'll cost you $32.00 the balance of the week, $21.50 after 3:00 p.m. On Tuesdays and Thursdays you can play before 9:00 a.m. for $25.00. Seniors, age 60 and up, can also play before 9:00 a.m. on Mondays and Wednesdays for $22.75. Clubs rent for $15.00. Green fees include a cart, and credit cards are welcome.

They have a snack bar offering cold beer and wine, plus a full-service pro shop and driving range. The range has grass tees and you can get a bucket of balls for $2.00 to $3.50. Lessons, and tournament planning, help are available.

Directions: Meriwood Golf Course is located a few miles east of Lacey, just south of I-5.

ORTING

HIGH CEDARS GOLF CLUB
14604 149th St. Ct. E.
Orting, WA
(360) 893-3171 or 845-1853

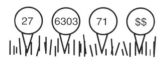

High Cedars has a great view of Mt. Rainier, and offers both an executive 9-hole and a championship 18-hole course. The 18-hole course plays through old growth maple and cedar trees, and around hazards formed by the Puyallup River. Its slope is 113 and the ratings 68.7 for men, 72.0 for women. Tee times are given seven days ahead; a credit card guarantee is needed for weekends.

The executive course is $10.00 for 9 holes or $14.00 for 18 on weekdays, $12.00 and $15.00 on weekends. The championship course is $22.00 and $30.00 Friday thru Sunday as well as holidays, and $16.25 and $21.50 the rest of the week. Twilight rates are $12.00. On weekdays, seniors can play the executive course for $9.00 and $11.00, or the 18-hole course for $13.00 and $16.25. That same rate applies to golfers age 10 thru 17. Clubs rent for $5.00 and $9.00, handcarts $2.50 and $4.00, and motorized carts $15.00 and $21.50. Credit cards are welcome.

They have a coffee shop where beer and wine coolers are available, a full-service pro shop, and a driving range with both covered and uncovered stalls. You can get help with tournament planning and arrange lessons. The range is open from one half hour before sunrise to shortly before sunset, has mat tees, and supplies buckets of balls for $2.50 to $4.00. They also have a new 18-hole grass putting course where you can play for $6.00. Children under 10 must be accompanied by an adult when on the putting course.

Directions: To reach High Cedars Golf Club, take Highway 162 north of Orting 1 mile.

YELM

NISQUALLY VALLEY GOLF COURSE
Yelm Highway
Yelm, WA
(360) 458-3332

This is a scenic course with an outstanding view of Mt. Rainier. The terrain is relatively flat with some hills, and very dry during the winter months. Open year round, reservations are taken only for weekend play. The course was built in 1976, and from the women's tees the total distance is 5,693 yards for a par of 72.

Green fees are $10.00 for 9 holes, or $17.00 for 18, all week long. On weekdays, seniors can play for $5.00 and $10.00. Clubs rent for $5.00, handcarts $2.00, and motorized carts $8.00 and $15.00. Facilities include a restaurant and lounge with a liquor license, plus a banquet area and pro shop. Help with tournament planning, and lessons, are available.

Directions: Take exit #116 off I-5, follow the Old Nisqually Highway to Reservation Road, take this to Yelm Highway and turn left to the course.

CENTRALIA

CENTRALIA PUBLIC GOLF COURSE
1012 Duffy St.
Centralia, WA
(360) 736-5967

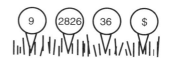

Formerly known as Armory Hills, this public course has a hilly terrain, lots of trees, and a new large pond. The slope is 121 for men and 125 for women, and the ratings 67.3 and 70.8. Weather permitting, it is open year round. Reservations are generally not needed during the week, but are recommended for weekend play. The women's par is 37 for 2,697 yards.

On weekdays you can play 9 holes for $6.00, it's $8.00 on weekends. If you want to play 18 holes it'll cost you $9.00 and $12.00. Clubs, handcarts, and motorized carts are available for rent. You'll find a full-service pro shop, and a restaurant that serves beer and wine. Credit cards are accepted for green fees.

Directions: Follow the city center signs from I-5 to Tower Street where you will turn left. Turn right on Maple, and at the top of the hill you'll find signs directing you to the course.

CHEHALIS

NEWAUKUM VALLEY GOLF COURSE
153 Newaukum Golf Dr.
Chehalis, WA
(360) 748-0461

Newaukum Valley is both challenging and pleasant. It's a good wet-weather course with rolling fairways. Offering 27 holes, each 9 is distinctly different. The course is open year round and tee times are advised March thru October. From the ladies' tees it's a total distance of 5,628 yards.

During the week, green fees are $10.00 for 9 holes or $15.00 for 18. On weekends they charge $14.00 and $19.00, but juniors can play after 1:00 p.m. on weekends for $10.00 and $15.00. You can rent clubs for $10.00, and electric carts are $18.00 for 18 holes. Facilities include a restaurant where you can get cold beer and wine, and a pro shop where you can arrange for lessons.

Directions: Take exit #72 off I-5 North, go left on Rush Road, turn right on Bishop, right on Jackson Highway, and drive 2.5 miles to the course.

RIVERSIDE COUNTRY CLUB
1451 N.W. Airport Rd.
Chehalis, WA
(360) 748-8182 or (800) 242-9486

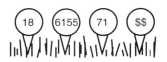

The Chehalis River runs along one side of this course, and ponds affect several holes. It's tree lined, fairly level, and has a beautiful view of Mount St. Helens. The slope is 117 and the ratings 68.3 for men, 71.0 for women. Par from the ladies' tees is 72 for a distance of 5,456 yards. Winter hours are 7:00 a.m. to dark, October thru March; the rest of the year they open at 6:00 a.m. Call ahead for tee times.

During the summer season you can play 18 holes Monday thru Friday for $17.00; it'll cost you $22.00 on Saturdays, Sundays, and holidays. Winter rates are $12.00 and $15.00. The twilight summer rate is $12.00, it's $10.00 in winter. Join the Men's or Ladies' Club and play weekdays for $12.00 in the summer, $10.00 in the winter. Seniors can also play Monday thru Wednesday for $12.00 and $10.00. Juniors, 17 years and under, can play 9 or 18 holes during the week for $10.00.

When space is available, anyone can play 9 holes in the winter for $10.00. Summer weekdays 9 holes will cost you $12.00, but you can only play after 2:00 p.m., on weekends and holidays and it'll cost you $14.00. Motorized carts rent for $15.00 to $20.00, and handcarts $2.00. Credit cards are welcome.

Facilities include a snack bar where beer and wine is available, plus a full-service pro shop and driving range. At the driving range you can get a bucket of balls for $3.00 to $6.00, depending on the size. It is open from daylight to dusk and offers grass tees. They can help with tournament planning and lessons.

Directions: Take exit #79 off I-5; the Riverside Country Club course is west of the airport.

RANDLE

MAPLE GROVE GOLF
Cispus Road
Randle, WA
(360) 497-2741

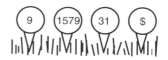

Maple Grove opened in 1987. The terrain is flat to slightly hilly, with some water hazards and sand traps. It has a nice view of the Cascade Mountains, and is open March thru November.

Green fees are $7.50 for 9 holes, $9.75 for 18, or $12.00 to play all day. During the week, juniors and seniors can play for $6.00, $7.50, and $9.50. Clubs rent for $3.00, handcarts $2.00, and they have a few motorized carts reserved for disabled golfers. Facilities include a restaurant that serves beer and wine, plus a full-service pro shop. Group lessons are available.

Directions: Located .5 mile south of Randle via Highway 125.

GLENOMA

IRONWOOD GREEN
8138 Hwy. 12
Glenoma, WA
(360) 498-5425

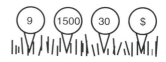

Ironwood is a flat executive course with narrow tree-lined fairways and small greens. Built in 1983, this course is tougher than you would imagine. Open year round, Wednesday evenings are reserved for the men's league, and Thursday evenings for the women's league. The women's par is 31.

You can play Ironwood all day for $10.00, or pay $5.50 for 9 holes, $7.50 for 18. Seniors pay $4.50 for 9 holes and $6.50 for 18. Clubs are available for $3.50, handcarts $2.50, and power carts $8.00 and $15.00. Facilities include a full-service pro shop, a small RV park, and a store. Golf lessons are available during the summer.

Directions: Located along Highway 12, in Glenoma.

CATHLAMET

SKYLINE GOLF COURSE
20 Randall Dr.
Cathlamet, WA
(360) 795-8785

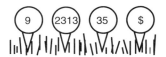

Skyline's 65 acres offer a great view of the Columbia River. The terrain is hilly, with sand traps and a pond. Open year round, elk and deer are often seen on the course. Reservations are not taken, but you might want to check the tournament schedule. Dual tees add variety when shooting an 18-hole game.

Green fees are $8.00 for 9 holes or $12.00 for 18 all week long. Clubs rent for $5.00, handcarts $1.00, and motorized carts $7.00 and $15.00. They have a banquet area and a limited pro shop where you'll find snacks, beer, and help with tournament planning.

Directions: Take Highway 4 to Cathlamet, turn right on Bogie Road, turn right again on Clover Street, and watch for signs.

LONGVIEW

GOLFGREEN GOLF CENTER
561 Seventh Ave.
Longview, WA
(360) 425-0450 or (800) 424-0450

Built in 1962, Golfgreen is open from 7:00 a.m. to dark every day but Thanksgiving and Christmas. The terrain is flat, and the greens small with undulating surfaces. Reservations are not needed. No walk-alongs are allowed on the course.

During the week, green fees are $4.75 for 9 holes or $9.00 for 18. On weekends it's $5.00 and $9.50. Clubs rent for $2.25 and handcarts $2.00. Motorized carts are not available. Golfgreen offers a full-service pro shop, lounge, snack bar, and miniature golf. The miniature course is $1.00 for 18 holes.

Directions: Leave I-5 north at exit #36 and take the first left after entering the city of Longview.

MINT VALLEY GOLF COURSE
4002 Pennsylvania
Longview, WA
(360) 577-3395

Mint Valley has both a 9-hole par three and a challenging 18-hole course. You'll find lots of water and sand on the 18-hole course to keep your game sharp. The slope is 127 and the ratings 71 for men, 70 for women. The total distance from the ladies tees is 5,231 yards. Designed by Ron Fream, and built in 1976, it's open year round. Tee times are available one week in advance.

Green fees on the 18-hole course are $13.50 for 9 holes or $18.50 for 18 on weekends; weekday rates are $10.50 and $14.00. On weekdays, and after 1:30 p.m. on weekends, juniors pay $8.00 and $10.00, seniors $9.00 and $11.00. Clubs rent for $8.00, handcarts $3.00, and motorized carts $11.00 and $22.00.

Young children are not permitted on the 18-hole course, and your 18 hole game must be completed in four hours or less. However, Mint Valley's easy-to-play par three course is great for beginners and young children. Adults can play all day on this one for $5.00; children 15 and younger play for free.

Facilities include a snack bar where you can get cold beer and wine, plus a full-service pro shop and driving range. At the range they offer both mat and grass tees and you get a bucket of balls for $3.50 to $5.50. They also give lessons and provide tournament planning assistance.

Directions: Take Highway 4 west 2 miles, turn right on 38th, after .5 mile turn left on Pennsylvania and follow to the course.

KELSO

THREE RIVERS GOLF COURSE
2222 S. River Rd.
Kelso, WA
(360) 423-4653

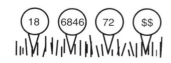

The Three Rivers course was built on Mount St. Helens ash. It has good drainage, and is playable year round. Reservations are taken one week in advance. During the summer you can get on the course at 6:15 a.m.; in the winter they open at 8:00 a.m. Three sets of tees are available, the total distance from the women's tees is 5,455 yards.

Weekend green fees are $14.00 for 9 holes or $17.00 for 18. During the week it's $11.00 and $15.00, and seniors, over age 62, pay $8.50 and $11.00. Juniors can play during the week, and after 1:00 p.m. on weekends, for $6.00 and $9.00. Clubs rent for $7.50, handcarts $2.00, and motorized carts $11.00 and $20.00. You'll find a restaurant where beer and wine is available, plus a driving range and full-service pro shop. Lessons, and help with tournament planning, are available. At the driving range you'll pay $2.50 to $5.00 for a bucket of balls.

Directions: Leave I-5 North at exit #36, Industrial Way, and head north to South River Road and the course.

WOODLAND

LEWIS RIVER GOLF
3209 Lewis River Rd.
Woodland, WA
(360) 225-8254

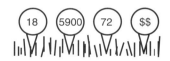

Lewis River is open year round, from dawn to dusk, unless closed by snow. This beautiful dry winter course has both flat and rolling terrain. The slope is 116 and the ratings 67.9 for men, 68.9 for women. Built in 1966, reservations are taken seven days in advance. The women's par is 73 for a total distance of 5,240 yards.

Green fees during the week are $12.00 for 9 holes, or $22.00 for 18. On weekends it'll cost you $15.00 or $27.00. Monday thru Friday, juniors and seniors can play 9 holes for $8.00, or 18 for $16.00. Credit cards are welcome. Facilities include a restaurant and lounge with a liquor license, plus a full-service pro shop and driving range. Lessons, and help with tournament planning, are available. At the driving range you'll find grass tees and pay $2.00 to $4.00 for a bucket of balls.

Directions: Take State Highway 503 east of town 5 miles.

RIDGEFIELD

TRI MOUNTAIN GOLF COURSE
1701 N.W. 299th St.
Ridgefield, WA
(360) 887-3004

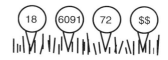

Built in 1994, Tri Mountain was designed by William G. Robinson. The view includes Mount St. Helens, Mt. Adams and Mt. Hood. Open year round, winter hours are 8:00 a.m. to dusk; the rest of the year they open at 6:00 a.m. You'll find rolling hills, four sets of tees, 84 bunkers and 11 lakes. Water comes into play on 12 holes. Reservations are taken one week in advance.

Weekday green fees are $10.00 for 9 holes or $18.00 for 18. On weekends they charge $12.00 and $22.00. Clubs rent for $5.00 and $10.00, handcarts $2.00 and $3.00, and motorized carts $10.00 and $20.00. Facilities include a snack bar which serves cold beer and wine, plus a full-service pro shop and driving range. At the range you can get a bucket of balls for $2.00 to $4.00. Lessons, and help with tournament planning, are available.

Directions: Leave I-5 North at exit #14, turn right onto 269th Street, left onto 11th Avenue, and left onto 299th Street.

BRUSH PRAIRIE

CEDAR GOLF CLUB
15001 N.E. 181st St.
Brush Prairie, WA
(360) 687-4233

There are water hazards on 14 of the 18 holes at Cedar Golf Club, and no parallel fairways. Open year round, tee times are taken one week in advance. The course is mostly flat, with two hills, fast greens, and mature trees. The women's par is 73 for a total distance of 5,050 yards.

Green fees for 18 holes are $16.00 during the week and $18.00 on weekends. Clubs rent for $10.00, handcarts $2.00, and motorized carts $20.00. Facilities include a restaurant and lounge with a liquor license, plus a banquet area, pro shop and driving range. At the range a small bucket of balls will cost you $2.50 and a large one $4.00. Lessons are available.

Directions: Leave I-5 at the Fourth Plain exit, go east, turn left on Ward Road, left on 152nd, and follow for 5 miles to the course.

NORTH BONNEVILLE

BEACON ROCK GOLF COURSE
Highway 14
North Bonneville, WA
(509) 427-5730

This course is located in the beautiful Columbia River Gorge, and offers outstanding views of Beacon Rock and snow-covered mountains. A flat course, it opened in 1971. Reservations are required on weekends, and are a good idea during the week as well. The distance from the women's tees is 2,540 yards.

Green fees are $9.00 for 9 holes or $18.00 for 18, seven days a week. Tuesday thru Thursday, seniors, age 62 and over, can play 9 holes for $7.00. Clubs rent for $6.00 and $10.00, handcarts $2.00 and $3.00, and motorized carts $9.00 and $18.00. Facilities include a restaurant where beer is served, plus a putting green.

Directions: Located along Highway 14, between Beacon Rock and North Bonneville.

VANCOUVER

BOWYER'S PAR 3 GOLF
11608 N.E. 119th St.
Vancouver, WA
(360) 892-3808

Bowyer's is mostly flat, with fir trees lining the fairways, and a nice view of Mount St. Helens. They are open year round and do not take reservations. They have a snack bar that also sells limited golf supplies. Children under 8 are not permitted to play.

Green fees for 9 holes are $6.50 all week long. On weekdays, 18 holes will cost you $12.00; it's $13.00 on weekends. Children, age 8 to 12, and senior golfers, can play during the week for $6.00 and $11.00. Credit cards are welcome. You can rent clubs for $1.50, handcarts are $1.50, and motorized carts are not available.

Directions: Leave I-205 southbound at the Orchards exit, follow Highway 503 for 3 miles to 119th Street. From I-205 northbound take the Vancouver Mall exit, turn right onto Fourth Plain, left at 117th Avenue, and take 119th Street to the course.

FAIRWAY VILLAGE GOLF
15509 S.E. Fernwood Dr.
Vancouver, WA
(360) 254-9325

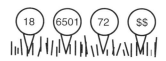

The Fairway Village course slopes gently towards the river. Built in 1981, it was designed by Bunny Mason, and is open year round. Summer hours are 7:00 a.m. to dusk, but they don't open until 8:00 a.m. during the winter. They are closed to the public Tuesday thru Friday until noon. Tee times are required. The total distance from the ladies' tees is 2,311 yards.

Weekday green fees are $10.00 for 9 holes or $17.00 for 18. Weekend rates are $11.00 and $18.00. Fairway Village is an adult community and seniors, 62 and older, can play during the week for $7.00 per 9 holes. You can rent handcarts for $1.00 and motorized carts are $11.00 and $17.00. They have no rental clubs available. Facilities include a full-service pro shop where lessons can be arranged.

Directions: Leave I-205 at the Camas exit, go east to 164th, north to McGilvrey, turn left after 3 blocks, and follow the signs.

LAKEVIEW GOLF CHALLENGE
2425 N.W. 69th St.
Vancouver, WA
(360) 693-9116

Lakeview is only for golfers who want a real challenge. It's not supposed to be easy, in fact, it was designed to improve your short game and changes constantly. Open year round, 8:00 a.m. to dusk, it has flat, rolling greens, two ponds, and lots of trees.

It offers a beautiful view of Vancouver Lake, and the greens are contoured with difficult slopes. You'll find trees directly in front of some tees and greens; the 8th hole has a small pond in the middle of the green, and the 6th hole has two bunkers. The course is posted each Thursday for its toughness. Some weeks it's easy (1) and other weeks the pin settings have been changed to very difficult (10). USGA rules and traditions have been ignored to create this challenge.

Green fees are $6.00 for 9 holes, or $11.00 for 18. Seniors can play during the week for $5.00 and $9.00. Clubs can be rented for $2.50 and handcarts $1.00. The course operates on the honor system, and reservations are not possible. They can provide help with tournament planning and will rent the course to groups.

Directions: Leave I-5 North on 78th Street, head west to Fruit Valley Road, turn left, drive .7 mile and go right on Whitney, follow .5 mile to the course.

PINE CREST GOLF COURSE
2415 N.W. 143rd St.
Vancouver, WA
(360) 573-2051

Pine Crest has rolling hills, beautiful trees, sand traps, and a view of both Mount St. Helens and Mt. Hood. They are open year round from 8:00 a.m. till dark. Reservations are not required.

Green fees are $6.50 for the first 9 holes, and $5.50 for the second, every day of the week. On weekdays, seniors pay $5.50 per 9 holes. Clubs rent for $2.00 and handcarts $1.75. They have a cute Bavarian-style clubhouse where you can get snacks as well as cold pop and beer. They also have a putting green.

Directions: Take the 134th Street exit off I-5, after 2 miles turn left onto 143rd Street, and follow to the course.

CENTRAL WASHINGTON

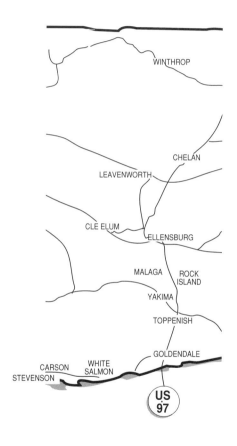

Central Washington
Table of Contents

WINTHROP

BEAR CREEK GOLF COURSE
Eastside County Road
Winthrop, WA
(509) 996-2284

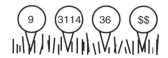

Bear Creek is real pretty, with snow-capped mountains in the distance, especially in the fall when the colors are changing. The course is challenging, some holes are on the hillside and others in the meadow, and your ball has to travel across the lake on one hole. The back nine at Bear Creek plays like a different course, the tee placement is so varied. The slope is 117 and the ratings 68.9 for men, 69.4 for women. The women's par is 37 for a total distance of 2,706 yards. You can play here April thru October, depending on the snowfall, from 8:00 a.m. to dark. Tee times are recommended on holidays.

Weekday golfers pay $11.00 for 9 holes or $16.00 for 18. On weekends and holidays it's $12.00 and $18.00. Juniors, those under 17, can play for half price on weekdays. You can rent clubs for $4.00, handcarts $2.00, and motorized carts $10.00 for 9 holes or $19.00 for 18. Facilities include a pro shop, practice green, and lunch counter.

Directions: Located 3 miles south of Winthrop, along Eastside County Road.

CHELAN

LAKE CHELAN GOLF COURSE
Golf Course Road
Chelan, WA
(509) 682-5421 or (800) 246-5361

The Lake Chelan course offers an outstanding view of the lake against a backdrop of towering mountains. The front 9 holes are flat and the back 9 hilly. Built in 1970, it is open from mid-March thru October. Reservations are needed seven days in advance. From the women's tees it's a total distance of 5,501 yards.

Green fees are $15.00 for 9 holes, $25.00 for 18. Clubs can be rented for $12.00 and $20.00; motorized carts are $12.00 and $22.00. Facilities include a restaurant where you can get beer and wine, plus a banquet area and pro shop. Lessons, and tournament planning help are available. At the driving range you can get a small bucket of balls for $3.00 or a large one for $5.00.

Directions: Take Manson Hwy. and follow signs to the course.

LEAVENWORTH

KAHLER GLEN GOLF COURSE
20890 Kahler Dr.
Leavenworth, WA
(509) 763-4025

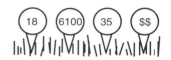

The signature hole at Kahler has a 507 yard dogleg and a 225-foot-long lake. Its terrain is mountainous, and the course is surrounded by a gorgeous natural forest. Designed by Randy Pelton, it is open April thru October. Reservations are taken two weeks in advance. Tournaments tie up the course the last weekend in July, and the 3rd weekend in September.

Green fees are $12.00 for 9 holes or $20.00 for 18 Monday thru Thursday. On weekends and holidays it's $15.00 and $25.00. Clubs rent for $6.00 and $12.00, handcarts $2.00 and $3.00, and motorized carts $11.00 and $22.00. Facilities include overnight accommodations, a snack bar that serves beer, and a full-service pro shop. A driving range is being added. Lessons, and help with tournament planning, are available.

Directions: Leave Highway 2 on Highway 207, drive 4 miles and follow the signs.

LEAVENWORTH GOLF CLUB
9101 Icicle Rd.
Leavenworth, WA
(509) 548-7267

This course is located in the mountains, and surrounded on three sides by the Wenatchee River. The scenery is gorgeous, and wildlife, including an occasional bear, is often spotted on the course. Open April thru October, depending on snowfall, the terrain is one of rolling hills. Built in 1947, the slope is 116 and the ratings 67.0 for men and 69.6 for women. The total yardage for women is 5,343.

Reservations are needed one week in advance for holidays; only a few days ahead the rest of the time. They begin taking reservations on Mondays for the following week. On Sundays, before 11:00 a.m., the course is open only to men. Women get the course to themselves on Wednesday mornings. Children 11 and younger are not allowed on weekends; those 9 and older can play during the week.

Green fees are $12.00 for 9 holes or $18.00 for 18. Motorized carts can be rented for $10.00 per 9 holes, clubs $15.00, and handcarts $2.00. Facilities include a restaurant where beer and wine is served, plus a snack bar and pro shop.

Directions: Located 1 mile west of town via Highway 2, then .6 mile south on Icicle Road.

CLE ELUM

SUN COUNTRY GOLF COURSE
E. Nelson Siding Road
Cle Elum, WA
(509) 674-2226

This challenging course is located in the beautiful Upper Kittitas Valley. The slope for men is 119 and the rating 68.8; for women it's 124 and 70.9. There are two sets of tees so golfers can play 18 holes with some variety. Open April 15 thru October 15, weekend hours are 6:00 a.m. to dusk; on weekdays they open up at 7:00 a.m. Reservations are taken one week in advance for weekend and holiday tee times.

On weekends, green fees are $10.00 for 9 holes or $15.00 for 18. Monday thru Friday you'll pay $8.00 or $12.00, and juniors play for $5.00 and $8.00. Clubs rent for $3.00 or $10.00 for a full set, handcarts are $1.00, and motorized carts $10.00 for 9 holes or $18.00 for 18. They offer a limited pro shop, a snack bar where you'll find cold beer, and a driving range. They can help with tournament planning and provide banquet facilities. At the driving range you'll find mat tees, and a bucket of balls cost $2.00. Sun Country also has its own campground where golfers can pitch a tent or park an RV.

Directions: Leave I-90 at exit #78 on Golf Course Road; the course is located 6 miles west of Cle Elum.

ELLENSBURG

ELLENSBURG GOLF CLUB
Thorp Road
Ellensburg, WA
(509) 962-2984

This semi-private course doesn't open to the public until 1:00 p.m. on weekends. Women have the course to themselves on Thursdays, but non-members are welcome after 1:00 p.m. The men get the course on Wednesdays, and non-members can play after 10:00 a.m. The rest of the time anyone can play.

Located along the Yakima River, it was built in the 1930s and has a lovely mountain view. Weather permitting, they remain open March thru mid-November. Tee times are given out one week in advance. The women's par is 73 for a total distance of 5,678 yards.

During the week, green fees are $9.00 for 9 holes or $18.00 for 18. On weekends they're $10.00 and $17.00. Juniors can play for $3.00 and $5.00 seven days a week. Clubs rent for $5.00, handcarts $1.50, and motorized carts $7.00 and $16.00.

Facilities include a full-service pro shop and a driving range, plus a restaurant, lounge and banquet facilities where liquor is served. They can help with tournament planning as well as lessons. At the driving range you'll pay $1.00 per 30 balls.

Directions: Take I-90 to Ellensburg, cross the river near the KOA campground, and follow Thorp Road to the course.

MALAGA

THREE LAKES GOLF COURSE
2695 Golf Dr.
Malaga, WA
(509) 663-5448

Built in 1953, the Three Lakes Golf Course is open year round. Reservations are taken a week in advance. This course is hilly and challenging, with tree-lined fairways that overlook the Columbia River. The surrounding area is full of orchards, making it a gorgeous place to play in the spring.

Green fees are $12.00 for 9 holes or $20.00 for 18. Juniors can play for $7.00 and $10.00. Clubs rent for $5.00 and $7.00, and motorized carts $12.00 and $20.00. Facilities include a restaurant offering beer and wine, plus a banquet area and driving range. At the range you'll pay $2.50 to $4.00 for a bucket of balls. They can also help you with tournament planning.

Directions: Take Wenatchee Ave. 3 miles south of Wenatchee.

ROCK ISLAND

ROCK ISLAND GOLF CLUB
314 Saunders Rd.
Rock Island, WA
(509) 884-2806

The Rock Island course is open year round, weather permitting. It has a nice mountain view, flat terrain, and enough water to make the game challenging. The total yardage from the women's tees is 2,884. Tee times are available only on weekends.

Green fees are $10.00 for 9 holes or $15.00 for 18, seven days a week. Seniors, age 60 and over, can save $2.00 on Tuesdays and Thursdays. Clubs rent for $3.00 and $5.00, handcarts $1.60 and $2.15, and motorized carts $10.00 and $18.00. Facilities include a restaurant with a banquet area, limited pro shop and practice area. Help with tournament planning is available.

Directions: Take Highway 28 9.5 miles southeast of Wenatchee.

YAKIMA

APPLE TREE GOLF COURSE
8804 Occidental Ave.
Yakima, WA
(509) 966-5877

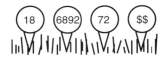

The 17th hole at Apple Tree sits on a tiny apple-shaped island. Opened in 1992, this challenging course is located on the site of a 100-year-old apple orchard and very scenic. The terrain is relatively flat with some hills, and weather permitting you can golf here year round, from sunrise to sunset. The slope is 124 and the ratings 70.7 for men, 72.0 for women.

Reservations should be made one week in advance, but if you're coming from out of town you can get them earlier. The women's par is 72 for a total length of 5,857 yards.

Monday thru Thursday green fees are $16.00 for 9 holes or $35.00 for 18. On weekends you'll pay $50.00 for 18 holes. Locals get a discount when playing 18 holes, so do golfers younger than 18 playing during the week, as well as those 60 and older who come on Monday or Tuesday. Clubs rent for $14.00, handcarts $4.00, and motorized carts $24.00.

Facilities include a restaurant, full-service pro shop, and a driving range with grass tees where balls are $3.00 to $4.50 a bucket. They can provide tournament planning assistance and arrange lessons.

Directions: Located in west Yakima. Take the 40th Avenue exit off Highway 12, go south to Washington Avenue, turn left at 64th Avenue, and right on Occidental which leads to the course.

FISHER PARK GOLF COURSE
Arlington & 40th Ave.
Yakima, WA
(509) 575-6075

Built in 1961, this city-owned course is open from March to November from dawn till dusk. Fisher Park is a beautifully landscaped spot with well kept-greens, and lots of evergreens and flowers. The terrain is easy to walk.

Green fees are $6.00 for 9 holes or $10.00 for 18 all week long. Juniors and seniors pay $5.00 and $8.00. Between 7:00 a.m. and 11:00 a.m. ladies can play for $4.00 on Tuesdays, men on Thursdays, and juniors on Saturdays. Clubs rent for $2.75 and handcarts are $2.00 per 9 holes. Lessons are available during the summer. Facilities include a putting green and a small pro shop where you'll find snacks and soft drinks.

Directions: Located in west Yakima.

SUNTIDES GOLF COURSE
231 Pence Rd.
Yakima, WA
(509) 966-9065

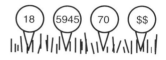

18 · 5945 · 70 · $$

Open year round, Suntides is fun with two creeks bringing water into play on 13 of the holes. The terrain is flat with some elevated tees. Reservations are only taken for Fridays and weekends, and the women's par is 71 for a total distance of 5,509 yards.

Green fees are the same seven days a week, $10.00 for 9 holes or $17.00 for 18. Clubs rent for $3.00 and $5.00, handcarts $2.00, and motorized carts $10.00 per 9 holes. Lessons are available, and you can get help with tournament planning. Facilities include a lounge and restaurant with a liquor license, plus a banquet area, driving range and pro shop. At the range a bucket of balls cost $2.50 to $4.00, depending on the size of the bucket.

Directions: Located 4 miles west of Yakima, along Highway 12.

WESTWOOD WEST GOLF COURSE
6408 Tieton
Yakima, WA
(509) 966-0890

9 · 2691 · 35 · $$

Westwood is the only Pacific Northwest golf course that produces and sells fruit. Each year they harvest 100 tons of apples. The course includes an orchard, and golfing during apple blossom time is beautiful. Westwood is open from dawn to dusk, year round, unless snow falls. Built in 1965, it has a combination of hilly and flat fairways, and two sets of tees.

Green fees are the same all week long; you can play 9 holes for $11.50 or 18 holes for $18.00. Golfers 60 and over can buy a monthly ticket for $75.00, plus tax, which allows unlimited play on non-holiday weekdays. Juniors can get the same monthly pass for $80.00, plus tax. Clubs rent for $4.00, handcarts $2.00, and motorized carts $10.00 per 9 holes. Lessons are available. Facilities include a pro shop, covered driving range, and practice area.

Directions: You'll find this course by heading west of town along Tieton Drive.

TOPPENISH

MT. ADAMS COUNTRY CLUB
1250 Rocky Ford Rd.
Toppenish, WA
(509) 865-4440

This course is flat with gentle draws, and offers a spectacular view of Mt. Adams. It has some of the most puttable greens in Central Washington and is open March thru November.

A semi-private club, it is not open to the public on Wednesdays and Thursdays until 1:00 p.m. The rest of the time it opens to everyone at 7:00 a.m. on weekdays and 6:00 a.m. on weekends. Weekend reservations are taken starting on Thursday, and weekday tee times are given two days in advance. The women's tees have a total distance of 5,873 yards for a par of 73.

Green fees are $11.00 for 9 holes or $17.00 for 18, all week long. Juniors can play during the week for half price. Clubs rent for $5.00 and $9.00, handcarts $1.25 per 9 holes, and motorized carts are $11.00 and $21.00.

They have a limited pro shop, restaurant, lounge, and banquet facilities with a liquor license. Both lessons and tournament planning are available. At the driving range you'll pay $3.00 for 40 balls or $4.00 for 80.

Directions: This course is located 2 miles south of Toppenish, via Highway 97.

GOLDENDALE

GOLDENDALE COUNTRY CLUB
1901 N. Columbus
Goldendale, WA
(509) 773-4705

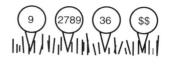

This is a semi-private club, but anyone who lives more than 15 miles outside of Goldendale can play for daily fees any day but Thursday. They do occasionally hold tournaments on weekends, so you might want to call ahead if you're travelling a long distance. This course has a wonderful view of Mt. Hood, Mt. Adams, and Mount St. Helens. The greens are small but interesting, and are kept in good shape. A creek comes into play twice. Open year round, weather permitting, they have two sets of tees. The women's par is 37 for a total distance of 2,546 yards.

Green fees are $10.00 for 9 holes or $18.00 for 18, seven days a week. Clubs rent for $5.00, handcarts $2.00, and motorized carts are $10.00 for 9 holes or $18.00 for 18. They offer a limited snack bar, banquet facilities, and a full-service pro shop. Lessons, and help with tournament planning, are available.

Directions: Take the Broadway exit at Goldendale, drive 1 mile west to the flashing yellow light, turn right, and go 1.5 miles.

STEVENSON

SKAMANIA LODGE GOLF COURSE
1131 Skamania Lodge Way
Stevenson, WA
(509) 427-2541

Designed by Bunny Mason, this year-round course opened in 1993. Cut out of a forest, and overlooking the Columbia River Gorge, you'll find spectacular views. Its rolling terrain includes natural areas and wildlife ponds; one pond contains a beaver lodge, and a few holes wrap around the ponds. Winter hours are 9:00 a.m. to 5:00 p.m.; they're open 7:00 a.m. to 8:00 p.m. the rest of the year. Lodge guests can get tee times when confirming their overnight reservations, others two weeks in advance.

Midweek green fees May thru October are $11.00 for 9 holes or $21.00 for 18. The rest of the week you'll pay $17.00 or $32.00. November thru April they charge $9.00 and $18.00 every day of the week. Credit cards are welcome. Clubs rent for $10.00 and $15.00, handcarts $3.00 and $5.00, and motorized carts $14.00 and $27.00. Facilities include a restaurant and a coffee shop that serves beer and wine, plus a full service pro shop and driving range. Help with tournament planning, and lessons, are available. The driving range has buckets of balls for $2.00 to $4.00.

Directions: To reach Skamania Lodge, take Highway 14 west of Stevenson, turn left on Rock Creek Road, and follow to the lodge and course.

CARSON

HOT SPRINGS GOLF COURSE
Carson Hot Springs
Carson, WA
(509) 427-5150

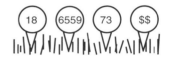

Here's a place where you can enjoy a rousing game of golf and then relax with a hot soak and massage. Completed in 1991, Carson's Hot Springs Golf Course has beautiful views of the Columbia Gorge and includes 6 lakes, 71 traps, and lots of trees. The terrain is level with some hills, and weather permitting, you can play year round. Tee times are recommended. The total distance from the women's tees is 5,365 yards.

Green fees for 18 holes are $16.00 during the week; on weekends you'll pay $19.00. Senior rates are $13.00 during the week and $14.00 on weekends. Clubs rent for $8.50, handcarts $3.50, and motorized carts $20.00. Amenities include a restaurant that serves beer and wine, plus banquet facilities, a covered driving range and pro shop. Tournament planning help and lessons are available.

Directions: Take Highway 14 to Carson, turn at the intersection, and follow the signs.

WHITE SALMON

HUSUM HILLS GOLF COURSE
820 Hwy. 141
White Salmon, WA
(800) 487-4537

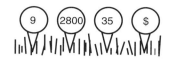

Built in 1958, Husum Hills is a scenic course with spectacular views of Mt. Adams and the White Salmon River Valley. The terrain is hilly but very walkable, the fairways are wide, and the greens small and fast. Reservations are advised on weekends. March thru October this course is open daily; the rest of the year they are open Wednesday thru Sunday only, weather permitting. The total yardage from the women's tees is 2,500.

Green fees are $9.00 for 9 holes, $17.00 for 18. Clubs are $4.00 and $8.00, handcarts $2.00 and $3.00, and motorized carts $9.00 and $17.00. You'll find a restaurant and lounge serving beer and wine, plus banquet facilities and a full-service pro shop. They offer lessons, and help with tournament planning.

Directions: Located 6 miles north of Highway 141's junction with Highway 14.

EASTERN WASHINGTON

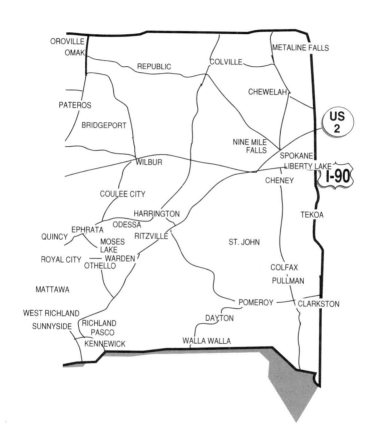

Eastern Washington
Table of Contents

OROVILLE

OROVILLE GOLF CLUB
Nighthawk Road
Oroville, WA
(509) 476-2390

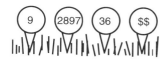

The Oroville Golf Club offers scenic river views and is surrounded by mountains. Its terrain is hilly, and they are only open March thru October. Tee times are available one week in advance. The course is occasionally closed for tournaments so it's wise to call ahead. Two sets of tees are available, and the women's par is 37.

Whether playing 9 holes or 18, they have a flat fee at Oroville Golf Club. On weekends you'll pay $18.00, during the week $15.00. You can rent clubs for $4.00, handcarts $2.00, and motorized carts are $10.00 per 9 holes. They have a full-service pro shop plus a snack bar where you'll find cold beer.

Directions: Located 2 miles west of Oroville via Nighthawk Road.

OMAK

OKANOGAN VALLEY GOLF CLUB
Golf Course Road
Omak, WA
(509) 826-9902

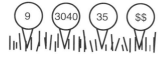

The Okanogan Valley course was built in 1946, is open from the middle of March thru October, and has a fairly flat terrain. This semi-private club is closed to the public on Sunday mornings, Wednesdays are reserved for men only, and Thursdays for the ladies. Tee times are required on weekends and holidays. It's an interesting course with wide fairways and small greens. Two sets of tees are available for playing 18 holes.

Green fees during the week are $10.00 for 9 holes or $15.00 for 18. On weekends and holidays it's $15.00 and $20.00. Juniors can buy an annual pass for $27.50. Clubs rent for $3.50, handcarts $1.50, and motorized carts are $11.00 for 9 holes or

$20.00 for 18. You'll find a small pro shop, snack bar, and cold beer. Lessons are available, and they have a small banquet area.

Directions: Situated on a flat above Omak, at the south end of the reservoir; simply follow the signs from town.

METALINE FALLS

PEND OREILLE GOLF CLUB
Golf Course Road
Metaline Falls, WA
No Phone

This is the least expensive place to play golf in the Pacific Northwest! Located in Washington's northeastern corner, it's a rugged course surrounded by forest. The terrain is flat with some hills, the fairways fairly wide, and the greens are sand. The view is great, and wildlife is occasionally seen on the fairways. Pend Oreille's official season is May thru September. The grounds are maintained by volunteers.

This course operates on the honor system. During the week the charge is around $2.00, and on weekends $3.00. It's a minimal-facility course and no rental equipment is available. Be sure to have exact change for the green fee box.

Directions: Located just off Highway 31, 3 miles north of town.

REPUBLIC

SHERIDAN GREEN GOLF COURSE
Swamp Creek Road
Republic, WA
(509) 775-2767

Sheridan Green began with five holes for area residents who didn't want to drive 50 miles to play golf. It now sports nine holes and two sets of tees. The terrain is pretty flat with some slope and is surrounded by pine trees. Weather permitting, it is open from late April until early October, between 7:00 a.m. and dusk.

You can play 9 holes at Sheridan for around $8.00. Clubs and handcarts rent for $2.00, and motorized carts $8.00. They have a snack bar and lounge, and can help with tournament planning.

Directions: Take Highway 20 out of town for 2.5 miles to Swamp Creek Road, turn right and drive an additional 1.5 miles.

COLVILLE

COLVILLE ELKS GOLF COURSE
1861 E. Hawthorne
Colville, WA
(509) 684-5508

The Elks operate this course April thru October, weather permitting. It is fairly challenging, offers rolling terrain, and three sets of tees. Reservations are not taken. The total distance from the women's tees is 2,865 yards.

Green fees remain the same all week long. To play 9 holes you'll pay about $10.00; juniors can play 9 holes for around $5.00. Clubs rent for $4.50, handcarts $2.50, and motorized carts $10.00 and $18.00. They have a full-service pro shop where you can arrange for lessons and get help with tournament planning, plus banquet facilities and a driving range.

Directions: Turn at the first stoplight and go to the top of the hill.

CHEWELAH

CHEWELAH GOLF CLUB
Sand Canyon Road
Chewelah, WA
(509) 935-6807

Chewelah has lots of trees, is flat, and easy to walk. You'll find a couple of lakes and some sand, making it a pleasant place to play. The course is open from April thru mid-November and offers three sets of tees. Reservations are taken one week in advance. The women's par is 74 for a total distance of 5,672 yards.

Weekend green fees are $12.00 for 9 holes or $16.00 for 18. During the week they're $10.00 and $14.00, juniors can play for $5.00 and $8.00, and seniors for $8.00 and $13.00. Season passes are available allowing everyone to play for reduced rates. Clubs rent for $5.00 and $7.50, handcarts $2.00, and motorized carts $12.00 and $22.00. Facilities include a driving range, limited grill, banquet facilities, and a lounge offering beer and wine. At the full-service pro shop they can help you with lessons as well as tournament planning. At the driving range you get a bucket of balls for $2.50 and $4.00.

Directions: Leave Highway 395 on Sand Canyon Road and go 3 miles.

PATEROS

ALTA LAKE GOLF CLUB
Alta Lake Road
Pateros, WA
(509) 923-2359

Alta Lake's front 9 was built in 1975, the back 9 in 1993. The slope is 126 and the ratings 71.6 for men, 71.2 for women. It is open March thru October, and reservations are needed on summer weekends and holidays. Situated in the beautiful Methow Valley, this is a British-version course. It has lots of trees, a view that includes both Alta Lake and the Columbia River, plus a creek that cuts across three fairways. The total distance from the women's tees is 5,620 yards.

Seven days a week green fees are $12.00 for 9 holes or $20.00 for 18. On weekdays juniors can play for half price. Credit cards are welcome. Clubs rent for $5.00, handcarts $3.00, and motorized carts $18.00. They have a limited pro shop and a snack bar that offers cold beer. Other facilities include a motel and swimming pool.

Directions: Take Highway 53 off Highway 97, turn left on Toppenish Road, and follow to Alta Lake Road and the course.

BRIDGEPORT

LAKE WOODS GOLF COURSE
Golf Course Road
Bridgeport, WA
(509) 686-5721

In 1995 the Lake Woods Golf Course was rated the second best 9-hole course in Washington. The terrain includes a few hills, lots of trees, narrow fairways, excellent greens, and is bordered by the Columbia River. Built in 1963, two sets of tees are available. The slope is 115 and the ratings 66.7 for men, 67.8 for women. Lake Woods is open from mid-March thru October. Tee times are not needed.

Green fees are $10.00 for 9 holes or $15.00 for 18 Friday thru Sunday, as well as holidays. The rest of the week it's $9.00 for 9 holes or $14.00 to play all day. Juniors, under 18, can play 9 holes mid-week for $5.00 or all day for $8.00. Credit cards are accepted for green fees. You can rent clubs for $5.00, handcarts $2.50, and motorized carts $18.00. They have a restaurant and snack bar where beer is served, plus a limited pro shop where you can get help with tournament planning. At the driving range you'll find grass tees and get a large bucket of balls for $3.50.

Directions: Located near Bridgeport State Park, off Highway 17.

NINE MILE FALLS

SUN DANCE GOLF COURSE
Nine Mile Road
Nine Mile Falls, WA
(509) 466-4040

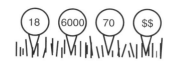

Sun Dance's tree-lined fairways and small greens provide quite a challenge if you're not accurate off the tee. Its terrain is relatively flat and easy to walk. The women's par is 72 for a total distance of 5,900 yards. They are open mid-March thru November.

Weekend green fees are $15.00 whether you play 9 or 18 holes. After 2:00 p.m. the cost drops to $12.00. On weekdays it's $10.00

for 9 holes or $13.50 for 18; seniors pay $9.00 and $10.00. Clubs rent for $7.50, handcarts $3.00, and motorized carts $10.00 per 9 holes.

Facilities include a restaurant and lounge with a liquor license, plus a full-service pro shop and covered driving range. At the range you'll pay $3.00 to $5.00 for a bucket of balls. Lessons are available.

Directions: Leave downtown Spokane heading west on Francis Avenue which soon becomes Nine Mile Road. The course is an additional 2.5 miles.

WILBUR

BIG BEND GOLF CLUB
Highway 2
Wilbur, WA
(509) 647-5664

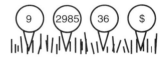

The Big Bend course is considered definitely one of the best 9-hole courses in Eastern Washington. It offers excellent greens, plus some hills and sand bunkers. The slope is 107 for men and 120 for women, the ratings 64.7 and 73.6.

Open March thru November, weather permitting, it's best to call ahead in case they are scheduled for a tournament. Built in 1964, the women's par is 37 for a total distance of 2,875 yards.

On weekends and holidays you'll pay $10.00 for 9 holes or $15.00 for 18. During the week it's $9.00 and $13.00, or you can play all day for $17.50. Clubs rent for $2.00 and $4.00, handcarts $1.00 and $1.75, and motorized carts $10.00 and $15.00.

Facilities include a lounge where liquor is served, plus a snack bar, banquet area, and driving range. At the range you'll find grass tees and can get a bucket of balls for $1.25. Lessons are available.

Directions: Located in the west end of Wilber, at the junction of Highways 2 and 174.

SPOKANE

DOWNRIVER GOLF COURSE
3225 Columbia Circle
Spokane, WA
(509) 327-5269

Downriver has narrow fairways, some trees, a few traps, lots of hills, and some pretty good par threes. Weather permitting, they are open from 6:00 a.m. to dark, April thru October. Reservations are taken one week in advance, and the course offers three sets of tees. From the women's tees the total distance is 5,592 yards for a par of 73.

Like many of Spokane's golf courses, this one has special rates for residents. County residents pay $13.50 for 9 holes or $16.75 for 18. Local juniors and seniors also play at discounted rates. Non-residents pay $17.00 for 9 holes or $22.00 for 18. Clubs rent for $10.00, handcarts $3.00, and motorized carts around $10.00 per 9 holes. Facilities include a restaurant and lounge that serves beer and wine, plus banquet rooms, a full-service pro shop and driving range. Lessons are available, as is help with tournament planning.

Directions: Take the Maple Toll Bridge exit off I-90, turn left at Northwest Boulevard, after the third stoplight turn left again onto Euclid Avenue, and follow the signs.

ESMERALDA GOLF COURSE
E. 3933 Courtland
Spokane, WA
(509) 487-6261

Esmeralda is a joy to play all year long with its rolling hills and beautiful maples, but you'll need good putting skills to break par. The course opens in mid-February and closes in mid-November. Reservations are taken seven days in advance for weekend play; during the week they only take reservations one day ahead. Built in 1956, the women's tees have a total distance of 5,600 yards for a par of 72.

Green fees are $13.00 for 9 holes, or $18.00 for 18, all week long. Juniors can play for $8.50 on weekdays. Clubs rent for $6.00 and $10.00, handcarts $2.00, and motorized carts $22.00. Facilities include a restaurant serving beer and wine, plus a pro shop and driving range. At the range a bucket of balls will cost you $2.00 to $4.00. Lessons can be arranged.

Directions: Go north on Division to Wellesey, turn right and go to Freya, turn right again heading south to Courtland, and turn left.

HANGMAN VALLEY GOLF COURSE
Hatch Road
Spokane, WA
(509) 448-1212

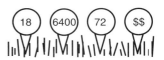

Hangman Valley is open from mid-March to early November, weather permitting. The terrain is rolling with lots of trees and fairly open fairways. It's a challenging, well-trapped course with medium-sized greens and some water. Reservations are taken one week in advance. They offer three sets of tees and the women's tees have a total distance of 5,699 yards for a par of 71.

If you live in Spokane County you'll pay $11.00 to play 9 holes or $14.50 for 18, seven days a week. On non-holiday weekdays resident seniors can play for $10.25 and juniors $7.75. Golfers from outside the county limits pay $14.50 for 9 holes or $19.50 for 18 every day of the week. You can rent a full set of clubs for $10.00, handcarts are $2.00 and $3.00, and motorized carts $10.50 per 9 holes.

Hangman Valley has a driving range where floating balls are hit directly into a lake. A bucket of balls will cost you $3.00 to $5.00. Facilities include a full-service pro shop, restaurant, lounge, and a banquet area where beer and wine is served. You can get help with tournament planning and arrange for lessons.

Directions: Leave I-90 on Highway 195, go 4.5 miles to Hatch Road, turn left, then right onto Hangman Valley Road, and drive 5 miles.

INDIAN CANYON GOLF COURSE
W. 4304 West Dr.
Spokane, WA
(509) 747-5353

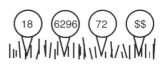

You'll find this Spokane course at the top of Sunset Hill. The terrain is hilly, and open from March thru October. Three sets of tees add variety, and from the women's tees the total distance is 5,318 yards for a par of 73. Indian Canyon was designed by Chandler Egan, the same man who designed Pebble Beach. It is operated by the Spokane Parks and Recreation Department, so local residents pay less than visitors.

Green fees for city residents are $13.50 for 9 holes or $16.75 for 18. Nonresidents pay $17.00 and $22.00. Local juniors can play 18 holes for $10.00, and the city's seniors pay $13.00 for 9 holes or $14.00 for 18. Clubs rent for $10.00, handcarts $2.00, and motorized carts $11.00 per 9 holes.

Facilities include a driving range, restaurant, lounge, and banquet area where beer and wine is served, plus a limited pro shop where you can get help with tournament planning and arrange lessons. At the driving range you'll pay $3.00 to $5.00 for a bucket of balls.

Directions: Leave I-90 at the Garden Springs exit and follow the signs.

PAINTED HILLS GOLF COURSE
S. 4403 Dishman-Mica Rd.
Spokane, WA
(509) 928-4653

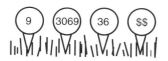

The Painted Hills course is easy to walk and open year round, weather permitting. You'll find an interesting flat terrain with seven white-sand traps and water on four holes. The slope is 120 and the ratings 70.1 for men, 71.0 for women. It was built in 1988, and each hole has four tees. The women's tees have a total distance of 2,621 yards for a par of 37.

Green fees are $10.00 for 9 holes or $15.00 for 18, all week long. Juniors and seniors can play weekdays before 3:00 p.m. for $8.00 and $12.00. Clubs are $7.50 and $10.00, handcarts $2.00, and motorized carts $5.00 per 9 holes. Facilities include a restaurant that serves beer and wine, plus a lighted driving range and full-service pro shop. The range is open until 10:00 p.m., April thru September, offers buckets of balls for $3.00 to $6.00, and mat tees. Help with tournament planning and lessons are available.

Directions: From I-90, take the Argonne exit #287 and head south 5 miles to the course.

PINE ACRES PAR 3
N. 11912 Division
Spokane, WA
(509) 466-9984

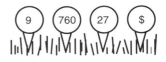

Pine Acres is Spokane's only par three course. Built in 1960, it is open March thru October. The terrain is flat and easy to walk. It's a good place for beginners, and those looking to practice their short game. Reservations are not taken; everyone plays on a first-come basis. Children under seven aren't allowed on the course.

Green fees are $5.50 for 9 holes or $9.00 for 18. Juniors and seniors can play during the week for $4.50 and $8.00. Clubs rent for $.25 each and handcarts $1.00. Motorized carts are not available. You'll find a discount golf shop, snacks, cold drinks, and a driving range at Pine Acres. Lessons are given during the summer; call for information.

Directions: Located 7 miles north of downtown Spokane, along Highway 395.

THE CREEK AT QUALCHAN
301 E. Meadow Ln.
Spokane, WA
(509) 448-9317

You play across the creek five times at Qualchan. Its front 9 is flat with some rolling hills, the back 9 tree-lined and hilly. In all, 5 ponds and 65 bunkers dot the course. There are four sets of tees; the shortest cover 5,535 yards. The course is open March thru November, from 7:00 a.m. to dusk. Tee times are given a week in advance for weekends and a day ahead for weekdays.

This course also has special rates for Spokane County residents; $13.00 for 9 holes or $16.50 for 18. County seniors can play for $10.50 and $13.00, and juniors pay $10.25 to play all day. Out-of-county golfers pay $16.50 for 9 holes or $22.00 for 18. Clubs rent for $6.00 and $10.00, handcarts $2.00, and motorized carts $11.00 per 9 holes. You'll find a restaurant with banquet facilities that serves beer and wine, plus a driving range and full-service pro shop. Lessons, and help with tournament planning, are available. A bucket of balls at the range is $2.50 to $4.50.

Directions: Leave I-90 on Highway 195 heading south; the course is about 5 minutes from downtown.

WANDERMERE GOLF COURSE
N. 13700 Division St.
Spokane, WA
(509) 466-8023

Wandermere has some of the toughest holes in the city. Built in 1929, it has a rolling terrain. When playing 18 holes you have to shoot across a river twice, and around three ponds. The slope is 119 to 126, and the ratings 68.6 for men and 72.2 for women. Open March thru October, from 5:00 a.m. to dusk, reservations are taken a week in advance for weekends, one day ahead for weekdays. The women's tees cover 5,760 yards for a par of 73.

Green fees will cost you $11.00 for 9 holes all week long. You'll pay $16.00 for 18 holes on weekends and $15.00 on weekdays. During the week golfers 60 and older pay $9.50 for 9 holes or $10.50 for 18, and juniors can play 9 holes for $9.50. Clubs rent for $7.00, handcarts $3.00, and motorized carts $11.00 and $22.00. Credit cards are welcome.

Facilities include a restaurant, lounge and banquet area with a liquor license, plus a full-service pro shop and driving range. Lessons are available, as is help with tournament planning. A bucket of balls at the driving range will cost you $3.00 to $4.00 depending on the size. You'll find both mat and grass tees.

Directions: Located 10 miles north of downtown Spokane via Deerpark Highway.

LIBERTY LAKE

LIBERTY LAKE GOLF CLUB
E. 24403 Sprague
Liberty Lake, WA
(509) 255-6233

Weather permitting, the Liberty Lake course is open year round. The front 9 is considered the most challenging in town; the back 9 is much shorter with rolling hills and lots of trees. They are open year round, and begin taking reservations on Tuesday mornings for the following seven days. The women's par is 74 for a total distance of 5,886 yards.

Green fees are the same all week long. County residents pay $11.00 and $14.50, others $14.50 and $19.50. Resident seniors play for $10.25, juniors $7.75. Clubs rent for $5.00, handcarts $2.00, and motorized carts $10.00 per 9 holes. Facilities include a driving range, plus a restaurant serving beer and wine, a banquet area, and full-service pro shop. At the driving range you can get a bucket of balls for $2.00 to $5.00. Lessons can be arranged.

Directions: Leave I-90 at the Liberty Lake exit and head south 1 mile before turning left onto Sprague.

MEADOWWOOD GOLF COURSE
Valley Way
Liberty Lake, WA
(509) 255-9539

Meadowwood was built in 1988, and designed by Robert Muir Graves. Open March 10th thru November 10th, it has 7 lakes, 52 large bunkers, and a rolling terrain. The slope is 126 and the ratings 74.2 for men, 73.8 for women. Reservations open up Tuesdays at 7:00 a.m. for the following seven days. The total distance from the women's tees is 5,880 yards.

Green fees are $14.00 for residents, $20.00 for non-residents. Clubs are available for $10.00, handcarts $3.00, and motorized carts $20.00. Children under 12 are not permitted on the course unless they have paid to play and are being supervised by an adult. Facilities include a restaurant that serves beer and wine, plus a banquet area, snack bar, full service pro shop, and 9-acre water range. At the range you'll find mat tees, and pay $2.00 to $5.00 for a bucket of balls. Lessons, and help with tournament planning, are available.

Directions: From I-90, take exit #296 and drive 1 mile south on Liberty Lake Road before turning left onto Valley Way. The course is just a short distance.

VALLEY VIEW GOLF COURSE
Golf Course Road
Liberty Lake, WA
(509) 928-3484

The Valley View course is open March thru December, weather permitting. Reservations are not necessary. The terrain is easy to walk and the area surrounded by rolling hills. This country setting offers a beautiful view of the mountains and has two sets of tees so you can play 18 holes with variety.

Weekday green fees are $8.50 for 9 holes or $12.50 for 18, but golfers younger than 18, or over 65, can play for $6.50 and $9.50. On weekends and holidays everyone pays $9.00 and $13.00. Clubs rent for a flat $4.00, handcarts $2.50, and motorized carts $6.00 and $10.00. You'll find a restaurant, lounge, and banquet facilities with a liquor license, plus a full-service pro shop and driving range. The range offers buckets of balls for $3.00 to $5.00. Lessons, as well as help with tournament planning, are available.

Directions: Located about 14 miles east of Spokane; take the Liberty Lake exit off I-90 and head south 2 blocks.

CHENEY

THE FAIRWAYS WEST TERRACE
W. 9810 Melville Rd.
Cheney, WA
(509) 747-8418

You'll find lots of water hazards and some of the finest greens available at The Fairways West Terrace. This course opened in 1987 and is closed only when snow is on the ground. The terrain is slightly rolling, and the women's tees have a total distance of 6,000 yards. Reservations open up on Saturday mornings for the following week.

You can play 18 holes here for $18.00 and 9 holes for a little less. Discounts are available to club members and seniors. They also give you a free round of golf with large pro shop purchases. Clubs rent for $10.00 and motorized carts $20.00. Facilities include a restaurant and lounge with a liquor license, plus a banquet area, full-service pro shop and driving range. A bucket of balls at the range will cost you $3.00 to $6.00, depending on how many you want. Lessons, and help with tournament planning, are available.

Directions: Located east of I-90's exit #272. At the exit go right on Hayford Road, turn left onto Melville, and follow to the course.

COULEE CITY

VIC MEYERS GOLF COURSE
Sun Lakes Park Resort
Coulee City, WA
(509) 632-5738

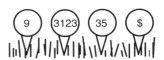

The Vic Meyers Golf Course is part of Sun Lakes Park Resort. Built in 1949, it is open year round, weather permitting. This is a beautiful course overlooking Sun Lakes, rocky bluffs, and scenic canyons. The terrain is hilly, and wildlife is often spotted on the course. From the women's tees the total yardage is 2,702.

During the week green fees are $9.00 for 9 holes or $13.00 for 18. On weekends it'll cost you $10.00 and $14.00. Club rental is $6.00, handcarts $2.00, and electric carts $12.00 and $20.00. They have a putting green, limited pro shop with snacks and cold drinks, and offer help with tournament planning.

Directions: Located 6 miles south of Coulee City on Highway 17.

HARRINGTON

HARRINGTON GOLF CLUB
Golf Course Road
Harrington, WA
(509) 253-4308

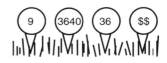

Harrington is a semi-private course, but the general public is welcome any time but Thursday evenings. Open March thru October, you'll find wide fairways, big greens, blind holes, and doglegs. A second set of tees give you a distance of 6,449 yards when playing 18 holes. The total yardage from the women's tees is 2,998 for 9 holes or 6,006 yards for 18. Reservations are taken one week in advance.

Weekday green fees are around $10.00 for 9 holes; juniors play for about half the normal rate and seniors save $2.00. On weekends and holidays everybody pays the same rate, about $12.00. Clubs rent for $4.00, handcarts $2.00, and motorized carts around $12.00 per 9 holes.

This is a pretty course in early summer when the wheat in the surrounding fields provides a lush, golden backdrop. Facilities include a restaurant, lounge and banquet facilities with a liquor license. They also have a full-service pro shop and driving range. Lessons, and help with tournament planning, are available.

Directions: Located in the town of Harrington.

ODESSA

ODESSA GOLF CLUB
Highway 28
Odessa, WA
(509) 982-0093

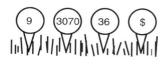

Built in 1967, the Odessa course is kept in excellent shape. Open March to November, weather permitting, the terrain has a few rolling hills, but is easy to walk. The slope is 113 for men and 121 for women, the ratings 68.8 and 72.9. You'll find wide lush fairways, elevated greens, and a few sand traps. The ladies' tees cover 2,894 yards for a par of 37. Tee times are not required.

Weekday green fees are $8.00 for 9 holes, $12.00 for 18, or $15.00 for all day. On weekends it's $9.00, $14.00 and $18.00. Seniors, 60 years and up, get $1.00 off the 9-hole rate, juniors, 11 and under, play for free on weekdays. Rental clubs are $3.00, handcarts $2.00, and motorized carts $20.00. Facilities include a pro shop where you'll find light snacks and cold beer.

Directions: Located at the west end of Odessa.

EPHRATA

OASIS PARK PAR 3
2541 Basin S.W.
Ephrata, WA
(509) 754-5102

Golf is both affordable and challenging at the Oasis Park Par 3 course. The terrain is flat with some hills, plenty of water, banked greens, and grass tees. Open dawn to dusk year round, they only close occasionally for bad weather.

You can play 9 holes for $3.75 at Oasis Park, or all day for $6.50. If you're under 16, or over 60, you can play 9 holes for $2.75, and the all-day rate is $4.50. Clubs rent for $2.50 when playing all day, and handcarts are $1.25. They have a limited pro shop where you can arrange for lessons, and get help with tournament planning.

Directions: Located 1 mile south of Ephrata, on Highway 28.

QUINCY

CRESCENT BAR RESORT
8894 Crescent Bar Rd. N.W.
Quincy, WA
(509) 787-1511

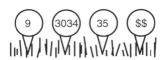

Crescent Bar Resort is open March thru November, weather permitting. The slope is 109 and the ratings 68.4 for men, 72.1 for women. Summer tee times are given one week in advance. This course offers three sets of tees, and the women's par is 36 for a total distance of 2,944 yards.

Weekday green fees are $12.00 for 9 holes, $18.00 for 18, or $25.00 for all day. On weekends you'll pay $15.00 for 9 holes or $20.00 for 18. Seniors, 60 and over, can play all day on Mondays for $10.00. Clubs rent for $10.00 and $15.00, handcarts $4.00 and $5.00, and motorized carts $15.00 and $20.00. The resort offers lodging, convention facilities, a restaurant/lounge with a liquor license, and a driving range. Tournament planning is available. The range has grass tees and charges $4.00 for balls.

Directions: Go west 7.5 miles on Highway 28 and follow signs.

QUINCY VALLEY GOLF
1705 6th Rd. 5 N.W.
Quincy, WA
(509) 787-3244

Quincy Valley has excellent greens, the terrain is flat, and there's a pond off the 3rd tee. Open year round, weather permitting, they

take reservations one week in advance for weekend play. The distance from the women's tees is 2,633 yards.

Weekday green fees are $10.00 for 9 holes or $13.00 for 18. On weekends it's $12.00 and $16.00. Clubs rent for $3.00 and $5.00, handcarts $2.00 and $3.00, and motorized carts $9.00 and $16.00. You'll find a restaurant with banquet facilities where beer is served, plus a full-service pro shop. Lessons, and help with tournament planning, are available.

Directions: Leave I-90 at the town of George and take Highway 281 toward Quincy. The course is 5 miles.

RITZVILLE

RITZVILLE GOLF COURSE
104 E. 10th St.
Ritzville, WA
(509) 659-9868

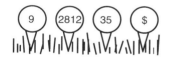

The Ritzville course is open mid-February thru mid-November, 8:00 a.m. to 8:00 p.m. Built in 1940, it has narrow fairways, tall trees, and small fast greens. Par from the ladies' tees is 36.

Green fees are $9.00 for 9 holes or $13.00 for 18, all week long. You can rent clubs for $5.00, handcarts $2.00, and motorized carts $9.00. Facilities include a restaurant where you'll find cold beer, plus a banquet area and full-service pro shop.

Directions: Located right in Ritzville.

TEKOA

TEKOA GOLF & COUNTRY CLUB
Farmington Highway
Tekoa, WA
(509) 284-5607

The Tekoa Golf and Country Club is a semi-private course and open April thru October. Built in 1960, it offers nice greens, a semi-hilly terrain, and excellent views of the surrounding wheat fields and mountains.

You'll pay $8.00 on weekdays, $10.00 on weekends and holidays, whether playing 9 or 18 holes. Clubs rent for $2.00, handcarts $2.00, and motorized carts $12.00 and $16.00. Facilities include a restaurant, and the staff can help you with tournament planning.

Directions: From Tekoa, head south .5 mile on Farmington Hwy.

ST. JOHN

ST. JOHN GOLF & COUNTRY CLUB
Golf Course Road
St. John, WA
(509) 648-3259

This is another one of those rare courses where you can play all day for one flat fee. For a long time this semi-private course had only six holes, but they recently added four new ones and eliminated one of the older ones. You'll find two par threes, six par fours, one par five, and a creek. The slope is 115 and the ratings 67.0 for men, 72.2 for women. It is open May thru mid-October.

The St. John course operates on the honor system. Rates are posted, and although they are raised occasionally, it'll cost you about $10.00 to play all day. If an attendant is on hand, you can rent a handcart for $2.00. Lessons are available from time to time.

Directions: This course is located right in St. John.

MOSES LAKE

SOUTH CAMPUS GOLF COURSE
1475 E. Nelson Rd.
Moses Lake, WA
(509) 766-1228

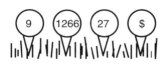

The South Campus Golf Course is flat, easy to walk, and surrounded by trees. Built in 1991, there is no water on the fairways. Open year round, weather permitting, early golfers can get on the course at 6:00 a.m. Reservations are generally not necessary.

At this par three course you can play 9 holes for $5.00 or 18 for $8.00 seven days a week. Seniors and juniors can play during the week for $4.00. Clubs rent for $1.00, handcarts $1.00, and motorized carts $6.00.

You'll find a full-service pro shop, driving range, snack machines, a lighted 9-hole putting course, plus help with tournament planning and lessons. At the 275 yard driving range you get a basket of balls for $2.50 to $3.50. The putting course charges $3.00 for 9 holes or $5.00 for 18.

Directions: Leave I-90 at exit #179 on Highway 17, turn right onto East Nelson Road and follow to the course.

ROYAL CITY

ROYAL CITY GOLF COURSE
13702 Dodson Rd. S.
Royal City, WA
(509) 346-2052

Royal City opened in 1991 and is a year-round course, weather permitting. It has rolling fairways, water on the 1st and 9th holes, and bent grass greens. The women's tees have a total distance of 2,850 yards.

Bargain day is Monday at Royal City; you can play 9 holes for $5.00. Tuesday thru Friday 9 holes will cost you $8.00 and 18 holes $11.00. On weekends you'll pay $9.00 and $13.00. Clubs are $3.00 for 9 holes or $5.00 for 18, and motorized carts $10.00 and $15.00. The pro shop is limited, but they offer cold pop and snacks. They can also help you with tournament planning. At the driving range you'll pay $1.00 to $2.00 for a bucket of balls. They also have an RV park.

Directions: Located at the corner of Highway 26 and Dodson Road, east of Royal City.

WARDEN

SAGE HILLS GOLF CLUB
Route 1, Box 289
Warden, WA
(509) 349-7794

This 25-year-old course is open February thru November, weather permitting, from 6:00 a.m. to dusk. It's a well maintained rolling course with three sets of tees, large greens, some traps, and water. Weekend tee times are given two days in advance. The distance from the women's tees is 5,665 yards for a par of 74.

During the week, green fees are $10.00 for 9 holes or $16.00 for 18. Seniors pay $9.00 and $15.00, and juniors $7.00 and $10.00. On weekends everybody pays $12.00 and $20.00. Clubs rent for $5.00, handcarts $2.00 and $2.50, and motorized carts $12.00 and $20.00. Facilities include a restaurant/lounge serving beer and wine, plus banquet rooms, a full-service pro shop, and a driving range where you get a bucket of balls for $2.50 to $3.50. Lessons, and help with tournament planning, are available.

Directions: Located near Potholes State Park, 12 miles south of Moses Lake, along Highway 17.

OTHELLO

OTHELLO GOLF CLUB
W. Bench Road
Othello, WA
(509) 488-2376

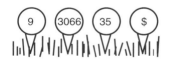

The Othello Golf Club is located in the heart of the Columbia Basin, and open year round. It provides a good challenge, a fairly flat terrain, and is easy to walk. The course is kept in great condition, and has two sets of tees. The women's par is 37.

During the week, green fees are $8.00 for 9 holes, or $14.00 for 18. On weekends you'll pay $10.00 and $15.00. You can rent clubs for $6.00, handcarts are $2.00 per 9 holes, and motorized carts $11.00 and $18.00. They have a lounge with a liquor license, banquet facilities, driving range, and a full-service pro shop. Help with tournament planning is available. A bucket of balls at the driving range is $2.00.

Directions: Head south on Bench Road for 1 mile, then west for 2 miles on West Bench Road.

COLFAX

COLFAX GOLF CLUB
Cedar Street
Colfax, WA
(509) 397-2122

This course was built in 1927 and is open year round, sunup to dusk. The slope is 117 to 120, and the ratings 67.9 for men, 67.9 for women. It's a flat, challenging course with sand traps at each hole. Tee times are recommended on weekends, and the women's par is 36 for a total distance of 2,817 yards.

You'll pay $10.00 for 9 holes or $15.00 for 18 any day of the week. You can rent clubs for $2.50 and handcarts for $1.50. Motorized carts are not available. Facilities include a full-service pro shop where you'll find light snacks and cold drinks, plus a driving range and a 30 by 60 practice net. The range offers mat tees and is open during daylight hours.

Directions: Located at the north end of town.

PULLMAN

WSU GOLF COURSE
N. Fairway Road
Pullman, WA
(509) 335-4342

This short course has a variety of different types of holes. Its greens are interesting and kept in good condition, and the total distance from the women's tees is 2,623 yards. The slope is 110 to 119, and the ratings 65.4 for men and 69.8 for women. The terrain is both flat and hilly, and the course offers a nice view. Open March to November, from 7:00 a.m. to dusk, reservations are not taken and no one under six is allowed on the course.

Green fees are $8.00 for 9 holes or $11.00 for 18, all week long. Students pay $7.50 and $10.00. Clubs rent for $4.00, handcarts $3.00, and motorized carts $12.00 and $20.00. They have a lounge, pro shop, driving range, and banquet facilities. Lessons are available, as is help with tournament planning. The driving range charges $2.00 to $3.50 for a bucket of balls, and offers mat tees in the spring and fall, grass tees during the summer.

Directions: Take Fairway Drive off Stadium Way; located behind the Washington State University baseball field.

MATTAWA

DESERT AIRE GOLF COURSE
505 Clubhouse Way W.
Mattawa, WA
(509) 932-4439

Desert Aire is a semi-private course with no restrictions on public play. They are open year round, have a slightly hilly terrain, and a view that includes the Columbia River. The back 9 opened in 1975, the front 9 in 1991. The slope is 111 for men and 115 for women, and the ratings 69.9 and 71.9. Par from the ladies' tees is 73 for a distance of 5,786 yards.

Weekday green fees are $12.00 for 9 holes or $16.00 for 18. On weekends and holidays it's $14.00 and $18.00. Seniors, age 55 and over, can play 18 holes on Mondays and Thursdays for $12.00. Between Memorial Day and Labor Day students, age 7 to 18, can play for $5.00 and $9.00 after 1:00 p.m. on weekdays and after 4:00 p.m. on weekends. You can rent clubs for $5.00 and $7.50, handcarts are $1.25, and motorized carts $10.00 and $15.00. They have a driving range with grass tees where you can get balls for $1.25 to $2.50 during daylight hours.

Directions: Located off State 243, near the Columbia River.

POMEROY

POMEROY GOLF CLUB
19th St. & Arlington Ave.
Pomeroy, WA
(509) 843-1197

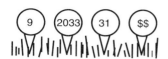

This city course is open year round. It has large greens, well-kept fairways, and the terrain is hilly, but easy to walk. You'll have to shoot up the hill on the 6th hole and down again on the 7th, but it helps to keep the game interesting. The slope is 94 and the ratings 59.9 for men, 63.3 for women. The women's par is 32 for a total distance of 1,977 yards.

Green fees are $10.00 for 9 holes or $12.00 for 18, all week long. Juniors can buy season tickets which give them special discounts. From November thru March this course operates on the honor system, so be sure to bring exact change. April thru October they have some golf clubs and handcarts available for rental, and motorized carts are $5.00 per 9 holes. You'll find a limited seasonal pro shop and a snack bar. Help with tournament planning is available.

Directions: Located 3 blocks off Main Street, in Pomeroy, near the city park.

CLARKSTON

QUAIL RIDGE GOLF COURSE
3600 Swallows Nest Dr.
Clarkston, WA
(509) 758-8501

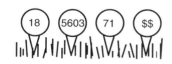

A second 9 holes were added to the Quail Ridge course in 1992. It was designed by Mark Poe. The original 9 holes were built in 1971. The slope is 113 and the ratings 66.9 for men, 66.2 for women. It has a rolling terrain and small greens. The total distance from the women's tees is 4,720 yards.

Quail Ridge offers a nice view of the Snake River and Blue Mountains. It is open year round, from 6:00 a.m. to dusk in the summer and 7:00 a.m. to dusk in the winter. Tee times are available one week in advance.

Green fees are $10.00 for 9 holes or $13.00 for 18 all week long. Juniors, age 15 and younger, can play for $5.00 and $7.00. Clubs are $5.00 and $6.00, handcarts $2.00 and $3.00, and motorized carts $12.00 and $20.00.

Facilities include a restaurant, lounge, and a banquet area where beer and wine is served. They also have a full-service pro shop, practice putting green and driving range. At the range you'll find mat tees and get buckets of balls for $2.75 to $5.00. The range is open from 6:00 a.m. to dusk. Help with tournament planning and lessons are available.

Directions: Follow Highway 129 south to Critchfield Road and head west.

DAYTON

TOUCHET VALLEY
Columbia County Fairgrounds
Dayton, WA
(509) 382-4851

This course is located in the beautiful Touchet River Valley, southeastern Washington's gateway to the Blue Mountains. Open from daylight to dusk, March thru October, the terrain is nice and flat. Although reservations are not taken, they occasionally close for tournaments so if you'll be driving a long distance you might want to call ahead. Four sets of tees are available.

Weekend green fees are $12.00 for 9 holes or $15.00 for 18. During the week they're $9.00 and $12.00. Juniors, those in eighth grade to age 17, pay $7.00; younger children pay $5.00. Clubs rent for $5.00, handcarts $2.00, and motorized carts $10.00 and $18.00. They have a limited pro shop, plus a restaurant, lounge and banquet facilities offering beer and wine.

Directions: Located 1 block north of Highway 12 at Dayton's west end, in the center of the Columbia County Fairgrounds race track.

WEST RICHLAND

WEST RICHLAND GOLF COURSE

4000 Fallon Dr.
West Richland, WA
(509) 967-2165

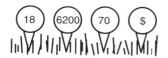

This challenging year-round course is right in West Richland. The terrain is fairly flat and easy to walk, and it borders the Yakima River on one side. The greens are small and reservations are given one week in advance for weekend tee times. Total distance from the women's tees is 5,800 yards.

Green fees are $8.00 for 9 holes or $9.75 for 18, seven days a week. Monday thru Friday seniors, 62 and older, can play for $6.75 and $8.75, and juniors for $3.50 and $5.00. Clubs rent for $4.00 and $5.00, handcarts $2.00, and motorized carts $10.00 per 9 holes. Facilities include a restaurant, lounge and banquet area serving beer and wine, plus a full-service pro shop and driving range. The range charges $1.75 to $3.75 for a bucket of balls. Lessons and tournament planning can be arranged.

Directions: From Bypass 240 take the Van Giesen NW exit, turn right onto 38th Street, and follow to the course. The total distance is about 1 mile.

SUNNYSIDE

LOWER VALLEY GOLF CLUB

31 Ray Rd.
Sunnyside, WA
(509) 837-5340

Lower Valley is open year round, has a fairly flat, easy-to-walk terrain, and a lovely view. It is both interesting and challenging, with wide fairways and small greens. Ten of the holes have water. The slope is 112 and the ratings 70.2 for men, 70.6 for women. The original 9 holes opened in 1946, the second in 1995. Three tees are found at each hole, and the total distance for ladies is 5,618 yards. Reservations are given one week in advance.

All week long, green fees are $11.00 for 9 holes or $16.00 for 18. Juniors, age 18 and under, can play all year for $75.00. Clubs rent for $10.00, handcarts $2.00, and motorized carts $10.00 per 9 holes. Credit cards are welcome. They have a full-service pro shop, snack bar, practice green, driving range, and provide help with tournament planning and lessons. At the driving range you'll find grass tees, and get a bucket of balls for $1.50 to $4.00.

Directions: Located 1 mile east of town, on Yakima Valley Hwy.

RICHLAND

HORN RAPIDS GOLF COURSE
2800 Horn Rapids Dr.
Richland, WA
(509) 375-4714

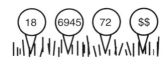

Horn Rapids was built in 1993 and will make you feel like you're playing in the middle of nowhere. It's a target-style course; the only one of its kind in Eastern Washington. You'll find no trees, just lots of desert roughs. The terrain is rolling, and water comes into play on the 9th and 18th holes. Open year round, weather permitting, from 7:00 a.m. to dusk, reservations are available one week in advance. They offer four sets of tees, and the total distance from the ladies' tees is 5,179 yards.

Green fees are $16.00 for 9 holes or $20.00 for 18 on weekends, $10.00 and $15.00 on weekdays. Clubs rent for $10.00, handcarts $4.00, and motorized carts $10.00 per person. They have a full-service pro shop, driving range, and a snack bar offering beer and wine. At the range you'll pay $2.00 for 25 balls. Lessons, and help with tournament planning, are available.

Directions: Located 2 miles out of Richland via Highway 240.

SHAM-NA-PUM GOLF COURSE
George Washington Way
Richland, WA
(509) 946-1914

Sham-na-pum will be closed until the summer of 1997, while they remodel the course. Prior to this closure Sham-na-pum was open year round, except during severe weather. The terrain was challenging and the rates reasonable.

Directions: Located just off George Washington Way.

PASCO

SUN WILLOWS GOLF COURSE
2035 N. 20th
Pasco, WA
(509) 545-3440

Sun Willows has 37 bunkers and 5 lakes. Located in the heart of the Tri-Cities, it offers a challenging back 9. The terrain is fairly flat and the course is open year round, weather permitting. Reservations are given one week in advance. Three sets of tees are available; the distance from the ladies' tees is 5,695 yards.

Green fees are the same seven days a week, $10.00 for 9 holes or $15.00 for 18. Juniors can play on weekdays for $8.00 and $10.00. Clubs rent for $10.00, handcarts $3.00, and motorized carts $12.00 and $24.00. Facilities include a restaurant/lounge and banquet area with a liquor license, plus a driving range and full-service pro shop. At the range you'll pay $3.00 to $5.00 for balls. Lessons, and help with tournament planning, are available.

Directions: Leave I-182 at the 20th Street exit and go north, turning right just past the Red Lion.

KENNEWICK

CANYON LAKES GOLF COURSE
3700 W. Canyon Lakes Dr.
Kennewick, WA
(509) 582-3736

Weather permitting, you can play year round at Canyon Lakes. The slope is 127 and the ratings 73.4 for men, 72.0 for women.

This is considered one of the best courses in the Pacific Northwest with its rolling fairways, fast greens, numerous bunkers and lakes. Designed by John Steidel, it opened in 1981. Reservations are available one week in advance. The women's tees have a total distance of 5,700 yards.

Green fees are $12.00 for 9 holes during the week and $15.00 on weekends. To play 18 holes you'll pay $20.00 all week long. Juniors, age 17 and under, can play 9 holes for $8.00 or 18 for $14.00. Clubs rent for $10.00, handcarts $2.00, and motorized carts $12.00 per 9 holes. Credit cards are welcome.

Facilities include a restaurant where beer and wine are served, plus a snack bar, driving range and pro shop. Lessons, and help with tournament planning, are available. At the driving range you'll find grass tees, and can get buckets of balls for $2.00 to $5.00.

Directions: Follow Highway 395 south to 27th Avenue and head east. Signs will direct you from there.

COLUMBIA PARK GOLF COURSE
2700 Columbia Dr.
Kennewick, WA
(509) 585-4423

The Columbia Park Golf Course is right on the Columbia River, and the summertime view is of hydroplane races and waterskiers. Open mid-February thru mid-November, this is an easy-to-walk course. It will challenge players of all skill levels but is a particularly good place for beginning players and family groups. The slope is 71 and the rating 51.1. Reservations are taken only on weekends.

During the week you can play 9 holes for $5.00 or 18 for $8.00. On weekends the rates are $5.50 and $9.00. Golfers who are 62 and older, or 17 and younger, receive a $1.00 discount. Clubs rent for $3.50 and $4.00, handcarts $1.50 and $2.50, and motorized carts are not available.

They have a snack bar, driving range, and a limited pro shop where you can arrange for lessons and get help with tournament planning. The driving range is open from 8:00 a.m. to dusk, has grass tees, and you get 25 balls for $1.50 or 60 for $3.00.

Directions: Located in Kennewick, beside Highway 240.

TRI-CITY COUNTRY CLUB
314 N. Underwood
Kennewick, WA
(509) 783-6014

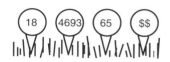

This semi-private course is open to the public, but you must call two days ahead for tee times. This is the oldest course in the Tri-Cities. It has rolling hills, and plenty of trees to block the spring winds. The 14th tee offers a spectacular view of the course, as well as the Columbia River and Blue Mountains. Open year round, they offers two sets of tees.

Weekday green fees are $17.00, on weekends it's $22.00. Juniors play for $7.50. Clubs rent for $7.50, handcarts $2.50, and motorized carts $20.00. They have a full-service pro shop, and can help with tournament planning or to arrange lessons.

Directions: Leave Highway 395 at the Kennewick/Umatilla exit, stay right, go left on Yelm, after 2 blocks turn left on Clearwater, and at the T go left on Underwood and follow to the course.

WALLA WALLA

VETERANS MEMORIAL GOLF
201 E. Rees
Walla Walla, WA
(509) 527-4507

This semi-flat course is short, tight, interesting, and has fast greens. Open year round, reservations are available on Mondays for the following weekend. The ladies' tees cover 5,732 yards for a par of 76.

Green fees are $11.50 for 9 holes or $16.00 for 18, seven days a week. Juniors pay $5.00 and $8.00, seniors $9.50 and $12.50. Clubs rent for $6.00 and $8.00, handcarts $2.00 and $3.00, and motorized carts $13.00 and $20.00. You'll find a restaurant, lounge and banquet facilities with a liquor license, plus a driving range and limited pro shop. At the range you'll pay $2.00 to $5.75 for a bucket of balls.

Directions: Leave Hwy. 410 at the second exit and follow signs.

INDEX

Marysville Golf Course - 68
McKenzie River Golf Course - 69
McNary Golf Course - 63
Meadow Lakes Golf Course - 94
Meadowlawn Golf Course - 63
Meriwether National Golf - 45
Middlefield Village Golf - 75
Milton-Freewater Golf - 107
Mountain High Golf Course - 97
Mountain View Golf Course - 52
Neskowin Beach Golf - 20
Nine Peaks Golf Course - 92
North Woodlands/Sunriver - 100
Oak Knoll Golf - 65, 84
Oakway Golf Course - 72
Ocean Dunes Golf Links - 24
Olalla Valley Golf Course - 23
Oregon City Golf Club - 51
Orenco Woods Golf Course - 46
Orion Greens Golf Course - 98
Paradise Ranch Inn Golf - 79
Persimmon Country Club - 44
Pine Cone/Resort @ Mtn. - 49
Pine Hollow Golf Course - 90
Pineway Golf Course - 67
Portland Meadows Golf - 38
Progress Downs Golf - 40
Pumpkin Ridge - 42
Quail Point Golf Course - 83
Quail Run Golf Course - 100
Quail Valley Golf Course - 34
Ranch Hills Golf Course - 57
Red Mountain Golf Course - 79
Resort at the Mountain - 49
River's Edge Golf Course - 98
Rivergreens Golf Course - 43
Riveridge Golf Course - 72
Riverwood Golf Course - 54
Rose City Golf Course - 39
Round Lake Golf Course - 103
Sah-hah-lee Golf Course - 41
Salem Golf Club - 64
Salishan Golf Links -22
Sandelie Golf Course - 48
Sandpines Golf Resort - 25
Sandstrip Golf Course - 60
Santiam Golf Club - 64

Seaside Golf Club - 18
Shadow Butte Golf Course - 112
Shield Crest Golf Course - 103
South Meadows/Sunriver - 100
Springwater Golf Course - 53
St. Helens Golf Course - 33
Stewart Meadows Golf - 83
Stewart Park Golf Course - 76
Stoneridge Golf Club - 80
Summerfield Golf Club - 47
Sunriver Golf Course - 100
Sunset Bay Golf Course - 27
Sunset Grove Golf Club - 50
Sutherlin Knolls Golf Course - 76
Thistle/Resort at the Mtn. - 49
Tokatee Golf Club - 70
Top O'Scott - 39
Tukwila OGA Course - 58
Trysting Tree Golf Club - 68
Umatilla Golf Course - 107
Valley Golf Club - 112
Vernonia Golf Club - 33
Widgi Creek Golf Club - 99
Wildwood Golf Course - 40
Willow Creek Golf Club - 110
Wilson's Willow Run Golf - 108
Woodburn Golf Course - 59

Senior rates - 21, 23, 25, 28, 33,
34, 36, 37, 38, 39, 40, 41, 43, 44,
46, 47, 48, 49, 50, 51, 52, 54, 56,
60, 61, 62, 63, 65, 67, 68, 71, 72,
73, 75, 76, 77, 78, 80, 81, 82, 84,
89, 92, 94, 102, 103, 108, 109, 110,
112, 122, 124, 129, 130, 131, 132,
133, 137, 138, 140, 141, 142, 143,
144, 146, 147, 148, 149, 150, 151,
152, 153, 154, 155, 156, 157, 158,
159, 160, 162, 163, 164, 165, 166,
167, 168, 169, 170, 171, 172, 173,
174, 175, 176, 177, 178, 179, 180,
181, 183, 184, 185, 187, 188, 190,
191, 193, 194, 196, 197, 198, 205,
206, 207, 210, 218, 221, 222, 223,
223, 225, 226, 227, 228, 229, 230,
233, 234, 236, 239, 242, 243

Goldendale Country Club - 209
Golfgreen Golf Center - 192
Grandview Golf Course - 130
Green Lake Golf Course - 148
Hangman Valley Golf - 222
Harbour Pointe Golf Club - 144
Harrington Golf Club - 228
High Cedars Golf Club - 187
Highland Golf Course - 122
Highlands Golf Club - 171
Horn Rapids Golf Course - 240
Horseshoe Lake Golf - 163
Hot Springs Golf Course - 210
Husum Hills Golf Course - 211
Indian Canyon Golf - 222
Ironwood Green - 191
Island Greens - 154
Jackson Park Golf - 149
Jade Greens Golf Course - 174
Jefferson Park Golf - 149
Kahler Glen Golf Course - 202
Kayak Point Golf Course - 140
Kenwanda Golf Course - 147
Lake Chelan Golf Course - 201
Lake Cushman Golf Club - 166
Lake Limerick Golf - 181
Lake Padden Golf Course - 133
Lake Spanaway Golf - 179
Lake Wilderness Golf - 169
Lake Woods Golf Course - 219
Lakeland Village - 167
Lakeview Golf Challenge - 197
Leavenworth Golf Club - 202
Legion Memorial Golf - 145
Lewis River Golf - 194
Liberty Lake Golf Club - 225
Lipoma Firs Golf Course - 177
Lobo Country Club - 147
Lopez Island Golf Course - 135
Lower Valley Golf Club - 239
Lynnwood Municipal Golf - 156
Madrona Links Golf - 176
Maple Grove Golf - 191
Maplewood Golf Course - 157
McCormick Woods Golf - 164
Meadow Park Golf Course - 172
Meadowmeer Golf Club - 151

Meadowwood Golf Course - 226
Meridian Greens Golf - 178
Meriwood Golf Course - 186
Mint Valley Golf Course - 193
Monroe Golf Course - 158
Mt. Adams Country Club - 208
Mt. Si Golf Course - 161
Newaukum Valley Golf - 189
Nisqually Valley Golf - 188
North Shore Golf Club - 173
Oaksridge Golf Course - 183
Oasis Park Par 3 - 129
Ocean Shores Golf Course - 124
Odessa Golf Club - 229
Okanogan Valley Golf - 215
Orcas Island Golf - 134
Oroville Golf Club - 215
Othello Golf Club - 234
Overlook Golf Course - 145
Painted Hills Golf Course - 223
Peaceful Valley Golf - 131
Pend Oreille Golf Club - 216
Peninsula Golf Course - 125
Pine Acres Par 3 - 224
Pine Crest Golf Course - 198
Pomeroy Golf Club - 237
Port Ludlow Golf Course - 143
Port Townsend Golf - 143
Quail Ridge Golf Course - 237
Quincy Valley Golf - 230
Raspberry Ridge Golf - 132
Ritzville Golf Course - 231
Riverbend Golf Complex - 155
Riverside Country Club - 190
Riverside Golf Course - 133
Rock Island Golf Club - 205
Rolling Hills Golf Club - 162
Royal City Golf Course - 233
Sage Hills Golf Club - 234
San Juan Golf Club - 136
Scott Lake Golf Course - 185
Sea Links Golf Course - 129
Semi-ah-moo Golf Course - 129
Sham-na-pum Golf Course - 240
Shelton Bayshore Golf - 182
Sheridan Green Golf - 216
Similk Golf Course - 136

Skamania Lodge Golf - 209
Skyline Golf Course - 192
Snohomish Public Golf - 148
Snoqualmie Falls Golf - 159
South Campus Golf - 232
St. John Golf Club - 232
Sudden Valley Golf Club - 134
Sun Country Golf Course - 203
Sun Dance Golf Course - 219
Sun Willows Golf Course - 241
Sunland Golf Club - 121
Suntides Golf Course - 207
Surfside Golf Course - 123
Tall Chief Golf Course - 160
Tapps Island Golf Course - 180
Tekoa Golf Club - 231
Three Lakes Golf Course - 205
Three Rivers Golf Course - 193
Tochet Valley - 238
Tri-City Country Club - 243
Tri Mountain Golf Course - 195
Tumwater Valley Golf - 186
Tyee Valley Golf Course - 150
University Golf Club - 173
Valley View Golf Course - 226
Veterans Memorial Golf - 243
Vic Meyers Golf Course - 228
Village Greens Golf Club - 165
Walter Hall Memorial Golf - 145
Wandermere Golf Course - 225
WA State Univ. Golf - 235
Wayne Golf Club - 153
Wellington Hills Golf - 154
West Richland Golf - 239
West Seattle Golf Club - 151
Westwood West Golf - 207
Willapa Harbor Golf Course - 123

Year round courses -17, 18, 19,
20, 21, 22, 23, 24, 25, 26, 28, 33,
34, 35, 36, 37, 38, 39, 40, 41, 42,
43, 44, 46, 47, 48, 49, 50, 51, 52,
53, 54, 55, 56, 57, 58, 59, 60, 61,
62, 63, 64, 65, 66, 67, 68, 69, 71,
72, 73, 74, 75, 76, 77, 78, 79, 80,
81, 82, 83, 84, 89, 91, 92, 93, 94,
95, 96, 98, 99, 101, 102, 103, 107,

108, 109, 110, 111, 112, 121, 122,
123, 124, 125, 129, 130, 131, 132,
133, 134, 135, 136, 137, 138, 139,
140, 141, 142, 143, 144, 145, 146,
147, 148, 149, 150, 151, 153, 154,
155, 156, 157, 158, 159, 160, 161,
162, 163, 164, 165, 166, 167, 168,
169, 170, 171, 172, 173, 174, 175,
176, 177, 178, 179, 180, 181, 183,
184, 185, 186, 188, 189, 190, 191,
192, 193, 194, 195, 196, 197, 198,
205, 206, 207, 209, 210, 211, 223,
225, 227, 228, 230, 233, 234, 235,
236, 237, 239, 240, 241, 243

Other books by KiKi Canniff

UNFORGETTABLE PACIFIC NORTHWEST CAMPING VACATIONS; Your Guide to Oregon & Washington's Most Spectacular Camping Regions. Each vacation covers a variety of things to see and do, as well as campgrounds for both RV and tent campers. *"There's a whole world of natural beauty to explore on the byways and backroads of Oregon and Washington. Nowadays, following those pathways is easier, thanks to the efforts of KiKi Canniff."* ' **The News-Times**. ($10.95)

NORTHWEST FREE - Volume 1; **The Best Free Historic Attractions in Oregon & Washington.** Includes the region's best ghost towns, covered bridges, aging lighthouses, museums, pioneer wagon trails, historic towns, archeological digs, Indian artifact collections, railroad memorabilia and more! *"KiKi Canniff is an expert on freebies."* **Woman's World Magazine.** ($10.95)

A CAMPER'S GUIDE TO OREGON & WASHINGTON; The Only Complete Guide to the Region's Non-membership RV Parks and Improved Tent Campgrounds. Perfect for campers who want showers, hookups or other civilized facilities. Each campground listing includes facilities available, trailer length, activities, and easy-to-follow directions. *"This handy guide belongs on every Northwest camper's 'must have' list."* **The Chronicle.** ($14.95)

FREE CAMPGROUNDS OF WASHINGTON & OREGON. This lightweight guide details the region's hundreds of cost-free campgrounds. A terrific book for folks who enjoy camping close to nature. *"...very well done, easy to read and to understand... the cost of this book is saved with the first campground used!"* **This Week Magazine.** ($8.95)

ABOUT THE AUTHOR

KiKi Canniff is a Pacific Northwest resident who has been writing books about recreation in Oregon & Washington since 1981. She is the Portland *Oregonian's* former campground columnist, and an avid camper who enjoys golf, hiking, travel, history, nature and exploring Pacific Northwest backroads.

ORDER COUPON

Please send:

___ NORTHWEST GOLFER/4th Ed. @ $14.95 ea.   _____

___UNFORGETTABLE PACIFIC NORTHWEST
    CAMPING VACATIONS @ $10.95 ea.   _____

___ NORTHWEST FREE/Historic @ $10.95 ea.   _____

___ A CAMPER'S GUIDE TO OR/WA @ $14.95 ea.   _____

___ FREE CAMPGROUNDS OF WA /OR @ $8.95 ea._____

Shipping   __3.00__

TOTAL ENCLOSED   _____

Name _____

Address _____

City/State/Zip Code _____

To order, send this coupon to Frank Amato Publications, Inc.,
P.O. Box 82112, Portland, OR 97282 – or call (800)541-9498.

G96

✂---✂

Please send:

___ NORTHWEST GOLFER/4th Ed. @ $14.95 ea.   _____

___UNFORGETTABLE PACIFIC NORTHWEST
    CAMPING VACATIONS @ $10.95 ea.   _____

___ NORTHWEST FREE/Historic @ $10.95 ea.   _____

___ A CAMPER'S GUIDE TO OR/WA @ $14.95 ea.   _____

___ FREE CAMPGROUNDS OF WA /OR @ $8.95 ea._____

Shipping   __3.00__

TOTAL ENCLOSED   _____

Name _____

Address _____

City/State/Zip Code _____

To order, send this coupon to Frank Amato Publications, Inc.,
P.O. Box 82112, Portland, OR 97282 – or call (800)541-9498.

G96